Badon and the Early Wars for Wessex, circa 500–710

*In the fifth century a new
route seems to have been struck, the West way, and
from the beech-clad islands and sandy links of the
Danish peninsula, and the broad flat pastures about
the river mouths between Elbe and Rhine, there
sailed westward many a ship-load of armed emigrants
from the great tribal leagues, Eotish, English, and
Saxon. For they had heard the news that there
were new homes to be won in the weakly defended
Roman diocese, and already bands of sea-rovers from
among them had harried the coasts on their own
account or fought over the land in the service of the hard-
pressed rulers of Britain. So all along the "Saxonic
shore," from the reedy broads south of the Wash to the
sandy dunes about the Humber mouth, and further
north up to the "Frisic Sea," the Firth of Forth, and
further west into the breaks of the Southdowns, up
the Belgic plain between the marshes and the wood,
into the fat meadow-lands of the Bajocasses and on
the warm Islands of the Channel Vectis and Caesarea
and the rest, they came and settled with their wives,
and children, and cattle, and set up new states and
flourished exceedingly*

EARLY BRITAIN – SCANDINAVIAN BRITAIN
by
W. G. COLLINGWOOD, M.A., F.S.A.
1908

Badon and the Early Wars for Wessex, circa 500–710

David Cooper

Pen & Sword

MILITARY

AN IMPRINT OF PEN & SWORD BOOKS LTD.
YORKSHIRE – PHILADELPHIA

First published in Great Britain in 2018 by
Pen & Sword Military
An imprint of
Pen & Sword Books Ltd
Yorkshire – Philadelphia

ISBN 978 1 52673 357 3

Printed and bound in England by TJ International Ltd, Padstow, Cornwall.

Pen & Sword Books Limited incorporates the imprints of Atlas, Archaeology,
Aviation, Discovery, Family History, Fiction, History, Maritime, Military, Military
Classics, Politics, Select, Transport, True Crime, Air World, Frontline Publishing,
Leo Cooper, Remember When, Seaforth Publishing, The Praetorian Press,
Wharncliffe Local History, Wharncliffe Transport, Wharncliffe True Crime and
White Owl.

For a complete list of Pen & Sword titles please contact

PEN & SWORD BOOKS LIMITED
47 Church Street, Barnsley, South Yorkshire, S70 2AS, England
E-mail: enquiries@pen-and-sword.co.uk
Website: www.pen-and-sword.co.uk

Or
PEN AND SWORD BOOKS
1950 Lawrence Rd, Havertown, PA 19083, USA
E-mail: Uspen-and-sword@casematepublishers.com
Website: www.penandswordbooks.com

Contents

Preface

Rome's abandonment of Britain in AD 410 had seismic consequences for the peoples who remained in the former Roman province. For many it was a catastrophe. For others, primarily those of a martial persuasion, it was an opportunity. Among those who seized the opportunity, apparently with considerable enthusiasm for the violence that ensued, were the ancestors of Alfred the Great, King of Wessex. On his orders, their story was written down in the *Anglo-Saxon Chronicle*.

A number of years ago I was instructing young army officers in tactics and doctrine. Out of the classroom we would conduct tactical exercises without troops, a grand name for a walk over a piece of land on which we would imagine how a modern-day battle might be fought. For one such discussion I had chosen Hambledon Hill in Dorset, primarily because it offered far-reaching views. To enliven proceedings, I introduced the students to what I knew about the Roman siege of the hillfort there, and the subsequent slaughter of the Durotriges, the ancient British tribe that had built it. Part of my preparatory reading had included Geoffrey Ashe's *A Guidebook to Arthurian Britain*. I fixated on a paragraph about another nearby hillfort, Badbury Rings, as a possible site for Arthur's famous victory at the Battle of Badon Hill. I was drawn to the words 'not in the path of any plausible offensive'. Knowing that the fort had been an early and particularly important objective in the earlier Roman campaign, I wondered what alternative plausible path the Anglo–Saxon offensive might have taken.

As I began to look for evidence of events that led up to the Battle of Badon Hill, I realised that examining its aftermath might also be instructive in trying to understand the battle in context. I sought to determine where and why battles occurred in the years that followed. I followed the trail of Ceawlin of Wessex in particular, who appeared to have achieved more than any other named leader in turning Germanic fortunes around after Badon. The *Anglo–Saxon Chronicle* calls him a West Saxon and records how he and his descendants established the kingdom of Wessex. Academics now dispute the *Chronicle's* version of the origins of Wessex, but few are prepared to try and provide a convincing and definitive view of what actually occurred. My view, after considerable time and effort expended, is set down in this book.

As my initial essay on Badon expanded it morphed over many years into the pages that follow. The book is essentially in two parts, with much background leading up to Badon in the first, and a more-or-less chronological account of Wessex battles in the second. Running through the whole are three major themes for the reader to bear in mind:

- That the Germanic rise to power in Britain manifested slowly in the earliest days as diverse warbands from post-Roman Britain and Europe fought localised wars over territory.
- That the British victory at Badon Hill was an early clash of larger armies, formed when warbands first began to form alliances out of necessity – in this battle the Germanic commander was out-thought and out-manoeuvred by his British adversary in a way that echoes other ancient battles that are better recorded.
- That Wessex, unlike Kent, Mercia and others, was not a kingdom established and then expanded by immigrant Germanic tribes; it emerged in more complex circumstances.

Introduction

We are Englishmen; that is one good fact.   – Oliver Cromwell

The English in Britain

The term Saxon was used freely in Britain from the seventh century onwards to describe all of the Germanic immigrant groups, including Frisians, Angles, Jutes, Saxons, Alamanni and Scandinavians. These settlers later came to describe themselves collectively as English and to describe the Britons as *wealhas*, meaning foreigners. The earliest recognisable kingdom of the English was established by Ecgberht of Wessex, who extended his rule to encompass Kent, Sussex, Surrey and Essex, thus usurping the hegemony that had been Mercia's. His reign, which ended with his death in 839, laid the foundations for his descendants to become kings of a more-or-less united England. The leading role of the House of Wessex in establishing England as a nation state is therefore a matter of record, but the history of the early West Saxons in Britain remains shrouded in mystery. Harold Godwinson of Wessex, the last English king, was killed in battle on 14 October, 1066. The *Anglo-Saxon Chronicle* relates that his ancestor Cerdic, founder of Wessex, arrived in Britain nearly six centuries before this. For many years, historians broadly surmised that the Celtic peoples were pushed wholesale from their territories to the western fringes of Britain through these times, but the archaeologists of today mostly reject this view and have posited alternative theories as to how the Germanic culture proliferated. The debate was split for a time between those who argued for social and trade links leading to gradual acculturation and those who believed that a multitude of leaders from the elite Germanic ruling classes were able to seize power and retain it through military might. Most scholars now agree that English rule was established in a multi-faceted manner that encompassed aspects of both theories and varied with time, place and the leaders involved.

From a military perspective, there was less complexity when the Romans seized power in Britain and also later when the Normans wrested the throne of England from Harold. These invasions of Britain, a millennium apart, were similar in so much as they both consisted of a series of planned and coordinated military operations that defeated effective resistance in a relatively short period of time. Both invasions had clearly defined strategic objectives that were pursued ruthlessly until success was achieved. On the other hand, the initial arrival to Britain of the Germanic tribes was neither planned nor coordinated and their military campaigns were opportunistic and *ad hoc*. The settlers had no particular strategic objectives in mind. Rather, their territorial expansion was driven by the need to acquire good agricultural land. Thus, their military actions, when successful, tended to result in incremental gains of territory. As they expanded in this way, they came up against British populations who were also prepared to seize or protect whatever they could by force. It was challenging for any group to survive and prosper amid the chaos that followed the Roman withdrawal from Britain in AD 410. Many of the Celtic tribes had been much reduced in power and influence by Rome and their fractured remnants had to compete for survival against each other, as well as against the Germanic newcomers.

The term Dark Ages refers generally to the period between the fall of Rome and the Renaissance. It has remained popular with scholars when describing the period in Britain's history between the collapse of Roman influence and the re-emergence of culture and learning under Christian leaders. Alfred of Wessex, the first monarch to describe himself as king of all of the Anglo-Saxons, is recognised as a major contributor to this cultural renaissance. In the late ninth century he directed his scribes to record the history of his peoples and his royal ancestors in a collection of annals known as the *Anglo-Saxon Chronicle*. However, the *Chronicle* is nowadays regarded by scholars with healthy suspicion, largely because the scribes were swayed by Alfred's need to emphasise his heritage and legitimacy as an English king. In the absence of other evidence, particularly before archaeology began to influence learning, historians who identified anomalies in the records struggled to piece together a wholly credible history of emerging England.

The desire to fill the knowledge gap was taken up foremost by military historians, partly because the earliest *Chronicle* entries focused heavily on battles.

In just a few decades leading up to the 1920s, numerous papers and books on Dark Age warfare in Britain were put forward by a 'Military Science' fraternity that included many serving and former officers of the armed forces. The prominence of this military scholarship was also enhanced by a wave of new studies of the European, Napoleonic and American wars, as well as the ongoing campaigns in the British colonies at the time. Competing theories on the 'Anglo-Saxon Conquest' invariably focused on how large armies might have manoeuvred across Britain and fought for strategically important towns and other objectives. Such an approach was understandable from scholars who were influenced by their studies of the great campaigns of old. In today's military parlance the popular idiom 'big hand, small map' is used to describe a commander who explains in the very broadest sense what he wants to achieve, thus he sweeps his hand across the map without ever dwelling on the minor detail. The same broad approach was applied initially to the military history of early England. However, as archaeology advanced, and new techniques were applied to an ever-increasing number of finds, many of the assumptions made by the practitioners of military science fell apart.

In the early twentieth century two authors in particular tried to make sense of the early wars between Germanics and Britons. Both published military studies of the early Anglo-Saxon campaigns in southern Britain. The evidence available to them consisted of written texts, primarily the *Anglo-Saxon Chronicle*, interpretations of those texts by Victorian scholars, and a smattering of archaeological research, much of which was carried out by enthusiastic amateurs. Major P.T. Godsal was particularly keen to paint a picture of Germanic armies engaged in a sweeping conquest of the Britons, a scenario that has been discredited in modern times by more rigorous study and archaeological evidence. The second author was the magnificently named Albany Featherstonehaugh Major who, in 1913, produced *Early Wars of Wessex: Being Studies from England's School of Arms in the West*, a very credible work that has recently been republished. Ground-breaking for its day, the study correlates the records of fighting to the details of the landscape on which the battles took place and the prevailing political situation. His reasoned assessments lacked the boldness of Godsal's works and were thus, somewhat ironically, less appreciated when published. Major was transparent in his desire to highlight what he saw as his competitor's shortcomings, which he ascribed to Godsal's reliance on written records alone. In fact, he went so far as to use his preface to *Early Wars of Wessex* to criticise Godsal's approach directly:

> *Recently another line has been worked by Major P. T. Godsal, who has endeavoured to reconstruct the early stages of the Saxon conquest by considering the military necessities and strategy involved in such a campaign. There is much in the brilliant romance which he has woven round the shadowy personalities of Ella, the first Bretwalda, and Ambrosius Aurelianus, which calls for criticism and tends to obscure undoubtedly valuable work; but any historical study on such unorthodox lines will ever be anathema to the scholar whose vision is bounded by what he can find within the four walls of a library. On the other hand, we may claim that the attempt to write history from documents only is likely to be equally dangerous. It is at any rate certain that, in studying the history of a period where written records are meagre and lacking in detail, a mere knowledge of the documents is of little value unless coupled with a careful study of the topography of the country and of the probable local conditions existing at the time.*

Major's book suffered from unfortunate timing, published as it was on the eve of the First World War. The niche genre of study that had been gaining popularity, and that he had exemplified, was shortly to disappear as it became unpopular for the British to acknowledge the Germanic side of their heritage. Academic historians turned their minds to other periods, as did the learned officers and their ilk of military writers. Retreating to their smoke-filled clubs they debated the folly of trench warfare and the potential for aircraft and armoured vehicles to render it a thing of the past. The early wars of Wessex and other Anglo-Saxon kingdoms were largely forgotten.

In recent years there has been a resurgence of interest in Dark Age warfare. Modern academics have analysed the contemporary written records with increased rigour and have exposed the fault lines that run through many of them. This has led to some revising of long-held assumptions about the early Germanic kingdoms. For the popular audience a vast swathe of fiction has been written that focuses often on the military affairs of the period. For all that, very few ideas have been advanced regarding where battles were fought and why. For the most part the debate on battle sites remains mired in the interpretation of place-names derived from the annals, rather than linking such interpretation to a careful study of topography and likely local conditions as espoused by Major.

In particular, the Siege of Badon Hill has become one of Britain's most discussed Dark Age battles, partly because it stands out as a rare and decisive victory for the Britons at a time when Germanic forces appeared to be far superior. It also gained popularity because of its association with King Arthur and in this mythological dimension there is little requirement to dwell on realism or the likely specifics of the battle. The most relevant lines of text devoted to this battle are those written by the British monk Gildas in the sixth century. These few lines in his famous polemic, *De Excidio*, have been analysed and interpreted for centuries, but the battle site and date remain unknown. Suggestions for the location range widely from Scotland to southern England, and dates anywhere between the mid-fifth and mid-sixth centuries have been proposed. Yet Badon is not alone among the battles of this period that are lost to us. Very few of the sites of Dark Age battles are known definitively. They are often guessed at, sometimes by academics but mostly by enthusiastic amateurs seeking to place their preferred localities into the historical narrative. Despite a plethora of books on Dark Age warfare, very few authors have posited locations other than through speculation. This may be due to the fact that many recent works lack the level of research that was considered essential by Major.

It is therefore apposite to reassess what we know of the Dark Age wars in Britain by reapplying Major's techniques, and to add a few more besides. Academics in recent times have provided much deeper studies of the period that Major and his contemporaries never lived to read. From a military perspective we can look not just at topography and conditions, but also inside the minds of the opposing commanders. Ancient war leaders were faced with very similar planning considerations to the generals who control armies today, making it possible to assess retrospectively their likely actions given the circumstances under which they operated. Through these methods we can arrive at a better understanding of where, why and how the Dark Age commanders in Britain conducted their campaigns.

List of Maps and Illustrations

Maps

Illustrations

Chapter One

The Fifth-Century Tribes of Britain

One does not inhabit a country; one inhabits a language. That is our country, our fatherland – and no other. — Emile M. Cioran

Roman Britain

The human inhabitants of the British Isles have left their mark on the landscape for millennia. The Neolithic period is the earliest to reveal a pattern of early settlement discernible from the distribution of enclosures, stone monuments, causeways, flint mines and burial mounds. The earliest areas of settlement expanded as native populations increased and even more so as others arrived, such as the Celtic peoples from mainland Europe who migrated to Britain from the late Bronze Age onwards. From his own accounts, entitled *Gallic Wars,* we know that Julius Caesar mounted two separate expeditions to Britain in 55 and 54 BC respectively. These operations are best described as armed reconnaissance, aimed at investigating what riches might be accrued from Britain for the Roman Empire. Caesar also wished to boost his popularity in Rome and, had he found an easy welcome, he would probably have seized the opportunity to claim the isles as a province of Rome at this time. Instead, both expeditions were curtailed due to a combination of poor luck, lack of resources and the resistance by some of the Celtic tribes of Britain. In the late August of 55 BC, Caesar's force, consisting of two legions, made landfall somewhere near Dover and had to fight immediately against British tribesmen even through the surf and onto the beaches. The ships carrying Caesar's cavalry regiment were beset by storms on the crossing and never arrived. The same storms damaged the legions' ships at anchor and the force that had begun to advance inland was ordered to return and help repair the fleet. Despite one faction of Britons having sued for terms, the Roman expedition foundered further when a large foraging party from VII Legion was ambushed and the day only narrowly won for Rome due to immediate intervention by

Caesar himself. For his second campaign Caesar employed five legions and made rapid progress, having made landfall on the eastern coast of Kent on 7 July 54 BC. Roman forces won a succession of pitched battles and assaults on hillforts and were at Wheathampstead, 75 miles from the beachhead, within one month of landing.[1] The Romans were nonetheless continually harassed by the British, who adopted guerrilla tactics of hit and run. As in 55 BC, the Roman fleet was again badly damaged by storms. Caesar's second campaign in Britain ended like his first, with his forces having come close to defeat. The lessons learned from these high-risk campaigns were undoubtedly studied by the Roman commanders who orchestrated the successful invasion of Britain nearly a century later.

The Claudian invasion of AD 43 was planned and organised in a deliberately ruthless manner to conquer the tribes of Britain and bring them under Roman governance. Colchester was an important initial objective, reached by way of an advance through Kent in which the Roman forces, knowing their own superiority in organised close combat, sought to bring the British tribes to open battle at every opportunity.[2] The strategy worked, and within a few months Roman forces were in control of modern-day Essex. Four legions, an estimated 40,000 to 50,000 Roman troops, defeated an alliance of British tribes estimated to have been 150,000 warriors strong. AD 44 saw the second deliberate operation of the campaign in which vigorous opposition from the Durotriges tribe in the Dorset area was crushed by Vespasian and his Second Legion Augusta. These early operations provided the firm foothold the Romans required for conquest, and by AD 49 they had secured a northern boundary from Colchester to the Bristol Channel. Scapula's subsequent victory over Caratacus in AD 51 established the absolute military superiority of Rome in Britain. Despite Boudicca's later rebellion and the protracted difficulties that Rome experienced in trying to control the northern territories, it is fair to say that the Roman conquest had succeeded within two years of the initial landings. Rome ruled the majority of the island of Great Britain for the next 350 years.

As the fifth century dawned, Roman dominance in Britain had been on the wane for some time as resources were increasingly diverted to other areas of the empire under threat. Finally, the need to withdraw forces to fight on mainland Europe led to a collapse of Rome's authority over the Britons in AD 410. The end of Roman rule has been argued to have offered an opportunity for British tribes to re-establish themselves in full and reclaim their old territories, but the extent to which this occurred is debatable, particularly when one considers the lasting changes established by the Romans.[3] Aside from the displacement, and in some cases the near destruction of ancient British tribes, a number of new groups had been allowed to settle, predominantly mercenaries and auxiliaries employed by Rome. The military prowess of these factions helped ensure their survival and enabled them to prosper, even after their erstwhile paymasters abandoned them. The presence of these groups over a protracted period of time and the influx of new opportunists from the fifth century onwards altered further the dynamics of the former British kingdoms. Germanic immigration to southern and eastern Britain in particular accelerated rapidly in the early fifth century, prompted by overcrowding in the European homelands and encouraged by the opportunities that arose in Britain through the lack of any central control. It was a time of opportunities to acquire land and power through force of arms. Predominantly, the immigrants sought cultivatable land on which to settle. They had to fight for it against the disparate peoples of the post-Roman British Isles, who were vying with each other for the same prize.

The influence of geography

In the fifth century, the changes wrought by mankind on the British landscape were less dramatic than they are today. Whilst the clearance of forests for agriculture had made its impact, a significant proportion of ancient woodland remained. Deciduous forests of beech, oak and elm stretched unbroken for hundreds of miles, including across the majority of the hilly regions south of the River Thames. The sea around the British Isles rose somewhere between 20 and 25 feet around the second to third century, and many low-lying areas that had been dry for centuries were inundated. Even with the relatively low density of settlement the availability of productive farmland was restricted, and areas of such land often resembled islands surrounded and divided by forests, waterways, marshes and barren uplands. These tracts of land suitable for agriculture were of the utmost importance to societies that survived mainly on the crops they grew and the animals they raised, especially through times of war-induced chaos when generating wealth through trade was more difficult.

The human population was relatively small and predominantly rural. Whilst there is no reliable record for population figures in Britain, a minimum estimate for the Roman period has been put at one-and-a-half million.[4] By the beginning of the Industrial Revolution, it was still only six million.[5] In human terms, the fifth-century boundaries between tribal territories were being re-established, replacing the artificial divisions made by Rome, and they were defined often by the edges of natural features that have since lost their significance. Lord Curzon's 1907 Romanes Lecture presented in Oxford was entitled 'Frontiers':

> *The last Natural Frontier to which I need here refer is the well-nigh obsolete barrier created by forests and marshes and swamps. The various Saxon kingdoms of England were, for the most part, thus severed from each other. When Caesar first landed in Britain, the head quarters of Cassivelaunus, the British leader, were placed at Verulamium, near St. Albans, which was surrounded by forests and swamps.*[6]

The sandy heaths and chalk downs that characterise much of southern Britain were as unattractive as swampland from a farming perspective. The extensive tracts of forest were also of no initial interest to Germanic settlers because they were too difficult to clear for a population that sought to establish itself quickly with limited manpower. Forests were also an unwelcome prospect for military operations, especially for outsiders fighting against an indigenous enemy that knew the terrain. Rivers have always been important territorial boundaries, and battle sites where neighbouring kingdoms clashed are often to be found close to their banks. Navigable rivers also provided good lines of communication for those who could use them. Waterways were a significant obstacle to movement by horse and on foot and this impacted on warbands and armies on the march. Very few bridges or causeways were in existence and those that were would have assumed significance in military affairs. Arguably the most important bridge in Roman Britain was that which spanned the River Thames at Southwark in London. Remains uncovered there include a timber box structure that has been assessed to be a pier base for a substantial wooden bridge built in the first century.[7] Even as early as the Bronze Age there is archaeological evidence for the existence of timber causeways such as that at Flag Fen near Peterborough, indicating that ancient Britons had mastered the technique of driving substantial logs upright into river beds. Such methods were effective at making standing crossing points, but construction was a complex and lengthy task and long-term maintenance was important if the structure was to survive. It is unlikely that such maintenance was sustained after the collapse of Roman rule and, thus, the rivers and waterways of Britain once more became significant obstacles to movement by land.

The first Germanic arrivals were experienced mariners and therefore able to exploit this aspect of Roman Britain's decline. They used flat-bottomed boats, evidenced by several finds of remains. This shallow hull design remained the rule for ships built to operate in the southern North Sea until the end of the age of sail.[8] The draft of these boats meant they were effective also on the navigable waterways of the interior. Therefore, rivers and estuaries were less of an obstacle for the new settlers compared with those among their potential adversaries, who had not needed to master seafaring or boatbuilding. We can discern from the written sources that Germanic use of ships was commonplace and the mobility they achieved on Britain's waterways was an advantage in times of war. In the Roman period, the fen and marsh areas of East Anglia were very sparsely populated, and the Romans had little regard for what occurred there, so long as rebellion did not fester. Thus, some areas were ceded through passivity during the Roman occupation, mainly to those immigrants who were at ease on the water. However, the same tacit acceptance was not extended to the Germanic pirates who menaced the seas around Britain at this time. Coastal raiding and attacks on shipping became endemic. Rome was forced to create bespoke defences, collectively known as the Saxon Shore, formed by a series of coastal forts in the South East, exemplified by the one built in the early third century at Reculver in Kent. The *Notitia Dignitatum* which, among other records, details Roman commanders and their units, lists the stations that were commanded by the *Comes Litoris Saxonici* (Count of the Saxon Shore). The existence of such a command has led some to believe that this series of defences was planned and coherent from the outset. However, archaeological evidence indicates that its constituent parts evolved over the course of some 200 years, and the defences are therefore much more likely to have provided bases for seaborne operations to protect Roman supply lines than they are to have formed a 'Maginot line' against barbarian raiders.[9] Either way, the collapse of this defence system once Rome abandoned Britain allowed the Germanic mariners greater freedom of movement, both on the sea and the interior waterways.

It was not only the politico-military climate that changed at this time. The relatively warm climate that prevailed through much of the Roman period ended some time around the fourth century, and colder times ensued in which farming became more difficult. The first Germanic groups to arrive in Britain established their farms in lower lying areas, in Kent and the Thames Valley for example, where the rich loam soils were best suited to their agriculture. However, at the same time that Germanic settlers were looking to exploit such regions, the colder climate was rendering the uplands ever harsher, thus reducing the availability of prime land for natives and newcomers alike. We can assess that this led to greater competition for the areas that could best support human existence.

Germanic farmers used oxen to pull ploughs across fields divided into strips and either planted crops of wheat, barley and rye, or left the strips fallow in rotation to allow the soil to recover. They also grew peas, cabbages, parsnips, carrots and celery, and grew and gathered fruits such as apples, blackberries, raspberries and sloes. Livestock consisted of goats, cattle, pigs and sheep. Farmers could not grow enough fodder to sustain many of their animals through winter, so most were slaughtered in autumn and the meat was salted or smoked to preserve it. The richest and best of the agricultural land, especially that which was already tilled and managed by Britons, was the most desirable commodity for the new settlers, and this land was a major factor in shaping the geography of conflict.

Across southern Britain, the hill country, particularly the chalk downs, assumed military significance because it was ideal terrain from which to defend and protect the fertile lower valleys and the populations that farmed them. These heights had been important since the Bronze Age for their defensive properties in times of inter-tribal conflict. The steep slopes provided excellent protection from attack and the high vantage points allowed visibility and early warning of military movement across hundreds of square miles. The hills and uplands of Britain are dotted and lined with the remains of ancient earthworks that were built for ceremonial and military purposes, many of which are remarkably well-preserved. Most date to the Iron Age, when the widespread construction of hilltop fortifications reached a zenith. Many of these hillforts remain spectacular today, given the height and complexity of the earthen structures, but they would have appeared even more dramatic when first constructed. Wooden palisade defences topped the concentric rings of earthen embankments. Gateways and entrances had to be accessed through complex alignments of these obstacles, designed to slow down, confuse and halt attackers.

In low-lying areas, where water features provided natural defences, design considerations for defensive works and fortifications were different. Unfortunately, marsh forts have not stood the test of time, often succumbing to inundation and overgrowth of vegetation. However, a relatively well-preserved example is found at Sutton Common near Doncaster, where the River Don marked the border between the tribes of the Coritani to the south and the Brigantes in the north. The fort is just under a hectare in size and, when constructed, was protected on all sides by deep marsh. A grand entrance leads to a large enclosure which is, in turn, linked to another by what appears to be a ceremonial walkway. This design, along with a lack of archaeological finds related to human habitation, suggests that the site may have been a symbolic or ceremonial place. However, because the building techniques closely resemble those of the hillforts and its location within the wetlands would have rendered the construction impregnable in time of war, a martial purpose for the site has not yet been ruled out by archaeologists.

Historians have speculated on whether there is any discernible pattern to these forts, strategic or otherwise. *The Wessex Hillforts Project*, published in 2006, identified 'clear preferred locations in the landscape and strong regional trends', helping to confirm the old tribal boundaries and, more importantly, identifying potential new groupings within them.[10] For example, the Durotriges, with their capital in Dorchester, were known to have minted coins at Hengistbury Head and the locations where these coins have been found have long provided a reasonably accurate picture of the extent of their territory. The density of their hillforts exceeds that of any other tribe and the distribution of these constructions has led historians to believe that the tribe was made up of a number of semi-autonomous clans. Some historians and archaeologists have speculated that the hillforts were status symbols constructed in times of food surplus, and that the chieftains competed to build the most imposing edifice. Yet, despite such theories, it can be assumed that the original builders were concerned primarily with the defence of their communities in time of war. Forts sprang up wherever natural hill features could best be improved for defence, just as the marsh forts improved on the natural obstacles provided by rivers and wetlands. Having been largely neglected for centuries, many hillforts were occupied anew and refortified in the Dark Ages, when the war between Britons and Germanics escalated.

Communities in Bronze Age Britain were connected by a network of ancient tracks that were used, as far as can be ascertained, for trade and communication. Many of the most important tracks tended to follow the higher ground and remained in use even after the Romans added roads that largely ignored terrain features and linked key towns by the most direct routes available. Roman roads were better constructed than anything that previously existed, but towards the end of the occupation, with towns falling into disrepair and no centralised government, the communications system began to deteriorate. Desire to travel also reduced as groups became increasingly invested in the protection of their own territory. In order to enhance security, some post-Roman kingdoms began to construct linear ditch and rampart defences, some of which stretch for many miles and appear today to be near incredible in scope. These were similar to the linear earthworks of the Bronze and Iron Age, which were used to mark out grazing rights between clans and tribes, but the newer constructions were higher and more complex and clearly for military use. It was also common for an existing feature, such as the remnants of an older embankment, to be extended. Like earlier builders, Dark Age engineers used natural features where possible to enhance the effectiveness of their constructions.

Perhaps the best known of these linear obstacles, and certainly the most extensive, is Offa's Dyke. It is Britain's longest ancient monument and it criss-crosses the England/Wales border up the Wye Valley to Monmouth, past Hay-on-Wye into the hills of Shropshire and then meanders on into the Clwydian Hills to Prestatyn. Asser, King Alfred's biographer, was the first to record the dyke, and his account points to tensions between King Offa of Mercia and the neighbouring princes of Powys as the reason for its construction. Work on the dyke in Offa's time commenced around 785, when labourers joined together two much older stretches of earthwork, one north and one south. This provided a contiguous embankment, which Asser described as stretching 'from sea to sea'. The dyke is aligned closely to the modern Welsh border and consists

of a rampart and a ditch facing towards the Welsh side. From a military perspective, its position appears to make the best of opportunities to provide surveillance deep into the Welsh countryside. When first built it is estimated to
have been about 90 feet wide, with a vertical dimension of up to 30 feet from
the base of the ditch to the top of the embankment. Many of the smaller dykes
constructed in the late Roman period and afterwards are much less noticeable
today than Offa's, but when surviving sections are traced across the map and
linked together their courses can often be seen to have delineated important
tracts of territory.

The ninth-century history of the region suggests that Offa's Dyke ceased
to have any relevance after a relatively short period, almost certainly because
the invasions of the Danes and their 'Great Heathen Army' presented Mercia
with a much greater threat than that which emanated from Wales. Work and
maintenance on the dyke was abandoned. It is perhaps fair to question the
military value of such constructions, citing the difficulty of defending across
such challenging frontages. But this misunderstands the strategies in place
at the time. We have to credit the Dark Age military commanders with the
ability to establish intelligence-gathering, surveillance and the means to react
effectively to a developing threat on their borders. The models for guarding
such a frontier, such as the Antonine Wall and Hadrian's Wall, had existed on
British soil for over half a millennium before Offa commissioned his defensive works. One can surmise that the considerable effort of construction
would not have been undertaken if the intent to use it militarily was not part
of an overall plan.

There is no written record to indicate how the British tribal territories of
the post-Roman period evolved and what their boundaries might have been.
Archaeological finds are also inconclusive. But particular sites can be identified that re-assumed importance or regained lost influence, particularly rural
military strongholds. In order to assess the distribution of post-Roman British
groups, it is necessary to look back at the period of Roman rule and chart how
the tribal areas of the Ancient Britons were affected by the Roman occupation.
By looking at why boundaries were likely to have shifted as Roman influence
faded, we can make some reasonable judgements regarding the geography of
the post-Roman British kingdoms that came under renewed threat in the fifth
century.

The ancient British tribes

Genetic links between peoples of the British Isles and the European mainland have been identified that date back tens of thousands of years, for example between Welsh and Irish Celts and the Basques of Iberia. Even without
such up-to-date science, the pre-Roman tribal boundaries in Britain have been
known to us for some considerable time, through written records and archaeological discoveries. A number of Britain's ancient tribes shared similar names
with other peoples across Europe. This is not always an indication that related
groups migrated into different regions, because often the names were derived
from a general description such as 'the people of the mountains'. Tacitus, a
Roman historian of the first century AD, remarked on the anthropology of the
British tribes:

> *Who were the original inhabitants of Britain, whether they were indige-
> nous or foreign, is as usual among barbarians, little known. Their physical
> characteristics are various, and from these conclusions may be drawn. The
> red hair and large limbs of the inhabitants of Caledonia point clearly to
> a German origin. The dark complexion of the Silures, their usually curly
> hair, and the fact that Spain is the opposite shore to them, are an evidence
> that Iberians of a former date crossed over and occupied these parts. Those
> who are nearest to the Gauls are also like them, either from the permanent
> influence of original descent, or, because in countries which run out so far to
> meet each other, climate has produced similar physical qualities.*[11]

Tacitus made this assessment on appearance alone, yet modern research confirms he was right to a degree. Once the tribal territories had been conquered,
the Romans divided Britain into administrative areas. For the most part they
delineated each area in accordance with the existing tribal boundaries and
administered it from a regional centre, a city or town called a civitas. We can
therefore be sure that whilst Rome had considerable influence on the way the
Britons were governed, the Roman rulers of Britain did not move populations
wholesale as a matter of policy. Therefore, in broad terms, the Britons who
had to confront Germanic immigration in the fifth century were of the same
stock as those who had succumbed to Rome in the first century. In the second

century, Ptolemy wrote down a set of coordinates that described Britain's geography as he understood it. Although his map of Great Britain is distorted, it is nonetheless recognisable and includes a list of tribes, a rough description of their territories, and the names and coordinates of their major settlements. Map 1 shows what we know today of these Roman administrative territories. The tribal areas are based on Ptolemy's map and other Roman records as interpreted by Rivet.[12]

Despite the Belgae territory having been established at a later date than the other territories (and under different conditions as will be explained), the importance of the natural boundaries already discussed becomes clear. Archaeological evidence broadly supports the map as shown, through a focus on finds of coins or other artefacts. Concentrations of such objects provide a high degree of confidence that the peoples associated with them were present in an area. But the significance of scattered finds is much harder to assess, given that such objects were widely traded. From a military perspective, it is most useful to focus on the natural boundaries between different groups, because that is where territorial disputes are most likely to have erupted.

The coming of the English

We know from archaeological evidence that, as the fourth century gave way to the fifth, Britain's population was already a mix of European peoples, predominantly Celtic but also including descendants of Romans and the auxiliaries or *foederati* hired to fight under their command. We can be reasonably sure from Roman records and supporting archaeological finds that the first significant Germanic populations arrived as early as the second century, when the Romans brought over warrior groups to help them maintain security. Sanctioned immigration of this nature was controlled by the Romans and was by invitation only, evidenced by their establishment of the Saxon Shore defences, designed to protect Britain against raiding, piracy and unwelcome immigration. The unfettered increase in settlers arriving from mainland Europe in post-Roman times added more bloodlines to the mix. To reflect this, historian Norman Davies labelled Britain as 'The Germanico–Celtic Isles' through this period.[13] One could reasonably assume that an event as dramatic as the establishment of Germanic rule in Britain was recorded accurately by earlier historians. Unfortunately, the

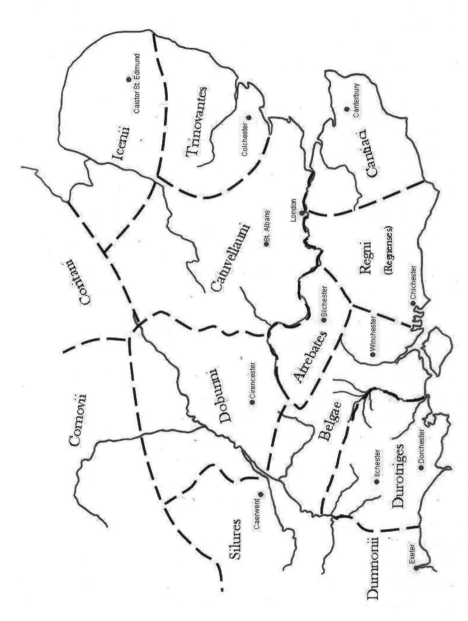

Map 1: Tribal Areas of Roman Britain

reverse is true. It is a period of Britain's history that has at worst been deliberately obfuscated or at best remains riddled with contradictions.

The best known contemporary record of early Germanic immigration to Britain, often referred to as the *adventus Saxonum*, is *De Excidio et Conquestu Britanniae* (On the Ruin and Conquest of Britain), a polemic written by Gildas, a monk who lived in south-west Britain:

> *Then there breaks forth a brood of whelps from the lair of the savage lioness, in three cyulae (keels), as it is expressed in their language, but in ours, in ships of war under full sail, with omens and divinations. In these it was foretold, there being a prophecy firmly relied upon among them, that they should occupy the country to which the bows of their ships were turned, for three hundred years; for one hundred and fifty----that is for half the time----they should make frequent devastations. They sailed out, and at the directions of the unlucky tyrant, first fixed their dreadful talons in the eastern part of the island, as men intending to fight for the country, but more truly to assail it. To these the mother of the brood, finding that success had attended the first contingent, sends out also a larger raft-full of accomplices and curs, which sails over and joins itself to their bastard comrades.*[14]

In his work, compiled in the mid-sixth century, Gildas excoriates the British leadership for their lack of moral fibre in difficult times and demonises the newcomers. The reference to three keels is of interest because the arrival of warriors in three ships occurs in origin stories told of the Picts, the Irish, the Goths and the continental Saxons. Some scholars construe that Gildas was using the figure three in a legendary way, and that he based some of his record on an Anglo-Saxon saga. The reference to a prophecy in the extract above goes some way to support such a perspective.

Other texts that help us to identify approximate dates for migrations to Britain were written by authors whose names are largely lost to us and are collectively known as the *Gallic Chronicles*, usually referred to by the year of their final entries, 452 and 511. These records are particularly useful because they illuminate wider European events. Tellingly, both versions portray the arrival of Germanic peoples to Britain in a negative light. The 452 version records that in 410 'the British provinces were devastated by an incursion of the Saxons', and that by 441 'the British provinces, which to this time had suffered various defeats and misfortunes, are reduced to Saxon rule'.[15] The 452 chronicle survives as a ninth- or tenth-century Carolingian copy and has been attributed to Prosper of Aquitaine who lived c. 390-465. His authorship of this text is unproven, but he is known to have made a written record of events covering the same period and the 511 version concurs on the dates. There is no reason to doubt the broad dates provided by either record, but the implication that all of the British provinces were overrun by 441 is highly misleading.

Modern historians continue to regard Bede as the best of the primary sources for the period. Also known as Saint Bede or the Venerable Bede, he was an English monk at the monastery of Saint Peter at Monkwearmouth and its companion monastery, Saint Paul's, in Jarrow. Both of these towns were in the Kingdom of Northumbria when Bede was compiling his works. His most famous work, *Historia ecclesiastica gentis Anglorum* (The Ecclesiastical History of the English People) was completed around 731 and later earned him the title 'The Father of English History'. His record indicates that Germanic immigration to Britain was initially encouraged:

> *In the year of our Lord 449 Marcian, forty-sixth from Augustus, became emperor with Valentinian and ruled for seven years. At that time the race of the Angles or Saxons, invited by Vortigern, came to Britain.*[16]

Bede's style of writing in the *Historia* seems to have been adopted by the authors of the *Anglo-Saxon Chronicle*. His works avoid the hyperbole associated with Gildas, which adds to his credibility, but it must be borne in mind that he was not located in southern Britain and was recording events long after they happened, using second-hand information. His focus was very much on the history and affairs of the English church, but his works also include some valuable accounts of the early pagan kings and their wars.

For detail and accuracy about the early Germanic kingdoms, we have long been encouraged to rely on either Bede or the *Anglo-Saxon Chronicle*. The latter was lauded by the Reverend James Ingram, who translated it in the early nineteenth century, as 'the second great phenomenon in the history of mankind'. He described it as containing 'many interesting facts relative to our architecture, our agriculture, our coinage, our commerce, our naval and military glory, our laws, our liberty, and our religion'.[17] Unfortunately, it has more recently been judged by academics to be rather dubious and, for the period of the *adventus Saxonum* at least, even argued to be 'largely worthless as history'.[18] Although the *Chronicle* relates events in a clinical and serious tone, it mixes myth with real events when describing the earliest Germanic arrivals to Britain. Many characters have their names associated erroneously with the conquests claimed for them. For example, we know that Wight is derived from the Latin *Vectis*, the Roman name for the Isle of Wight, not from the name of a chieftain called Wihtgar, as the *Chronicle* suggests. Furthermore, dates of earlier recorded events are nowadays considered unreliable by academics. A relevant example concerning the arrival of the first West Saxon leader to Britain is offered by Kirby in his acclaimed survey of Anglo-Saxon history from the sixth to the eighth century, *The Earliest English Kings*:

> *The* Anglo-Saxon Chronicle *attempts a framework for West Saxon history which is unacceptable. The annals place the arrival of Cerdic in 495 and again in 514 and he is said to have succeeded to the kingship in 519 (though Aethelweard, translating the Chronicle in the late tenth century, offers an alternative date of 500).*[19]

One possible reason for the errors, among several explanations of the discrepancies, is that the annalists tried to count backwards from a known point such as 871, when Alfred was enthroned, subtracting the total numbers of regnal years for each successive king. Another possibility is that they used the Dionysian Easter table cycles – cycles of nineteen years – to provide periods in which sequences of events occurred. In other words, they had little idea of exact dates so they tried to simplify the chronology by packaging key events into a sequence that fitted the narrative. Kirby summarises neatly the problems that this causes for any study of the period:

> *The indications are, therefore, that there were a number of alternative schemes for West Saxon chronology by the late ninth century and that none is demonstrably historical. The year 532 for Cerdic's arrival is no more acceptable than 495 or 514 because it depends on the assumption that West Saxon history really was dominated by a single line of kings after Cerdic,*

*ruling in succession, that all their names were known, and that all the reg-
nal figures were correctly preserved. Variants in regnal years in the West
Saxon Genealogical Regnal List and evidence for a multiplicity of kings
show that this was not the case.*[20]

It is clear that the problems inherent in studying the primary sources must be
borne in mind. However, incorporating what we can learn from Bede with the
Anglo-Saxon Chronicle does provide us with a recognisable and acceptable picture of the earliest Germanic kingdoms, except in the case of Wessex, where it
is nowadays clear that the story has been manipulated or is otherwise obscure.

Thomas Hardy's nineteenth-century Wessex is perhaps best-known to us.
His fictional locations are based on places ranging from the Devon-Cornwall
border to Oxford, and along the southern coastline to Portsmouth. By the time
of Alfred's reign, which commenced in 871, Wessex had already absorbed most
of Devon and its northern limits encompassed Bath, Berkshire and southern
parts of Oxfordshire and Gloucestershire. In geographical terms, the borders
of Alfred's Wessex were therefore quite similar to those recognised by Hardy.
But how did they evolve to be so?

The consolidation of a recognisable West Saxon kingdom was a culmination
of a long drawn out and complex series of events in which the whole southern
region of Britain played a part. Until recently, based on written sources, historians had described the expansion of West Saxon influence as progressing
steadily north and west from Hampshire, following the arrival of the early West
Saxon leaders from abroad. It is now clear that this idea is incorrect. To better
understand the emergence of Wessex, it is necessary to combine the information available from the written sources, Bede and the *Chronicle* in particular,
with a consideration of the likely interaction of groups across the whole of
southern Britain, from the Roman period onwards.

Myres, author of the widely acclaimed book *The English Settlements*, was
the first to put forward evidence that both peaceful immigrations and violent
conquests took place, sometimes simultaneously, in different areas of Britain.
In particular, he noted that the earliest immigration along the east coast merited separate consideration to the arrival of Germanic militaristic groups in
Kent and Sussex. He contrasted the slow expansion of the Anglians, primarily as cultivators, with the more warlike events south of the River Thames.[21]

Recent genetic research has shown that neither of these circumstances resulted in the disappearance of the Britons as was generally supposed by historians up to the early twentieth century. They assumed that, whether through conquest or peaceful settlement, the Germanics displaced the Britons wholesale. In an international study published in 2003, Capelli and others sought to provide a more complete assessment of the paternal genetic history of the British Isles. They concluded that the impact of the Anglo-Saxons in the fifth and sixth centuries was minimal when compared to the much larger Danish migrations that commenced in the late eighth century. The major impact from Danish genes remains visible today in the north-east of England, whilst the German/Danish element south of the Thames is limited and the male ancestry of this area 'appears to be predominantly indigenous'. Samples with the smallest German/Danish element all come from areas (Wessex, Sussex and Kent) reputedly settled by Saxons and Jutes.[22] A similar picture arises from the results of another study led by geneticist Mark Thomas of University College, London, published in 2006, which suggested that intermarriage was restricted by the ruling Germanic elite to keep Anglo-Saxon overlords separate from the native Celts who, despite being the majority, were forced into a system of servitude.[23] The suggestion is that Germanic people south of the Thames were in the minority and relied on military superiority to dominate. The process of acculturation, whereby native Britons were tolerated and gradually absorbed into the new English population including through intermarriage, was slower to take effect here than elsewhere in the British Isles.[24]

Archaeological evidence supports the idea that post-Roman Britons did not undergo social collapse. Rather, they resumed a pattern of life that had been established before the Roman period. This included the re-establishment of rural seats of power, indicating a general rejection of Rome's urban centres as places of government. Towns had never been a feature of the pre-Roman landscape. Urbanisation reached a peak in Roman strongholds in the years before AD 300. But the idea of an urban lifestyle simply never caught on with the native British, who preferred to gather temporarily to barter and exchange produce than concentrate and settle in urban centres. As Roman influence waned, many of their towns were abandoned and in disrepair by the fifth century.

The conclusion to be drawn from this brief look at ancient records versus modern research is that early writers described an Anglo-Saxon conquest of

Britain that we now know to be rather simplistic. In order to begin to understand the evolution of the Germanic kingdoms in post-Roman Britain, we need to look in detail at how the Celtic tribal areas evolved through the Roman period and thereafter how they began to absorb the Germanic peoples.

The peoples of post-Roman Britain

From a military perspective it is important to bear in mind that the number of warriors available to the Germanic groups who arrived in Britain was relatively small in the immediate post-Roman period. The term 'warband' is certainly more appropriate than 'army' in most cases. Any deliberate military undertakings would have been carefully decided upon because warbands could ill-afford to lose warriors in meaningless fights. Leaders through these times gained much of their standing via prowess in battle, which is oft emphasised as a trait of the Germanics. Maintaining a position of leadership primarily entailed ensuring that the group survived. Prosperity and lasting glory could only be achieved once security was assured. This was equally applicable to the post-Roman British. What we know of the various groups who fought for control in the south and are therefore most pertinent to the history of early Wessex, is summarised in the following paragraphs.

It has become fashionable for historians to mention kingdoms and sub-kingdoms of the Britons when referring to post-Roman Britain. Unfortunately, there are very few clues as to the nature of these entities or the status of their leaders. The tribes of old were no longer as discernible as they had been prior to Rome's intervention, having been conquered, dispersed or inter-bred with. It is most likely that these kingdoms and sub-kingdoms were amalgamations of related peoples, or more disparate groups. For the most part they probably coalesced under the leadership of warlords in the interests of mutual protection.

As a result of his expeditions in 55 and 54 BC, Caesar concluded that the inhabitants of Kent, the Cantiaci, were 'the most civilised of all these nations'. The first indigenous British coins were probably minted in Kent around the end of the second century BC, after the concept of coinage had been introduced to Britain by the sophisticated Belgae tribes from France and Belgium, who had also established settlements in southern Britain at this time. Caesar is said to have warned the neighbouring Catuvellauni against any aggressive acts but their leader, Cassivellaunus seems to have ignored this advice. Some time after Caesar's departure, and prior to the Claudian invasion of AD 43, the Catuvellauni appear to have conquered and then ruled over both the Trinovantes and the Cantiaci. There is some evidence that suggests this act precipitated the Claudian invasion. All of the evidence proposes that the British tribes of Kent accepted Roman rule and prospered under it. However, once deprived of Rome's protection they were probably left more vulnerable than most to the early Germanic incursions, a situation not helped by their geographical position.

The *Anglo-Saxon Chronicle* entry about the first significant Germanic landings in Kent is probably borrowed from Bede. We can say this because some of Bede's dates were awry by one year, for example the joint rule of Marcian and Valentinian started in 450 but Bede logged it as 449, the same year he posited as the start of the *adventus Saxonum*. The incorrect date for this event is nonetheless replicated in the *Chronicle*:

449. And in their days Hengest and Horsa, invited by Vortigern, king of the Britons, sought out Britain in the landing-place which is named Ebba's Creek, at first to help the Britons, but later they fought against them.[25]

Ebba's Creek (*Ypwines fleot*) is Ebbsfleet in East Kent. Kent was settled by Jutes, acknowledged by Bede as being equals in power to the Angles and Saxons. Bede identifies the northern Jutland peninsula as their homeland, consistent with Tacitus, who named the same location as the land of the Eudoses, later called the Iutae (Jutes). Other theories postulate that the Jutes were more closely associated with the Saxon and Frankish peoples, including the possibility that they migrated south from Jutland before the period of immigration to Britain. This fits equally well with a fifth-century arrival to south-east Britain, because modern Flanders, directly across the English Channel from Kent, was Frankish territory at the time.

It was important for the *Chronicle* authors to ensure that all of their kings could claim direct descent from Woden, a semi-mythical ancestor-god. Hengest and Horsa (stallion and horse) are described in the *Chronicle* as the great-great-grandsons of Woden and, thus, their place in history as opposed to myth is unclear. Horsa is believed to have been killed at Aylesford fighting the Britons under Wurtgern, a name or possibly a title meaning 'high lord' or 'great leader' nowadays usually written as Vortigern. The *Chronicle*, as is often the case when things seem to have gone awry for the Germanics, avoids mention of a result, leading to the assumption that the battle at Aylesford may have been a defeat for the Jutes. Nevertheless, Hengest and his son Oisc are recorded as having continued to advance steadily north to Crayford, whereas the British are recorded as having fled to London. Barbara Yorke, Emeritus Professor of Early Medieval History at the University of Winchester, draws attention to the likelihood that the origins of Germanic Kent, as described in the primary sources, owe much to myth and legend, but also that there is some reliable basis for Bede's account regarding Jutish expansion along the south coast of Britain.[26] Land in Kent was almost certainly handed to Jutes/Franks by the British leadership in return for military service. Whilst there are many gaps and problems of authenticity in the written records, most scholars agree that these mercenaries turned on their British employers, an insurrection that resulted in the initial establishment of Germanic rule over parts of Britain.

Once a Germanic presence was established independently in Kent, we can identify three options for its further expansion: north across the Thames into Essex and East Anglia; inland along the Thames Valley; or west along the south coast. Archaeological finds, such as jewellery recovered from graves, indicate the latter and reveal the spread of Jutish people westward to the Isle of Wight and parts of southern Hampshire. By the later sixth century, the influence of the *Oiscingas* (descendants of Oisc) also spread north into Essex and East Anglia through intermarriage.[27] Germanic Kent was for a long period split into two kingdoms, East and West, and both were relatively rich, through continuing trade links with the Franks, who may even have been overlords of the Jutes in Kent into the sixth century.[28]

Any power the Cantiaci had retained in Kent through being faithful servants to Rome was finally lost when the Romans withdrew and the Germanics arrived in strength. The Germanisation of Kent was a result of the unforeseen consequences of inviting foreign mercenaries to a region that had long since lost any ability to control them. The military strength of the Cantiaci had been eroded over the centuries, first when they were defeated by the neighbouring Catuvellauni and then again under Roman rule. Whether a British Vortigern was the unwitting architect of a Saxon revolt in Britain or whether mythology has provided this picture, the fact remains that Kent was one of the first Germanic kingdoms in Britain, and it was able to wield considerable military power from the outset.

If we accept the narrative of the *Anglo-Saxon Chronicle*, the rise of Germanic power in Kent precipitated a domino effect, whereby Anglo-Saxons steadily conquered the rest of the South East and central-southern Britain, including much of the territory that would later become the large and powerful kingdom of Wessex. Central-southern Britain was perhaps the most volatile and fractured part of post-Roman Britain. It witnessed significant and continuous fighting for control of territory by diverse groups. Despite such turmoil, or arguably because of it, Wessex, the kingdom we might call the crucible of England, emerged in this very region.

In pre-Roman times, a tribe the Romans called the Dobunni occupied the southern part of the Severn Valley and the Cotswolds. Once the tribe was subservient to Rome, Cirencester was established as the civitas for this client kingdom. This action deliberately fractured the original Dobunni tribal region. Gardner made a considered assessment of the fate of the tribe:

> *By AD 43 the south-western tidewater peninsula, from Dorset to Gloucester, was divided between three tribes, the Durotriges of Dorset and south-east Somerset, the Dumnonii of Devon, Cornwall and part of west Somerset and the Dobunni of Gloucestershire and north Somerset.*
>
> *According to Seutonius, Vespasian with his II Legion Augusta, conquered two of these tribes 'with extreme prejudice'. One was presumably the Durotriges to judge by the evidence of a massacre at their great oppidum of Maiden Castle, while the other could well have been the Southern Dobunni, who are major candidates for a similar sort of catastrophe at Worlebury. The Northern Dobunni are thought to have come separately to terms with Aulus Plautius, and thus avoided any recriminations.*
>
> *This apparent division of the Dobunni is reflected in the subsequent Civil Administration as the Imperial authority created a new Canton (of the Belgae) which included north Somerset and was administered from as far away as Winchester. The subservient Gloucestershire Dobunni were allowed their own local civitas at Cirencester (Corinium Dobunorum), thus perpetuating the division between the two sections of the tribe.*[29]

It is significant that this particular division was never repaired. The Wansdyke, an extensive earthen embankment similar to Offa's Dyke, was constructed in the post-Roman era, and marks a clear northern boundary for a militarily powerful region to its south. The territory controlled by the kingdom (or alliance of groups) that built the Wansdyke stretched beyond the original southern Dobunni lands, designated as Belgae territory by Rome. It later became the heart of Wessex, with the West Saxon royal vill initially established at Somerton long before Winchester became the capital. At first glance, it may seem odd that this situation came about, given that the region immediately to the south of the Wansdyke was the homeland of those peoples most stubbornly resistant to early Germanic attempts to invade. Yet, as we shall see, the dynamics of the emergence of Wessex were complex and a 'defenders versus invaders' scenario is nowadays far too simplistic to be taken seriously.

The Atrebates of central southern Britain appear to have been a federation of smaller tribal groups, possibly related to the Atrebates of northern Gaul. At the time of the Claudian invasion they had been clients of Rome for some time. Their territory in Britain was centred on the modern counties of West Sussex, Hampshire and Berkshire, a significant part of Alfred's Wessex. The leader of the Atrebates, Togidubnus, was put in place by the Romans as a client king. His warriors may have fought alongside the Romans against Boudicca, resulting, according to Tacitus, in the gift of land to Togidubnus on the grounds that he had been 'a most faithful ally'.[30] This land may have been to the west of traditional Atrebates territory. An inscription found in Chichester refers to Tiberius Claudius Togidubnus as a 'great king in Britain'. At some point after his death, his kingdom was divided. The northern part retained the Atrebates name and its capital at Silchester, whereas in West Sussex, Chichester became the civitas for the territory of a Celtic tribe called the Regni, who were formerly part of the federation led by the Atrebates.

Stuart Laycock, author of the 2009 book *Warlords – The Struggle for Power in Post-Roman Britain*, proposes that the fate of the Regni, or Regnenses, was similar to that of the British inhabitants of Kent. In Laycock's view this occurred because the Regni may have invited Ælle, king of the South Saxons, to bring warriors and fight on their behalf, only to find themselves betrayed then subjugated by their erstwhile allies.[31] Whether this theory regarding the birth of Sussex has more validity than the traditional view that Ælle simply conquered the Regni is still a matter of debate. However, it is clear that the Germanic kingdom of Sussex was established on territory formerly controlled by the Regni. British peoples from the Sussex region, including the Regni, were killed or displaced by the South Saxons and any who survived the fighting are recorded as having fled north into the Wealden Forest. It is most likely they would eventually have sought refuge in British territories to the north and west, around places such as Winchester and Silchester where warriors with recent combat experience and knowledge of the Saxon foe would have been welcomed.

So who were the South Saxons that gave Sussex its name? According to the *Anglo-Saxon Chronicle*, they landed in Britain in 477 and the consolidation of their Sussex territories under their leader, Ælle, took fourteen years. The end of British resistance in this region was marked by the battle at Pevensey in 491, where Ælle's forces are said to have slaughtered the Britons to the last man. In all likelihood, the majority of the surviving British population remained in place but was subjugated or enslaved. Ælle is named by Bede as the first of the English kings to have held sovereignty over 'all the southern provinces that are divided from the northern by the river Humber'.[32] Such a widespread influence for Ælle is doubtful, given the time he took to establish his rule in Sussex and the lack of any recorded exploits elsewhere. Yet Bede clearly identifies him as a superior leader, even though his territory in 491 was probably limited to a small coastal region between Pevensey and Southampton Water. From this we can surmise that he wielded enough power to attract other Germanic groups to his cause. Ælle's initial options for expanding his territory were limited, primarily because of the physical barrier provided by the Wealden Forest to the north of his coastal kingdom. One possible remnant of Ælle's original northern boundary is the 'Devil's Ditch', 2 miles north of Chichester. Probably constructed originally by the Atrebates tribe in the Iron Age, it is one of a number of earthworks that show evidence of later modifications dating to the medieval period. In the *Chronicle* account, Saxon progress inland from the channel coast was abetted by numerous other Germanic arrivals including Beda, Mela, Port, Stuf, Wihtgar, Cerdic and Cynric. Their collective heroics suit the narrative required by King Alfred, but academics today consider these names to be no more authentic than those of Hengest and Horsa. Wihtgar, for instance, is clearly based on a misunderstanding by the chroniclers, because *Wihtgaraburg* means 'fortress of the inhabitants of Wight' rather than 'Wihtgar's fortress'. What we can say is that there is evidence of Germanic settlements in Ælle's time along the Kent and Sussex coast, but only as far west as the Hampshire Avon. This indicates that the river was a barrier to further expansion. It is a small river, not an extensive natural barrier like the Wealden Forest, and not a physical barrier to progress like the mighty Thames, Humber or Great Ouse. It was a barrier because it was a territorial boundary defended strongly by military forces, the like of which the Anglo-Saxons had not yet encountered in Britain.

Cerdic and Cynric, the first leaders named as West Saxons in the *Chronicle*, are said to have landed in 495 and are credited with leading the annexation of British territory in the lands immediately to the west of Ælle's Sussex:

> *508. Here Cerdic and Cynric killed a certain British king, whose name was* Natanleod, *and 5 thousand men with him – after whom the land as far as* Charford [Cerdices/Cerdic's ford] *was named Netley* [Natanleaga]. [33]

One reason academics doubt the *Chronicle*'s reliability for this period is the apparent repetition of events. Shortly after 508, two more events of significance are recorded, the first of which in 514 appears to repeat the 495 arrival of the West Saxon leaders. The second record is also repetitive and seems designed primarily to emphasise the early and rapid establishment of West Saxon rule:

> *519. Here Cerdic and Cynric succeeded to the kingdom of the West Saxons; and the same year they fought against the Britons at the place they now name Cerdic's Ford. And the royal family of the West Saxons ruled from that day on.*[34]

Archaeological evidence suggests that the Germanic advance was halted at the Hampshire Avon for some thirty years.[35] We can be sure that Charford was an important location, but much less sure that it had any connection with the West Saxons so early on. Once the story of the West Saxons is taken up, the *Chronicle* doesn't mention the South Saxons again until over a century has elapsed, and it provides no clue as to what became of them in the intervening years. We are left to infer that the West Saxons took up the cudgel and were the main players in the conquest of the Britons once Ælle was gone. It is often speculated that Ælle was killed at the Battle of Badon Hill, yet the specific circumstance is unknown, as is the identity of his successor.

The limited conclusions we can make regarding the fight for control of central-southern Britain are first that the South Saxons suffered a severe setback in the Hampshire Avon region, evidenced by their disappearance from subsequent records. Second that the suspect nature of the earliest records of the West Saxons means that the scribes either lacked information or were fabricating, to conceal what was in reality a period of successful British resistance. The most likely scenario seems to be that Ælle was indeed defeated at Badon and that the reign of West Saxon kings was established a good deal later than 519, probably not as a result of any victory at Charford, as will later be explained.

If the *Chronicle* account of the West Saxon landings and conquest of southern Britain is indeed incorrect, then we must look for other clues in order to ascertain how Wessex was established. The evidence available indicates that the ancestors of the kings of Wessex are actually to be found further north, in the Thames Valley. Thus, for a full picture, we must look at the British tribes north of the Thames and how they lost their influence to the Germanics.

The division of former Dobunnic territory enforced by Rome left the Cotswolds and the uppermost parts of the Thames Valley populated by groups that, for the early Roman era at least, can be described as the Northern Dobunni. This area is therefore of particular significance and presents a conundrum, because the early line of Wessex kings appears to have originated here amongst a people called the Gewisse. Yet there is no record of the fate of the Dobunni in the post-Roman upheavals and, therefore, we cannot know what relationship, if any, they had to the Gewisse. In the late sixth century, the westward expansion of the Gewisse under Ceawlin, an early Wessex king according to the *Anglo-Saxon Chronicle*, brought them into what was by then the territory of the Hwicce people in the Gloucester region. The Hwicce and the Gewisse, their possible origins and the warfare that took place across the traditional Dobunni lands are discussed in greater detail in later chapters.

To the east of Dobunni territory (see Map 1), we find the lands of the Catuvellauni, the British tribe who led the resistance to Caesar's first expedition in 54 BC. Their conquest of the Trinovantes and Cantiaci, tribes favoured by Rome, is thought to have prompted Rome's intervention into British affairs in AD 43. Once again it was this tribe that led the resistance to the Roman occupation under their leaders Caratacus and Togodumnus. However, they were eventually crushed and thereafter appear to have accepted Roman rule and even adopted some aspects of the Roman lifestyle, such as urban living. St Albans became a thriving Roman town and London was established at a previously unoccupied site on the north bank of the Thames. As archaeological record shows, Rome's introduction of *foederati* and foreign auxiliaries led to a mixed population in this former British tribal region. It was a simmering pot of warrior peoples, all of them able to meet threat with violence, just the sort of elements that might have expected to prosper because of their military prowess after Roman rule collapsed. Perhaps we find in this volatile mix some pointers to the origins of the mysterious Gewisse, forefathers of the kings of Wessex.

By 571, much of the former territory of the Catuvellauni was controlled by the Gewisse, led by Ceawlin and his fellow warlords, apparently the strongest military power in the region at this time. Understanding how this transition came about is vital if we are to piece together how descendants of the Gewisse kings, based in the Thames Valley, came to consolidate Wessex 200 years later from a power base in Somerset. Both the Gewisse and the West Saxon kings have secured a place in history as founders of Wessex, but the military actions that contributed to this geographical shift of the Wessex power base have proved to be a longstanding enigma for historians. We will return to this in later chapters.

Moving further east from the territory of the Catuvellauni, a tribe called the Trinovantes inhabited a region north of the Thames Estuary, across modern Essex and South Suffolk. Another, the Iceni, occupied what is now Norfolk, parts of North Suffolk and Cambridgeshire. The Claudian invasion helped to restore a measure of power to the Trinovantes following their earlier defeat by the Catuvellauni. Nonetheless, it was the Trinovantes who allied with the Iceni to rebel against Rome in AD 60 under Boudicca. The resulting defeat ensured the end of any significant military power for both tribes. This left a power vacuum in these lands, which Germanic settlers, particularly the Angles, were seemingly able to exploit as Roman power began to wane. The Anglian peoples were later to combine to form the powerful kingdom of Mercia, an alliance that came very close to killing off the kingdom of Wessex in its infancy.

The homeland of the Angles was in the neck of the Jutland peninsula. Arriving in Britain by sea, their ships would have made landfall on the east coast, somewhere between the Humber and the Thames. Most of the Angles arrived incrementally into the estuaries, marshes and fens of East Anglia. Caistor St Edmund, the Roman town of *Venta Icenorum*, is the Romano-British predecessor of the modern county town of Norwich. It was originally the base of the Iceni. It suffered from Germanic raids from the third century onwards, evidenced by the construction of its rampart defences, which date to c. 240–275. There is also archaeological evidence that Germanic settlers lived in small communities in this region from the mid-fourth century. Laycock argues that these settlers occupied strategic spots around the borders of the traditional Catuvellauni and Trinovantes homelands, reflecting a role to help British tribes defend themselves.[36] The Anglian kingdoms of Norfolk and Suffolk were established by the end of the fifth century, at which point the British tribes of old were no longer in evidence.

The archaeology of Essex and East Anglia helps us to measure the spread of Germanic influence. There are concentrations of burials stretching from the north shore of the Thames Estuary to the coastal regions of Norfolk, Cambridgeshire, Lincolnshire and Humberside, but little indication of a Germanic presence in many parts of the interior. Peter Hunter Blair, in his 1963 book *Roman Britain and Early England, 55 B.C. – A.D 871*, suggested that the economic and agricultural conditions of the interior regions were not particularly conducive to settlement:

The chief problem presented by the evidence relating to the settlement of Essex is to reconcile the marked scarcity of pagan burial grounds with the abundance of place-names indicative of settlement in the pagan period. The coast may have been difficult of access because of the many off-shore shoals and sandbanks, and much of its interior may have been unattractive because of its heavy clays. Perhaps the circumstances which gave a poverty-stricken appearance to large parts of Essex in Romano-British times were still prevalent in the fifth and sixth centuries.[37]

Faced with such conditions, it is unsurprising that Germanic immigrants sought to expand away from the fens and wetlands. Archaeological finds associated with certain groups are particularly useful and concentrations of objects, like jewellery and runic items, tell a story. Anglian women wore distinctive ornamental sleeve-fasteners on their dresses, and the distribution of these artefacts is concentrated in areas associated with the kingdoms of the Angles: East Anglia, Mercia and Northumbria. The pattern of settlement these finds reveal is one in which the new arrivals spread gradually inland, initially along the estuary shores and river banks of present day East Anglia and Lincolnshire. The southern boundary of these objects can be defined quite accurately as a line from Ipswich running west to the Bedford/Luton area, where there is a particular concentration in the upper reaches of the Great Ouse River. The negligible finds of such fasteners south of this region indicates that in the early sixth century the Anglian kingdoms were spreading only slowly inland from the east coast. A relatively peaceful occupation seems to have occurred here, at least until the sixth century. However, the Angles later proved to be among the most aggressive and expansionist tribes, especially the Mercians, whose key role in shaping events in Wessex will be examined in due course.

The spread of Germanisation, visible through the archaeology of the South East, took longer to reach the west of Britain. What would later become the heartlands of Wessex were steadfastly British through the sixth century. The Dumnonii, who occupied much of modern-day Somerset and Devon, were most likely an amalgamation of smaller Bronze and Iron Age tribes who had settled in the South West Peninsula. On the arrival of the Romans, they seem to have offered little or no resistance. In turn, the Romans did not garrison the area in any great strength, indicating that Dumnonia was considered stable. The Dumnonii did not embrace the Roman way of life as extensively as some other tribes, and seem to have carried on according to their own traditions throughout the occupation. They did not use coins or establish any large settlements. Exeter was the civitas for Dumnonia, the Brythonic (British) name of which was Dyfneint (pronounced Dove-naynt), from which the modern county name Devon is derived.

A tribe called the Durotriges inhabited Dorset and parts of southern Wiltshire and Somerset. Like the Dumnonii, they appear to have been a federation of smaller tribal groups. They minted coins, but the currency never bore the name of any ruler. The Durotriges continued to occupy hillforts for some time after other groupings had abandoned them, and their tribal area contained by far the highest density of forts in all of Britain. From these defensive bastions they fought extremely hard against the Roman invaders, but could not match the firepower, discipline or engineering skills of the Roman forces. Archaeological finds indicate their resistance at the Maiden Castle and Hod Hill forts in particular. However, they collapsed relatively quickly, and many historians believe they were victims of genocide. Following their defeat, the remnants of the Durotriges were forced to become part of a territory with Dorchester as its civitas. Ilchester was also an important centre and probably a second civitas for the northern Durotriges.[38]

East and north of the Durotriges were the Belgae, administered by the Roman civitas at Winchester. The Belgae were a group of mixed tribes from France and Belgium who had begun to settle in southern England as early as c.110–100 BC. They had Germanic traits, having originated among German tribes who later crossed the Rhine to settle in Gaul.

They gradually extended their settlements into Hertfordshire and Essex, as far as the Catuvellauni territory. This indicates that as relatively new arrivals they were able to integrate across other traditional tribal areas. This may have been partly because the Belgae were the most advanced of the tribes in Britain. Their movement into and across Britain was an expansion rather than a mass migration or conquest. Yet in 1610, William Camden described them as having a more aggressive disposition, 'gat them over into Britaine for to spoile, and in a warlicke manner to invade the country'.[39] By the time of the Roman conquest, they had already developed close trading links between Britain and Gaul. The Belgae territory was a Roman invention, which rewarded the Belgae for their loyalty and helped to divide the more troublesome British tribes such as the Dobunni. Ptolemy names *Aquae Calidae*, which translates as 'hot waters' and is identified as Bath, as part of the Belgae territory, supporting the idea of a deliberate wedge having been driven between the Dobunni and the Durotriges roughly along a line later defined by the Wansdyke. By 688, King Ine's Wessex encompassed most of the former territories of the Durotriges and the Belgae, and in his time the border with Dumnonia became a new front-line in the struggle for control of southern Britain.

Finally, we come to Wales, there to find neighbours and enemies of early Wessex. The Silures of southern Wales were among the fiercest resisters of the Roman occupation, until they were subdued during the governorship of

Sextus Julius Frontinus, c. AD 74–78. The Silures region did not become fully Romanised until early in the second century, when its civitas, Caerwent, was established on a previously unoccupied site. Tacitus refers to the Silures as 'a naturally fierce people'. Their geographical position and interactions with neighbouring kingdoms – Dumnonia in particular – mark them as important players in the emergence of Wessex.

Summary

The new wave of Germanic immigrants to fifth-century Britain settled in the south and east initially, either as newcomers or, in some cases, joining earlier settler groups. The degree of cooperation between the various Germanic groups and their loyalty to their British hosts is debatable, but the circumstances of their arrival are certainly too complex to be described as a conquest. Yet at some point in the latter half of the fifth century, the tensions between Britons and Germanics escalated. Localised conflicts became more widespread. Much of the initial fighting was most likely driven by random events that forced groups to defend their interests, but some leaders also embraced the chaos as an opportunity, as Yorke describes:

> *The breakdown of centralized authority during the subRoman period allowed power to pass into the hands of those who had military forces at their disposal, and various Anglo-Saxon leaders, some of whom may well have had forefathers who had been brought to Britain to provide military protection for the Romano-British, were able to seize the initiative and to establish kingdoms for themselves and their successors.*[40]

Groups who found themselves unable to muster sufficient military strength were in a difficult spot, especially when their territory was adjacent to stronger neighbours. As a result of this complex and chaotic situation, alliances must have been forged both voluntarily and by force.

As the fifth century drew to a close, the increasing Germanic presence in the southern and eastern coastal regions was looking to expand across the nearest available farmland. British peoples of varying influence and strength still controlled the majority of territory, but they were under pressure from raids, internecine conflict and the general lack of security that had prevailed since the collapse of Roman authority. Germanic war leaders and their forces threatened to advance into exclusively British areas. Early scribes and historians introduced terms like 'barbarian invasions' to describe the growing Germanic presence in Britain. However, this phrase and others like it are no longer considered appropriate or accurate. Compared with the prosperity of the Roman years, it is easy to see why Gildas chose to describe the chaos and war that ensued when the Romans departed as 'the ruin of Britain'. From a Germanic perspective, it could just as easily be described as the making of England.

Chapter Two

The Hampshire Avon Frontier

Man has drawn artificial lines on the chest of the Mother Earth, which have no significance, except for the sake of war and clashes between countries.   – Girdhar Joshi

Badon Hill and the written sources

Gildas provides a British perspective on the escalation of violence as the early Germanic presence in southern Britain grew in strength. In his polemic, he describes a desperate situation for the Britons, who were seemingly unable to mount an effective resistance until they were victorious at the Battle of Badon Hill:

> *After a certain length of time the cruel robbers returned to their home. A remnant, to whom wretched citizens flock from different places on every side, as eagerly as a hive of bees when a storm is threatening, praying at the same time unto Him with their whole heart, and, as is said,*
>
> Burdening the air with unnumbered prayers,
>
> *that they should not be utterly destroyed, take up arms and challenge their victors to battle under Ambrosius Aurelianus. He was a man of unassuming character, who, alone of the Roman race chanced to survive in the shock of such a storm (as his parents, people undoubtedly clad in the purple, had been killed in it), whose offspring in our days have greatly degenerated from their ancestral nobleness. To these men, by the Lord's favour, there came victory.*
>
> *26. From that time, the citizens were sometimes victorious, sometimes the enemy, in order that the Lord, according to His wont, might try in this nation the Israel of to-day, whether it loves Him or not. This continued up to the year of the siege of Badon Hill, and of almost the last great slaughter inflicted upon the rascally crew. And this commences, a fact I know, as the forty-fourth year, with one month now elapsed; it is also the year of my birth.*[1]

Bede interpreted Gildas as having meant that the siege at Badon took place forty-four years after the arrival of the Germanics, but the sentence referring to the year is open to other interpretations and the meaning of it has never been resolved, despite much scholarly debate.[2] Some believe Gildas meant that the battle occurred forty-four years previous to the time in which he wrote this, but that exact time is unclear. Forty-four years after the coming of the Saxons to the south coast would suggest a date somewhere in the 490s, whereas the same period 'before his time of writing' extends the possibilities up to c. 520. Moving the *Chronicle* dates around according to different interpretations of the Easter cycles makes little difference to this broad timeframe. The circumstantial evidence of the reverse migrations and a *Welsh Annals* record that states the battle was in 516 together add weight to an argument for a date after the 490s. Any later than the 520s would negate the very credible idea that the Germanic switch of emphasis to Theodoric's campaign in Thuringia was partly a result of their reversal of fortune in Britain around this time. The next discernible period of heavier fighting between Germanics and Britons seems to have begun in the 560s, so there is no conflict between Badon having been fought as late as 520 and Gildas having written his works towards the end of the period of peace he describes.[3]

In relation to the emergence of Wessex, a precise date for the battle is irrelevant because there is no record of Gewisse or West Saxon involvement. The importance of this battle is that it was the first successful defence by Britons of territory that they would later cede to Wessex. Defining its place in history helps greatly towards understanding how the campaigns that followed eventually forced the end of British rule in the region, allowing the most influential of all Saxon kingdoms to emerge. It is enough to assign the siege of Badon Hill a date in the late fifth or early sixth century, around the time that aggressive attempts to expand by Germanic groups reached a decisive moment. Gildas' record is unique because he writes about the battle as a recent event, before folklore and legend crept in and reduced the credibility of subsequent accounts. He may be short on detail, but his description of the general situation agrees well-enough with what few facts are known.

The words used by Gildas, 'the cruel robbers returned to their home', indicate that Germanic military operations in Britain at this time were expeditionary, seasonal and subject to interruptions. This weighs against a scenario whereby Germanic armies advanced rapidly across British territory. The 'return to home' did not involve leaving the shores of Britain, but saw them withdrawing to those regions they had already secured. Breaks in campaigning were essential for warriors to work their settled lands. The planting and harvesting of crops and the need to survive through winter took precedence over fighting for much of the year. In the early years of Germanic involvement in Britain, military operations are unlikely to have been mounted too far from the home base, and most of the fighting would have occurred in those zones that became frontiers between British and Germanic dominated territories. Expeditionary raids by boat might sometimes have achieved greater reach, but would have involved smaller forces and been riskier than border scuffles. Similarly, incursions overland, deep into enemy territory, would have presented the same serious challenges that Caesar had faced, namely protecting the expeditionary force and the logistic support required to sustain it. Alternatively, raiding was a relatively quick and opportunistic activity, with the aim to plunder treasure, slaves and food. Therefore, Gildas guides us reasonably well when he describes the Germanic military activity as the work of 'cruel robbers'. It is highly likely that a multitude of armed groups were engaged in raiding. However, the serious business of expanding territory was conducted in the frontier regions and required a more enduring military presence.

The *Welsh Annals*, or *Annales Cambriae*, written c. 970, record events from 447 to 957 and it is thought that the authors may have derived their information from earlier sources, possibly from their own interpretation of Nennius, a Welsh monk and scribe of the ninth century most famous for ascribing twelve battles to Arthur. These annals appear to add some valuable detail about Badon, but the mythical content renders them unreliable:

516: The Battle of Badon, in which Arthur carried the Cross of Our Lord Jesus Christ for three days and three nights on his shoulders and the Britons were the victors.[4]

The word 'shoulders' might well be a mistranslation of 'shield', a more likely symbol-bearing object for a war leader, Christian or otherwise. The stated duration of the battle is an interesting conundrum. 'Three days and three nights' is often thought to exemplify the convention of saga writing

– everything in threes, three kings, three ships, etc – and therefore indicative of the annalists borrowing from other sources. On the other hand, a three-day duration would be realistic for a siege, the term used by Gildas, which implies a battle wherein the defenders are behind fortifications that the attackers must breach. The *Welsh Annals* also record a second battle at Badon in 665 (its possible locations will be considered in due course). Research by David Dumville, a British medievalist and Celtic scholar, and others into the authenticity of the *Welsh Annals* has concluded that the Arthur entries were probably added in the tenth century.[5] Academics mostly accept that the Arthurian entries have little validity, which obviously doesn't help anyone trying to use them to identify real battle sites. This is a particular disappointment because many of the older records in the *Welsh Annals* refer to events and personalities that are accepted as historically authentic. For example, the Annals record the onset of a plague in 537 along with the battle at Camlann, and they record the death of King Maelgwyn of Gwynedd from a 'yellow plague' in 547. Research into ancient tree-growth has shown that a change in climate occurred from c. 535, a meteorological phenomenon that could have contributed to an outbreak of plague.

In fact, there are countless blind alleys to explore if one tries to use Arthur as a basis for research. Academics and amateur scholars have attempted to link Arthur to real people and places, yet these efforts have led to a confusing multiplicity of Arthurian legends, what Dr Caitlin Green, a historian of late Roman and early medieval Britain, has described as a 'monstrous regiment of Arthurs'.[6] The difference between fact and fantasy can be difficult to discern in many books and articles. Mike Ashley is a prolific British bibliographer, author and editor. Most of his works are in the fields of science fiction and fantasy, but there are also works of gravitas like *British Monarchs*, published in 1998 and sub-titled *The Complete Genealogy, Gazetteer, and Biographical Encyclopedia of the Kings & Queens of Britain*. In this we are told that:

> *What is significant is that Oisc is the only English king named at the Battle of Badon where Arthur was victorious. Since Aelle was, at this time, regarded as the sovereign English ruler, Oisc was evidently fighting under his command, but Arthur destroyed the Saxon armies and we may presume that Oisc was killed.*[7]

In a later publication, *The Mammoth Book of King Arthur*, Ashley adds another character to the roll of battle:

> *I am not convinced that the Octha who fought at Badon, according to the story in* The Dream of Rhonabwy, *is the same as Aesc (or Oisc) from whom the rulers of Kent were descended.*[8]

Unfortunately, there is scant substance to any of this. *The Dream of Rhonabwy* was written somewhere in the late twelfth century and may be derived in part from earlier Welsh interpretations of the Arthur stories. Based on Arthurian legend, Ælle is often cited as having been defeated and/or killed at Badon, sometimes along with Oisc and one or more of their sons. However, there is no substantial evidence for this. It remains folklore and, thus, any search for historical events surrounding a 'real Arthur' is no more than a distraction. In seeking the location of Badon Hill and other lost battle sites, we have to accept that very little informa-tion can be derived from the written sources. Effort is better directed towards the search for other evidence, in particular to identify the pressure points in time and space that ignited the wars between the Germanic newcomers and the post-Ro-man peoples of Britain. Geographical pressure points would have included those natural boundaries that represented a 'line in the sand' for the Britons, where no further territory would be ceded without a fight. In terms of time, we can use the written sources and archaeology together, at least to derive a sequence of events and assess rough dates for when the key boundaries were contested.

Evidence in the landscape

The livelihood of the Germanic settlers relied on land that needed to be tended. Raiding adjacent lands for booty and slaves was relatively straightforward com-pared to capturing or defending territory, which required significant organisation and forward planning. Archaeological finds have revealed facts about where the first Germanic inhabitants settled and, of equal importance, where they did not. Map 2, derived from C.J. Arnold's *An Archaeology of the Early Anglo-Saxon Kingdoms*, indicates small areas of dense settlement in Kent and Sussex, compared to a more extensive geographical spread in the Anglian kingdoms.[9] This demonstrates that the kingdoms of Kent and Sussex in particular were constrained in the early days

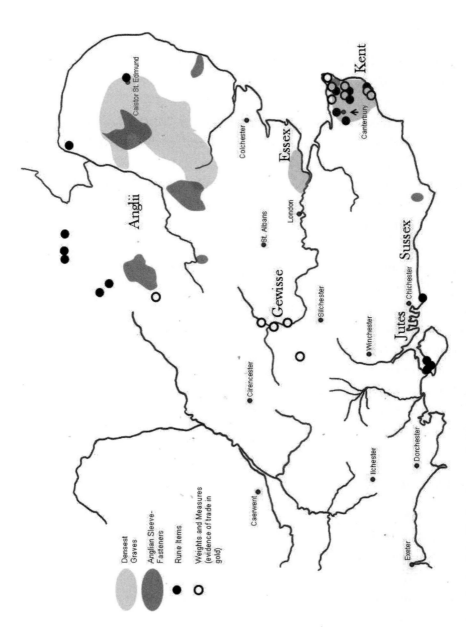

Map 2: Archaeology of the Early Germanic Kingdoms

of Germanic settlement, by geographical features as already described but also, in all likelihood, because adjacent lands were defended robustly. Also noteworthy is the identification of a wealthy settlement in the Thames Valley with Germanic traits, often assumed to be the Gewisse. Were these people newly arrived Anglo-Saxons? The sum of available evidence says they were not, an assumption that will be explained later, insofar as explanation is possible.

It is clear that the forests of the High Weald divided the Kent and Sussex kingdoms and defined the borders of both for some time. The Weald had been a valuable resource for the Ancient Britons and the Romans, who mined it extensively and cut it for firewood, mostly to support a well-developed iron-making industry. The Romans managed such woodland actively, including its regeneration, even introducing new species of trees. When this type of management resumed it continued into the medieval period. However, it was not an activity associated with the early Germanics. The physical barrier of the Weald offered a natural defence for the Britons and ensured that the early Saxon and Jute occupation was confined to a coastal strip:

> *The southern part of Hampshire became more closely tied to a South Coast system that stretched loosely from Kent to Wight than to one that looked north. The northern chalklands and the Silchester clays were more affected by developments in the Upper Thames Valley.*[10]

The Hampshire Avon stands out as a geographical pressure point, a frontier of strategic importance in the fifth century, along which battles were fought between Germanics and Britons. Together these battles made up a military campaign which, from the Germanic perspective, aimed to expand the 'South Coast system'. We know from the archaeology that the pattern of expansion of the Germanic kingdoms in Kent and Sussex described in the *Chronicle* is broadly accurate. That this expansion was slow and incremental reflects the significant amount of time required by the Germanic expeditionary forces to settle and secure their own areas. Any group seizing an area by force would need to ensure security prior to settling the lands with their families. Only once a new community was self-sufficient and safe could its warriors contemplate further military expeditions.

In 1913, Major had already identified that the Germanic expansion was concentrated along the south coast. He also identified the need to consolidate and the strategic value of the Hampshire Avon as reasons why the Germanic advance stalled there for a significant period:

> ... *there was the imperative need to settle, consolidate and cultivate the new-won lands. The earlier stages of the Saxon conquest were precisely similar in detail to the later Danish occupations of parts of England, and we have very definite statements that Danish advances ceased while the chiefs were apportioning and tilling their conquered districts. Wessex at this time had reached a frontier which was defensible against the Britons, and at the same time hard to pass. The land within it was sufficient for the time, and there was no reason why the hazard of a further extension of territory should be incurred. The statement of the definite assumption of king-ship at this time is clear evidence that the period of aggression had been succeeded by the wished-for period of organisation.*
>
> *It is noteworthy that a full generation elapsed before any further advance on the part of Wessex is recorded.*[11]

Major is following the *Chronicle* when he refers to the further advance by Wessex, but the doubt that nowadays hovers over anything derived from the written sources must be borne in mind. What he does go on to illustrate accurately is the difficulties the settlers faced in maintaining the momentum of their military efforts despite the pressures on them to do so once populations began to outstrip resources. In so doing he introduces his own views on the Battle of Badon Hill:

> ... *the increase of population in the thirty years would make expansion as imperative to the Saxons of Wessex as to any overpopulated Danish district, which must needs send its sons on the Viking path. This feature of the long inactivity of Wessex between 519 and the victory at Searobyrig in 552 has been very largely overlooked, but it is most important so important indeed that there is no need to seek for a British victory to account for the halt. It must be realised that the Wessex hosts were by no means enormous, that they were only able to win their way onward step by step, and that they were at a very great distance from any reinforcements. They had come to win a new home, and had won it. They were able to hold what*

they had won [in] Hampshire but any immediate attempt at extension of territory must have been out of the question.[12]

Major is referring to the Battle of Badon Hill when he states 'there is no need to seek a British victory to account for the halt'. Later in his book, he mentions the possibility of a battle at Badon Hill, but opines that any attempt to place it on the map or date it would amount to mere speculation. In rejecting the idea of a decisive battle at Badon, Major put himself directly at odds with Godsal, his contemporary Edwardian author. Godsal was convinced that, from their earliest landings, Germanic groups worked together to raise large armies to attack strategic objectives, mainly towns. He argued that London was the single most important military objective for a combined Germanic force of Jutes, Angles and Saxons:

The site of the city of London, whether occupied by a town or not, must have always been, as it is to-day, the strategic centre of England. After London, then, the river Thames must always have been the dominant strategic feature of the country, as the fleet and army that held the course of that river could, by means of a judicious use of it, choose its own time and place for fighting. Without saying a word against the courage and energy of the English and their Saxon brothers (for the Saxons were more than mere allies), it may be confidently stated that if after the crushing victory of Crayford they did not proceed to take London, and thenceforward, as time and opportunity allowed, push up the course of the Thames, then as soldiers, in the higher and professional sense of the word, they were contemptible. Apart from the paralysis that the capture of London would bring to the defence of the British, we have to consider the abject folly of invaders who would neglect to secure this noble port of entry and place for their fleets to refit and equip.[13]

Godsal's argument demonstrates military knowledge. However, it transmogrifies Major's more realistic idea of small armies with restricted ambitions into one led by grand military strategy. Julia Crick, a professor of palaeography and manuscript studies, once described Godsal's ideas as 'fundamentally misguided'. Godsal's assessments are certainly difficult to reconcile with the likely military activities of the age. Major, on the other hand, presented a cogent argument and a more credible narrative. However, it is also important to note that Major's dismissal of a decisive battle in the Hampshire Avon region ignores the most compelling argument for it – that Ælle and his South Saxons disappear abruptly both from history and from the archaeological record at the end of the fifth century. That alone requires explanation.

Most experts now agree that Germanic military operations in the fifth and sixth centuries were prosecuted by relatively small forces, and that Germanic colonisation by force was characterised by sporadic aggression, rather than by protracted, large-scale warfare. The evidence points to a state of enhanced military preparedness in most tribes, and warfare was characterised by short, localised campaigns. This was in part because significant reinforcements were required before launching a new offensive, and each such action was limited in its aims by the combat power available. The number of warriors available was itself determined by the overall population. Yet as populations increased, so did the need for more territory to support them. Along the southern coast of Britain, Germanic consolidation of territory westwards as far as the Hampshire Avon is an identifiable tipping point. It represents a point at which a combined Germanic military force was capable of prosecuting a more ambitious campaign, and also a time at which such a campaign became necessary to relieve overcrowding.

The period in which the Hampshire Avon was both a boundary and a focal point for conflict coincides with the time of Ælle's rule. Bede's record of Ælle's status, as a leader who held *imperium* over other Germanic kingdoms, points to his likely dominance over the settled groups along the south coast.[14] It is therefore probable that he did lead those groups in their military efforts, in which they collectively faced the numerical superiority of the Britons west of the Hampshire Avon. Ælle's campaign, the first identifiable joint enterprise by Germanic groups, provides the most likely scenario for Badon Hill.

Post-Roman Britain and the 'Celtic Revival'

The picture of how Germanic settlement developed east of the Hampshire Avon is relatively clear. What we must now determine is what was happening in the neighbouring British territories. If we can discern how the Britons organised themselves for war, then we can better assess the likely course of the subsequent conflict. Gildas described the devastation and squalor of Britain after Roman rule. While there are no written records to contradict his account, some archaeological evidence shows that Celtic art was resurgent in Britain at this time, suggesting that civilisation had not entirely collapsed. Grinsell is among those who have investigated the abidance of Celtic traditions, as the Roman presence in Britain declined:

> *One of the earth-fast water-jars from Linwood had a hand-made lid formed specially to fit it, and this lid was incised (before being fired) with a remarkable design embodying a man with outstretched arms, a man on a horse resembling the Uffington White Horse, and a woman drawn in a 'Celtic Art' style. The whole of this design suggests survival or revival of Celtic art towards the end of the Roman period – for which there is evidence from other sources.*[15]

Other recent archaeological discoveries suggest that the culture of the Britons in some areas remained relatively undisturbed from the fourth century to the sixth, particularly in the west and north of Britain.[16] However, it cannot be asserted that a similar benign situation existed in the South East, where the increasing presence of the Germanics was causing friction. A lack of cohesion among the British groupings in Kent, Sussex and Hampshire no doubt contributed to their ineffectiveness to resist attacks, but it is also likely that the immigrants were already too numerous and established to be countered easily. This situation would have been noted by British leaders in the South West, where we know that extensive preparations for war were made. Evidence of the re-occupation of older rural strongholds, and the construction of new defensive works, reinforces the picture of escalating tensions. Faced with the turmoil brewing on their borders, military leaders would have considered the advantages of cooperating with neighbours. In order to assess where they might have formed alliances, it is necessary to piece together the fragmentary evidence that exists, and to make judgements based on the geography of their territories.

Attempts by historians to bring clarity to this period often infer that Roman administrative territories remained in place until the establishment of the first recognisable Anglo-Saxon kingdoms, but that is unlikely and misleading. Given that the Belgae territory was a Roman invention, for example, we should not assume that its artificially created boundaries were recognised after Roman rule ended. Because they aligned with natural features, some older tribal boundaries might have regained significance when Rome's urban centres were abandoned or neglected. The post-Roman kings and war chiefs seem generally to have favoured the rural-based lifestyle that Britons had embraced before the Roman occupation. Leaders reverted to rural seats of power and their territories were likely bounded by defensible features rather than lines on the map created for administrative purposes. However, the degree to which the ancient tribal territories were re-established must be measured against the effects of hundreds of years of new immigration and foreign rule. There were many new groups arriving to Britain and this, following on from the subjugation and fragmentation of the ancient British tribes under Rome, ensured that many changes were irreversible. This was particularly true in the former lands of those tribes who had suffered most from Rome's invasion and occupation of Britain, such as the Durotriges and Dobunni.

It helps to look at traditional areas of settlement to form an idea of the possibilities for new territorial boundaries, or the reversion to old ones. In central southern Britain, areas of habitation can be traced back to Neolithic times, by looking at the distribution of burial mounds. Through the Iron Age, the high chalk downs continued to provide habitation for large numbers of people, and the tribal territories of southern Britain with their numerous hillforts began to take shape. The post-Roman period gave rise to new and extensive earthworks that are not aligned with the Iron Age or Roman era boundaries. Among the most significant of these earthworks, which indicate where new territorial boundaries emerged in the post-Roman period, are Bokerley Dyke and Wansdyke.

The Bokerley territory

The earliest sections of Bokerley Dyke are described by archaeologists as having originated in the Bronze Age. Construction continued into the Early Iron Age. The dyke defines a boundary between areas that show markedly different patterns of land division related back to the Bronze Age.[17] Other Bronze Age boundaries, including several sections of a dyke called Grim's Ditch, criss-cross this particular area. In some cases, these older works were partially dismantled to provide materials for an enhanced Bokerley Dyke, probably constructed in three stages over some seventy-five years in all, with the initial build occurring c. AD 325-30.[18] Coin finds indicate that it was completed, to the length still

visible today, around AD 400. The earthwork is bivallate, the larger bank is on
its south side, and therefore it can be defined as a defensive line for a territory
in southern Dorset. This territory appears to have been defined by its occupants as Roman influence waned. It would have encompassed the high chalk
region of Cranborne Chase, the valleys of the Allen, Tarrant and Stour rivers,
and numerous Iron Age hillforts, including large constructions at Hod Hill,
Hambledon Hill and Badbury Rings. The line of high ground that Bokerley
Dyke follows extends south-east within 3 miles of the Hampshire Avon, a probable eastern boundary for the territory. To the south, it is assumed that the
territory of the Bokerley peoples would have extended all the way to the sea.

Two important pieces of evidence suggest that early Germanic incursions
had an effect on this territory. The first is the status of Hengistbury Head, a
promontory to the south of Christchurch Harbour, where the Hampshire Avon
meets the sea. The Head, named after Hengest, is one of the oldest maritime
sites of importance in Europe. Between 1979 and 1984, evidence of ancient
quarrying for gravel was discovered along the shoreline, which appeared to
have been carried out in order to extract ballast for ships crossing the English
Channel as early as the first century BC.[19] The Head was also important
throughout the Iron Age, providing a sheltered harbour, a ready supply of
charcoal from the nearby forest areas for smelting, and an abundance of iron-
stone doggers – small boulders with a layered structure that can contain as
much as thirty per cent iron by weight. Trade in iron from Hengistbury peaked
in pre-Roman times before declining through the Roman occupation, probably because the Romans preferred to transport the raw material for processing
in a more efficient and centralised manner. Iron extraction at the site ended
abruptly with the Roman withdrawal from Britain, despite an abundance of
doggers still available, indicating that the promontory became unsafe as raids
and piracy by Germanic forces increased.[20]

The second piece of evidence for Germanic pressure on the Bokerley region
is provided by the original Hampshire county boundary, one of the many border lines that were established when the Germanic kingdoms took shape. In
places along the Avon, the expected natural boundary, the border diverts to
take in territory west of the river. The old boundary of Hampshire enclosed
Bournemouth and ran as far north as the small hillfort at Dudsbury on the
River Stour, suggesting that a Germanic incursion upriver may have pushed

back the early frontier with the British. This reinforces the evidence of early Germanic annexation of Hengistbury Head, not for its iron or gravel reserves, but because it was an easily defended location with a safe harbour, which provided access to the navigable stretches of the rivers Stour and Avon.

Another major deviation of the Hampshire boundary occurs in the Fordingbridge/Charford area. Major attributed this to Saxon gains as a result of a battle at Charford, recorded in the *Chronicle* as having been fought in 519:

> *The result of the battle remains evident in two tongues of Hampshire territory, which run up north-westward into Wiltshire beyond and opposite Charford. The northernmost of these extends for about two miles and a half beyond the river and comprises North Charford and Breamore Downs. It is bounded at the extremity by a section of Grim's Ditch, an earthwork which may have been an ancient tribal boundary, though its date has not been determined and its exact course and object is uncertain. The name seems to indicate that the Saxons found it already in existence and did not know its makers. The southernmost of these two tongues extends up the valley of the Rockbourne and over Rockbourne Down for some five miles from the river. It cuts the probable course of an eastern section of Grim's Ditch, and its furthest point N.W. just touches the northerly section. Its southern boundary just before reaching Grim's Ditch runs through the centre of the little camp at Damerham Knoll. Between these two strips of Hampshire Whitsbury Down thrusts eastward a finger of land, barely a mile across, crowned with the stronghold already described.[21]*

The stronghold referred to is Castle Ditches at Whitsbury. Major points out that Charford as the 'point of attack' for this Saxon offensive was chosen because the forest to the south and east met the open chalk downs to the north-west, making it a natural place to breach the Avon barrier. Castle Ditches is one of the largest hillforts close to the Avon. It was refortified in the sixth or seventh century and the only evidence found of its occupation in this period was Romano-British.[22] It was an important objective for the Germanics, as they tried to push back the frontier.

Another obvious and important objective lies further south. Named *Vinocladia* by the Romans, the most extensive and important Iron Age hillfort nearest the Avon is Badbury Rings. It lies near Wimborne in Dorset, just less than 10 miles west of the Hampshire Avon and 16 miles from Charford. Three embankments and ditches enclose more than 17 acres. Several important ancient routes converged at Badbury Rings, including the track from Salisbury, which turned west and continued to Dorchester. To the south, Badbury was linked by Roman military road to Lake Farm and to Hamworthy, where Vespasian made landfall. Lake Farm was the forward assembly area and logistic base for Vespasian's campaign. Badbury Rings was the first hillfort he captured from the British.[23] Having secured Badbury Rings, the Romans continued the road from Lake Farm northwards, but immediately north of the hillfort it forked into three, an unusual construction except where roads had an exclusively military purpose. The three roads, to Hod Hill, Bath and Sarum, were likely to have been constructed to enable Vespasian's campaign to subdue the Durotriges in AD 47.[24] Hamworthy, a defensible promontory within Poole Harbour, was just as ideal and attractive in the Dark Ages as it had been in Roman times, offering benevolent tides and extensive sheltered mud flats. Poole Harbour's importance for the seafaring Germanics cannot be overlooked. Its northernmost creeks reach within 5 miles of the land routes that converge at Badbury. The capture of Badbury Rings and its immediate surroundings would have reaped two additional bonuses – control over Poole Harbour and the nullification of Bokerley Dyke as a defensive obstacle. Bokerley Dyke countered a land-based threat from the north, and it is usually assumed to have played a role in resisting the spread of the Germanics into Dorset. It was evidently constructed by a militaristic Romano-British grouping that held out against Germanic expansion for a considerable period of time. Such resistance would not have been possible in this area had Badbury Rings fallen, because that would have allowed the Germanics to bypass the Bokerley defences.

Many historians agree on the significance of the Hampshire Avon as a flashpoint in the conflict between the Germanics and the Britons. Among them is Edwin Guest, a Victorian era English antiquary who published numerous papers on Roman-British history. He made a detailed study of place-names that supports the military evidence and identifies the Hampshire Avon as part of a frontier zone between the Germanics and the British. He argues that the frontier remained in place for a considerable period from the early sixth century. He also suggested that Badbury Rings was a likely location for Badon Hill, and rejected Bath and other previously named sites as unlikely.[25]

The Wansdyke territory

Wansdyke is an impressive bank and ditch earthwork. Its two discrete sections span 40 miles between the Dundry Hills near Bristol and Savernake Forest south of Marlborough. It is orientated such that its defenders would have occupied the territory of northern Somerset and Wiltshire to its south, and would have used it to protect themselves against an enemy coming from the Cotswolds and Upper Thames Valley to the north. Also known as Woden's Dyke, it is most often described as having been constructed by post-Roman Britons as a defence against the Anglo-Saxons. Archaeological finds support this and suggest that the majority of the dyke was probably built between 410 and 500. Given its location, the 'Britons' who constructed it would have included a significant number of descendants of the advanced Belgae peoples, who had been integrating in the region for centuries. Its earliest origins may date to Roman times and its fairly crude construct of turf and timber is similar to that of the Antonine Wall in Scotland. Certainly, it was already in existence when Ceawlin, named in the *Chronicle* as a West Saxon king, is also said to have defeated the British at nearby Dyrham in 577. Godsal, like some other early authors, was mistaken in his belief that the newly arrived Anglo-Saxons were responsible for its construction.[26]

Although separate sections of Wansdyke were not necessarily built at the same time, their alignment shows that they delineate a single boundary. The two main sections are linked by a Roman road, and it is possible that the dyke was intended to be completed along this path. The eventual plan may even have been to extend it westwards to the Bristol Channel. The gap between the two complete sections aligns with the course of the Bristol Avon in a manner that appears deliberate. The dyke, as an obstacle, complements the river such that together they provide a defensive boundary. Whatever the exact original plans for its course and construction, Wansdyke was clearly an important line of demarcation and a defensive structure. It would have required a large, well-organised workforce for construction and maintenance, and a properly coordinated military effort to patrol and defend it effectively.

Scholars continue to debate the origins of Wansdyke, but it is now widely accepted that it marks the northern boundary of a territory occupied by post-Roman Britons. It is aligned with the northern boundary of the Iron Age Durotriges tribe, and its eastern limit is on a discernible ridge of ground close to the source of the River Bourne, which flows south to join the Hampshire Avon at Salisbury. This suggests that those rivers continued to provide a natural eastern boundary for the post-Roman territory, just as they had in the Iron Age for the Durotriges. Amesbury, on the Avon, was recorded in a Saxon charter in c. 880 as *Ambresbyrig*, which translates as 'the stronghold of Ambrosius', recalling the British war leader hailed as a saviour of the Britons by Gildas.

Wansdyke's unfinished state can be explained in part by the evolving situation in the fifth and sixth centuries, when the threat posed by neighbouring British kingdoms was overtaken by the greater threat of Germanic invasion. It was likely built originally to help demarcate and protect the peoples inhabiting the territory to its south from rival British groups to the north. Its scale suggests that a rich and powerful people were behind it. Yet if Ambrosius Aurelianus had managed to unite the Britons in the former Roman territories of the Atrebates, Belgae and further west, as Laycock suggests, then Wansdyke's role as a frontier would have lost much of its relevance because the groups it had separated were now allied.[27] In consequence, by the early sixth century, as the new Germanic threat materialised along the Hampshire Avon, the military emphasis shifted and work on the dyke was probably abandoned at this time. The Bristol Channel to the west and the Hampshire Avon to the east are obvious borders for a British territory originally bounded by the dyke. This obstacle later reassumed significance as a British defensive structure when the focus of conflict shifted to the Thames Valley region.

The case for the existence of a militarily powerful British group or alliance in the region of Wansdyke is strengthened when one considers the defeat of Ceawlin of Wessex in 592, which probably took place at Woden's Barrow, as will be discussed in detail later. Woden's Barrow lies on a chalk ridge that overlooks the Pewsey Vale near Alton Barnes. Wansdyke follows another ridge feature three-quarters of a mile away to the north. As the dyke descends eastwards to lower ground, it remains overlooked by the highest of the chalk ridges extending east from Woden's Barrow. Seeking to move south into this region, Ceawlin likely came into conflict with the same alliance of peoples that had formed under

Ambrosius. Their ancestors had proved too strong for Ælle and his allies and were still powerful and organised enough to defeat Ceawlin. The Bokerley and Wansdyke territories may have been separate entities when the Romans departed, but common interest seems to have made the peoples there into allies against the emerging Germanic threat. The strength of this alliance explains in part how Dorset was retained under British control until the late seventh century.

The Central South

East of the Hampshire Avon and north into the Thames Valley, we can identify a number of British groups who came under immediate Germanic threat in the sixth century. British resistance appears to have been solid in Winchester (*Caer Gwinntguic*) and Silchester (*Caer Celemion*). Archaeological evidence demonstrates that the Silchester Britons held out through the fifth and into the sixth century, despite incremental Germanic encroachment. Winchester's proximity to the coast and the emerging threat from the South Saxons is reason to suspect its early demise as a British kingdom, but it presents something of an enigma. There is evidence that the town peaked in the third century and, thereafter, declined in common with other urban centres as the post-Roman Britons re-adopted the rural lifestyle that had been their preference before Romanisation took hold. However, rather than being abandoned in post-Roman times, Winchester was refortified:

> At Winchester, for example, the main south gate of the Roman city was so effectively blocked in two stages during the fifth and sixth centuries by walling and a ditch dug across the road, that all traffic from the south had for many years to enter by a minor gate further east, later known as Kingsgate ... Before it was put out of use in this drastic way the south gate road (Margary 42b) would have been the direct route between Venta and the late Roman fortress at Clausentum (now Bitterne) nine miles away near the mouth of the Itchen. It looks as if there came a moment in these dark centuries when the rulers of Venta and Clausentum were on opposite sides in some unrecorded sub-Roman conflict.[28]

Burials from the period in the Lankhills cemetery at Winchester are of a military nature and include late Roman military artefacts. From a strategic perspective, British Winchester in the immediate post-Roman period would have been under considerable threat from Germanic raiders utilising the Meon and Solent as waterways. The town would have been dangerously isolated once more cohesive land-based military operations were initiated by nearby Germanic groups. Finds close to the town at Twyford Down are Saxon and are thought to be from the seventh century. They include approximately eleven burials, many accompanied by grave goods including beads, daggers and a scramaseax, the dagger favoured by Germanic warriors from which the appellation 'Saxon' is derived. Three or four other Anglo-Saxon cemeteries of the same period are also to be found in and around Winchester.

By the time of the earliest Anglo-Saxon burials found at Winchester, it is clear that Britons in the South East and Thames Valley regions had been living alongside groups of Germanics like the Belgae for a considerable time. The levels of enmity present and the pattern of Germanic settlement (specifically how it was divided between hired mercenaries, other invited groups and unwelcome invaders) is unclear. There is archaeological evidence that a moderately sized community of Anglo-Saxons was settled at Abingdon in c. 425, and the Middle Seaxe grouping was establishing a presence on the fringes of London as early as the mid-fifth century.[29] British defences around Silchester were expanded between 410 and 450, indicating a growing threat that was probably Germanic.[30] British groups remained in Berkshire, Wiltshire and northern Hampshire – roughly the former Atrebates territory – into the seventh century. Archaeology reveals few early Saxon finds in these territories, but there is evidence of British military burials, including what are thought to be combat casualties.

North of London, the British kingdom of *Cynwidion*, encompassing much of Northamptonshire and Bedfordshire, had a significant British presence into the seventh century. It appears to have been founded by Cynfelyn, son of the Pennine king Arthwys, who moved south into the Chiltern Hills in the fifth century. His son later altered the name to *Calchwynedd* or Chalk Hills to reflect the kingdom's location. This kingdom came under considerable pressure from its inception. The *Iclingas*, forefathers of the powerful Mercian kings, were spreading south. Other Angles were immediately to the east. Evidence suggests that despite this pressure, there was a Celtic presence in the area well into the seventh century. Celtic settlement in the London area dates back earlier than 500 BC, but the present city expanded from a wooden bridge constructed by Roman engineers near to the site of the present-day London Bridge. London was an important haven and operating base for the post-Roman Britons, who resisted the Jutish occupation of Kent. There is little to be found in London by way of Anglo-Saxon artefacts and it seems likely that it remained in British hands until the latter part of the sixth century.

Sussex and the south-east pocket

British territories around Silchester, and across Dorset and Wiltshire, stood firm against the Germanic incursions at least into the sixth century, probably because they were part of a 'western alliance' under the leadership of the Ambrosius dynasty. Dumnonia and Siluria were still some way west of the threat, but their interests would have been served by a strong British defence of the whole region, and thus they might also have contributed troops. Ælle, seeking to expand his fledgling coastal kingdom of Sussex, would have seen that he could not win a war outright against an enemy as powerful and organised as that led by Ambrosius. Nevertheless, he would have considered his forces more than capable of continuing to make incremental gains because he had sufficient combat power to cherry-pick a piece of territory and thereafter defend it robustly. The decision facing him was whether to try and make such progress northwards to reach the Thames region or westwards along the coast. Both courses of action involved a degree of risk, but the former was discernibly the most dangerous. A move north risked pitching his forces against Silchester and into the chaos of several factions fighting for supremacy in the Thames basin and surrounding areas. To achieve success, Ælle's army would have to undertake a long inland journey, away from their coastal sites in Sussex and cut off by inhospitable forest from those established territories. The alternative, an offensive against the British in the South West, offered the chance of a more measured and incremental campaign with the all-important coastline close at hand.

The potential rewards for any of the Jutish peoples in Kent joining a venture led by Ælle are clear. Kent was a powerful and established kingdom, yet it was also constrained, geographically by the Thames Estuary and the Weald, and militarily by the enduring British presence around London. This explains in part why its leaders continued to further their interests alongside their Anglian cousins to the north, effectively bypassing London. Also, Kent could not afford a war against

Sussex under Ælle, a new and powerful neighbour. It therefore had to strike a delicate balance, protecting its own position whilst seeking to avoid any tensions with the increasingly hemmed-in South Saxons. The Jutes, further along the south coast, were in a similar situation, and perhaps viewed collaboration with Ælle's Sussex as their best hope for security and expansion. Evidence that the Jutes, already identified as settling in the Isle of Wight and south Hampshire, maintained close links to Kent has been emerging for some time:[31]

> *The scatter of objects reported now as being found in the Itchen valley south of Winchester at St Cross and Shawford, such as a supporting-arm brooch, hints at 'Anglo-Saxon' culture arriving well back in the fifth century even in an area previously thought to lack any such evidence (Stedman 2003; id. 2004). It may not be the objects themselves, however, that define identity so much as the way that they were worn; Stoodley considers that there is enough variation between the women's graves in north and south Hampshire to show that the latter had stronger links to East Kent, giving credibility to the 'Jutish' affiliations of the area known to Bede.*[32]

Based on the lack of any mention of Ælle and his South Saxons in the *Anglo-Saxon Chronicle* for the time that coincides with the aftermath of the battle at Badon Hill, Sussex appears to have collapsed and failed to recover for several generations. We can be fairly sure that the lack of any mention of the battle in the *Chronicle* points to a heavy defeat for the Germanics, despite Sussex having been initially one of the most dominant and militarily successful of the early Germanic kingdoms. Kent, and any other Jutish allies, seem to have been less badly affected. This points perhaps to them having supplied warriors in support of the effort without gambling everything on the result like the South Saxons seem to have done. Certainly, the Jutes appear to have flourished through these post-Badon times and were able to consolidate their territories along the south coast as far as Christchurch Harbour, but no further west, which reinforces the theory that the Britons west of the Hampshire Avon were conspicuously strong.[33]

There is no doubt that the situation along the south coast changed once Germanic forces reached the Hampshire Avon. They were unable to make significant further headway against a strong and well-organised British resistance.

There is no record or suggestion that any campaign progressed significantly westwards across the Hampshire Avon, and it seems that this frontier remained a focus for friction far into the sixth century. Around the time of Badon, we can see that Ælle and his Germanic neighbours were being held in check by British forces and by the natural barrier of The Weald. They were effectively trapped in what we can call a south-east pocket. To break out would probably have required the combined strength of an alliance, the formation of the largest Germanic army yet seen in Britain. A campaign led by Ælle to break out of the pocket can be argued, making the likely location of Badon Hill along the south coast in the environs of the Hampshire Avon frontier. It is impossible to pinpoint exactly when this campaign happened, but the context, specifically the known spread of Germanic dominance along the south coast, indicates a date that coincides with the siege mentioned by Gildas.

Summary

Map 3 illustrates the assessed situation immediately prior to the Badon campaign, when the hitherto successful Germanic expansion was stalled by resistance from the Britons. The approximate borders of the Wansdyke and Bokerley territories have been assessed by using the alignments of the defensive earthworks and the approximate known boundaries of Dumnonia and *Caer Celemion*. On the British side of the Avon, the hillfort defences and Bokerley Dyke held firm, but a Germanic presence that had been building in strength for some time managed to breach the frontier in places. Thus, some ground west of the river was ceded by the British, specifically lands upriver from Christchurch Harbour and in the Charford region. A significant battle became inevitable once the Germanics attempted to push deeper into the lands west of the Hampshire Avon. Military logic dictates that such an attempt would have been made in the immediate area of the gains already established in order to build on earlier success. Once we embrace these assumptions and use them to narrow the search for Badon, Badbury Rings stands out as a likely site for the battle because it became crucial to the defence of a frontier that was under threat. In the next chapters we will examine in more detail how the conflict along this frontier progressed.

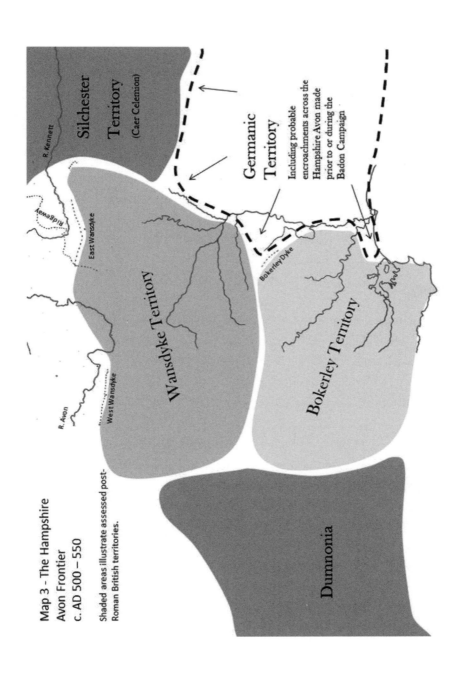

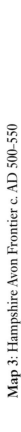

Map 3 - The Hampshire
Avon Frontier
c. AD 500 – 550

Shaded areas illustrate assessed post-
Roman British territories.

Map 3: Hampshire Avon Frontier c. AD 500-550

Chapter Three

Doctrine, Organisation and Tactics

Notions of chance and fate are the preoccupation of men engaged in rash undertakings — Cormac McCarthy, *Blood Meridian*

Military doctrine

In order to thoroughly assess the campaigns and battles of post-Roman Britain, it is essential to first understand the thought processes and considerations that led military commanders to act as they did. Only then can we assess whether the result of any particular military action was due to effective planning and execution, or to chance and fate. The essential elements of military planning, and the principles behind them, have changed little in three millennia of recorded conflict. This is why commanders of today still study ancient campaigns and battles. In the twenty-first century, many of the more developed armed forces embrace the concept of 'effects-based operations', a strategy derived from what they call a manoeuvrist doctrine. Whilst the terminology may be relatively new, the basic ideas that underpin this doctrine have been familiar to commanders since ancient times.

Effects-based operations are planned and executed from a perspective whereby commanders first study their enemy before deciding their own plan. Through reaching a detailed understanding of what the enemy is trying to achieve and how he is likely to go about it, the commander constructs his plan by envisaging the circumstances and conditions that will arise on the battlefield. From this he decides on some specific effects that will thwart the enemy plan and the actions his own forces must undertake to achieve those effects. He also pays attention to the environment, particularly the terrain and weather where combat operations are expected to take place. When planning, he will try to deduce how the enemy is likely to fight across any particular geographical area based on the information and intelligence he has obtained about the enemy's capabilities and *modus operandi*. If necessary information is missing, he will direct his surveillance and reconnaissance assets to find it. The end result of this process is a combined analysis of enemy forces and environment, which helps the commander to decide how best to outwit and defeat his opponent.

In written sources, the kings who fought in post-Roman Britain are often lauded for their victories. Yet there is negligible information about how, as commanders, they planned and executed their campaigns and battles. Occasionally, the texts hint at aspects of their characters. For instance, the *Anglo-Saxon Chronicle* emphasises the efforts of Ida, the first Northumbrian king, in building 'Bamburgh, which was first enclosed with a stockade and thereafter with a wall'.[1] We can surmise from this perhaps that Ida had some gift for defensive engineering, but there are precious few such clues as to how kings and war leaders behaved. In order to assess their effectiveness, we must form a view of their likely motives and their means of achieving their military aims. Then we must match these against the known achievements of the kingdoms and the peoples they led. Through an understanding of the forces they commanded and what was involved in the tasks that they undertook, we can perhaps add to the sparse information provided by primary sources.

History tells us that the most successful military commanders were often masters of thorough planning, but of paramount importance was their ability to make timely and effective decisions. At Salamanca in 1812, Wellington had already planned to withdraw his army to avoid being outflanked. But on seeing that the French Army had become strung out and vulnerable whilst marching parallel to his own, he instead committed immediately to the attack, which brought him victory. Such manoeuvres are as old as time. At Gaugamela in 331 BC, Alexander forced the Persian army to keep pace with his Macedonians in a parallel march, and then attacked as soon as a gap opened in the Persian lines. Such lessons endure precisely because they remain relevant. A primary aim of effects-based planning is to help the modern commander defeat his opponent in the swiftest and least costly manner.

In today's British military doctrine, effects are defined as the consequences of actions. For example, DISRUPT; DELAY; DESTROY. (It is common practice in modern military writing, for example in written orders for an operation, to write the effect in capital letters.) The effects are achieved on the enemy through various activities, all of which are subject to the actions and reactions of the enemy and the influence of the environment. The effects that the commander wishes to achieve guide his planning and help him and his staff to decide how best to employ the available combat power. A vitally important part of the commander's preparation for battle is the crafting of his 'concept of operations'. This concept always includes a clear statement of the commander's intent, defined as 'a succinct summary of the effects he intends to achieve over the enemy and the environment, related in time and space'. Once his intent has been made clear, the commander will define a scheme of manoeuvre, which is a short but broad description of how his forces will move and operate. He will also clarify what is to be the main effort (the single most crucial task or effect) and he will name the subordinate commander charged to conduct it. The main effort will normally be the most decisive act that the commander considers it necessary to achieve in order to obtain victory.[2]

The statement of intent is usually supported by a schematic, which need only be a simple diagram that the commander uses to show his subordinates what he wants each of them to accomplish. It helps them understand how their actions relate to each other and where they need to be synchronised in order to achieve the desired effects. This is not new. Throughout history, effective commanders like Hannibal have known that use of overwhelming force is not the only way to succeed. Instead, they have been adept at identifying those effects that will lead to the enemy's collapse. At the battle of Cannae in 216 BC, Hannibal predicted how the numerically superior Romans would fight and then he trapped them using a double envelopment manoeuvre that has been lauded by military experts ever since. Such a commander, with the ability to get inside the mind of his opponent, can second-guess the enemy courses of action and counter them more easily. The enemy thus becomes dislocated and unable to respond quickly, their plan unravels and initiative and momentum are lost. It follows from this that an early and important focus for the commander and his staff following a manoeuvrist doctrine will be on reconnaissance and the gathering of information and intelligence. This will be achieved by analysing known information and by tasking reconnaissance forces to gather that which is not known.

Today, the terrain and accompanying climatic conditions where operations take place are referred to as the battlespace. Commanders have long paid heed to the conditions in which they expect to fight and have tried to seek advantage whenever possible. In many cases, the environment has introduced an element of random luck. Cassius Dio, a Roman senator and historian, detailed the tactics used by the Germanic commanders Arminius and Segimer on mainland Europe in the autumn of AD 9. Leading an alliance of tribes known to have included the Cherusci, the Bructeri and the Marsi, Arminius and Segimer wiped out three Roman legions led by Varus in forests near mod-ern-day Osnabrück. Roman losses numbered roughly 23,000, against estimated losses for the Germanic tribes of roughly 7,000, in what came to be known as the Varian disaster:

> *The next day they advanced in a little better order, and even reached open country, though they did not get off without loss. Upon setting out from there they plunged into the woods again, where they defended themselves against their assailants, but suffered their heaviest losses while doing so. For since they had to form their lines in a narrow space, in order that the cavalry and infantry together might run down the enemy, they collided frequently with one another and with the trees.*
>
> *They were still advancing when the fourth day dawned, and again a heavy downpour and violent wind assailed them, preventing them from going for-ward and even from standing securely, and moreover depriving them of the use of their weapons. For they could not handle their bows or their javelins with any success, nor, for that matter, their shields, which were thoroughly soaked. Their opponents, on the other hand, being for the most part lightly equipped, and able to approach and retire freely, suffered less from the storm. Furthermore, the enemy's forces had greatly increased, as many of those who had at first wavered joined them, largely in the hope of plunder, and thus they could more easily encircle and strike down the Romans, whose ranks were now thinned, many having perished in the earlier fighting.*[3]

Varus suffered bad luck with the weather and there is no doubt that the Germanic tribes were better able to exploit the conditions and the terrain. It is less clear to what degree this was down to good Germanic planning or poor decisions by Varus. The record of Germanic waverers joining 'in the hope of plunder' indicates a somewhat haphazard development of events. The campaign serves well as an example of the chaos that can occur in combat due to random factors, but we must look elsewhere to demonstrate the deliberate application of effects-based operations in the ancient world.

Chaeronea

Philip II of Macedon was able to manipulate his enemy in a deliberate fashion and was skilled in using his forces to achieve victory in battle, even when they were outnumbered, and success looked unlikely. One of his greatest triumphs was the Battle of Chaeronea, fought on 2 August 338 BC. Macedonian intervention had brought about the end of a period known as the Third Sacred War, in which the Greek City States to the south of Macedonia had fought each other. With its military dominance established and Greek power diminished by civil war, Macedonia was in a position to exploit this opportunity to expand its influence. This threatened Persia, who sent troops to assist the towns of Byzantium and Perinthus. Athens and Thebes declared war on Macedonia at the same time and Philip was forced to break-off his campaign to address this new threat.

Philip needed to break the best army that Greece could muster in order to maintain his ambition to march southwards on Thebes and Athens. He confronted the Greek Army as it deployed in an attempt to block him on the plains near the town of Chaeronea. The Greeks deployed in a line with mountains to their left and an area of boggy ground and river on their right, deliberately blocking Philip's intended route. Philip assessed that the key to victory in these particular circumstances was the destruction of just one enemy unit, the Theban Sacred Band. The Band was the stuff of legend, an elite group of 300 men comprising pairs of lovers who would fight to the death to protect one another. They had never been broken in combat. Philip reasoned that defeating the Band would likely cause a general collapse of the Greek Army. Philip's Macedonian force totalled 32,000. In theory, particularly as he was obliged to attack in order to progress his campaign, he was at a disadvantage facing the combined Athenians and Thebans at some 35,000-strong on their chosen terrain.

The effects that Philip assessed would be decisive were made clear to his commanders prior to battle:

- BREACH the Greek line
- DESTROY the Sacred Band

Philip's schematic might well have been sketched into the sand, as his commanders stood around him on the eve of battle. It would have looked something like the diagram in Figure 1. The sketch is deliberately uncluttered. The whole point of an intent schematic is that it can be easily understood by those who must carry out the plan. Philip's subordinates would have been clear about their starting dispositions and were well-drilled in how to assemble for battle in good order. On the right, Philip would be deliberately visible leading a feint against the Greek left flank. In the centre, his infantry would advance at an oblique angle, an innovative tactic thought to have been first developed by Philip. Key to this scheme of manoeuvre was that the tightly packed formations of the enemy would react in the way he desired. The Greek left would be tempted into a pursuit if they could be fooled into thinking their enemy's commander was beaten. This would create space on the Greek left and begin to loosen the cohesion of the Greek lines. To enhance this effect, the oblique advance would cause the Greek centre to move crabwise as the Greek commanders sought to align their troops for combat in the way they were accustomed. The overall effect would be to separate the main body of the Greek Army from the more disciplined and elite Sacred Band. Once this was achieved, Alexander was tasked with the main effort, to lead his cavalry through the gap and surround and destroy the Sacred Band.

The battle unfolded exactly as Philip wanted (see Figure 2). He led the right flank of his army in person as planned. This included his *hypaspists*, a royal guard of mobile infantry that ensured his presence on this part of the battle-field could not go unnoticed. He deliberately appeared to fail in his attack and turned and fled with his men in apparent disarray. It was a perfect feint. Seeing the opposing king in such a state, the Athenians on the Greek left launched a wild pursuit. This, together with the Greek centre's attempts to meet the oblique advance, opened a gap in the Greek line just as Philip had intended. Alexander, only 18 years old, charged into the gap at the head of his famed com-panion cavalry, who encircled and destroyed the Thebans on the Greek right. The Sacred Band put up a predictably brave defence, but once surrounded and isolated they were no match for cavalry. As Philip had anticipated, the defeat of this one unit precipitated a general collapse in morale and the Greek Army broke and fled the field. On the battlefields of antiquity, cohesion was every-thing. Massed ranks standing firm were the key to success. But if just one part of such a tight formation broke, the whole army could become destabilised. This was particularly the case when 'ordinary' troops saw an elite unit collapse.

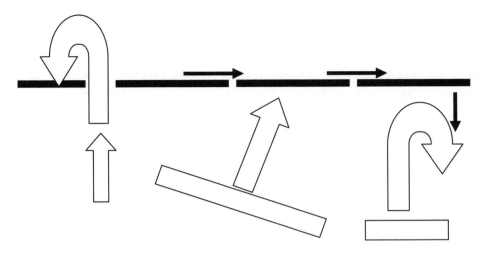

Figure 1: Philip II's Intent Schematic for the Battle of Chaeronea

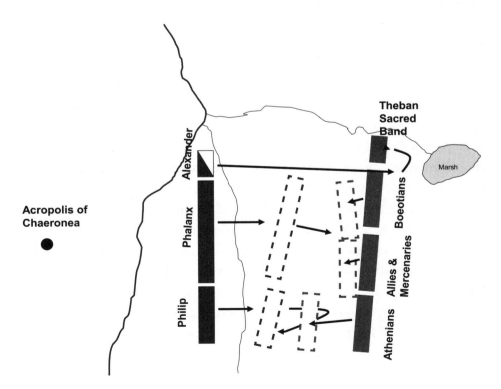

Figure 2: Battle of Chaeronea

There was more to Philip's victory than knowing which part of the Greek lines to attack in strength. He had advanced the technology of the time with lighter armour for his troops to enable faster manoeuvring, and longer *sarissas* (spears) to provide better reach in close combat. His light infantry, cavalry and the phalanx were well-coordinated in battle and able to perform a series of manoeuvres, including feints, oblique charges and encirclements, deliberately combined to confuse a slower and less imaginative opponent. In order to achieve this, he trained his troops hard and effectively. They were mentally and physically tough. All of this ensured he could achieve the effects he desired in battle. Chaeronea is an example of the ancient application of what we call manoeuvrist doctrine today.

Developing a military plan

Military planning takes place at three distinct levels – tactical, operational and strategic. Chaeronea was a battlefield success, a tactical victory that allowed Philip to continue his operation. The operational level is that 'at which campaigns and major operations are planned, conducted and sustained to achieve strategic objectives within theatres or areas of operations'.[4] Svechin, a Russian military theorist, explains that 'tactics form the steps from which operational leaps are assembled; strategy points out the path'.[5] Activities at the operational level link tactics to strategy by establishing campaign objectives in pursuit of a strategic intent. In 1544, King Henry VIII laid siege to Boulogne. At the operational level, his campaign objective was the return of this region of France to English rule. Yet Henry's efforts formed part of a much more ambitious scheme. The strategic intent was for England, in alliance with the Holy Roman Empire under Charles V, to subjugate the whole of France.

The early Germanic warbands in Britain cannot be said to have followed any cohesive military strategy, nor can the British, at least initially. However, as Germanic numbers grew and British resistance stiffened, both sides were forced to look at the bigger picture and focus on planning at the operational level. For those on the offensive, a sustainable and realistic plan was required to capture new areas to settle. The geographical areas that the Germanic commanders deliberately targeted can be considered their campaign objectives.

Having determined his desired effects, today's commander will then provide broad guidance to his staff officers, who will develop the details of the plan. Consideration will be given to the specific part of the enemy's structure or deployment on which each effect is to occur. This will include: analysis of the enemy intent and how best to thwart it; the known and likely enemy dispositions; enemy strengths (to avoid); and enemy weaknesses (to exploit). From this analysis, a commander will prioritise tasks in his plan and consider how he might be constrained in achieving them. At Chaeronea, the plan to feint on the right, advance obliquely in the centre and break the Sacred Band on the left amounted to three tasks. Each task was assigned to a separate element of the Macedonian Army. Consideration of the resources available is vital to ensure that each element of the force is properly supplied and equipped to achieve its nominated task.

Once the tasks are determined, they need to be synchronised to deliver the effects with maximum efficiency. Some activities will be simultaneous, often to enhance surprise or to deliver shock action. Others will be sequential, particularly when one task depends upon the completion of another. For example, Philip had to create the split before Alexander could launch his cavalry, whereas the oblique advance and feint were simultaneous actions. Once the tasks and their coordination are made clear, necessary control measures are imposed, such as defining the boundaries between units, giving a time by which a task must be complete, or limiting an action deliberately. For example, a line on the ground may be defined as a 'limit of exploitation' in order to keep the overall force cohesive, thus avoiding problematic actions such as the unplanned and over-exuberant pursuit of a fleeing enemy.

As the plan develops, a number of different courses of action will usually come to the fore. Each will be assessed for strengths, weaknesses and feasibility. A key consideration will be whether enough troops are available. If not, the problem may need solving strategically, for instance by accepting a level of risk in one area to ensure that another is supported to the maximum. An experienced commander will also consider what contingency plans he needs to make if events don't unfold as planned. Given enough time, he will plan to counter enemy actions that he considers unlikely but possible. He will formulate his own plan based on the most likely enemy course of action, and will bear in mind what the enemy might do in the worst possible case. This will usually lead him to form a reserve force. The placing of the reserve force is vitally important – it must be situated in a place of relative safety and be able to move swiftly to battle when it is needed.

With all of these considerations in mind, let us look at the military capabilities of the Dark Age British and Germanic commanders to assess how they might have planned and conducted their campaigns.

Romano-British forces

Successful military commanders have long heeded the lessons of history. The notable accomplishments of Roman forces on the battlefields of antiquity inevitably influenced military action for centuries to come. It is safe to assume that a post-Roman British commander would have drawn heavily upon handed-down expertise and experience in order to establish, equip and train military units. The traditional ferocity of the Celts can only have added to the potential for a remarkably capable military force.

The late Roman Empire had given rise to military forces of supreme professionalism and these were increasingly drawn from the stock of the occupied territories. Roman auxiliary forces were well-trained and disciplined, drilled in the Roman way of warfare but also fiercely proud of their tribal heritage and specialist skills. For example, Batavian cavalry were renowned for their ability to cross rivers and are thought to have played a key role under Aulus Plautius in AD 43, when they crossed the River Medway during a critical engagement that secured the earliest Roman gains in Kent. This surprise manoeuvre was instrumental in neutralising the threat from the federated British force, which was forced to withdraw north of the Thames. It is likely that such specialist skills were preserved amongst the post-Roman British and that their basic military structure was similar to that of the later Roman frontier armies, known as *limitanei* or *riparii*. This structure was a mix of infantry and cavalry in variously sized units that were assembled together according to role and task. Significantly, the late Romans had made a policy of keeping infantry and cavalry in separate units, rather than embedding mounted troops with infantry units as had previously been the case. It was also late Roman practice to divide units of *limitanei* into sub-units in order to occupy a number of small fortified bases. The landscape of southern Britain with its hilly terrain and Iron Age forts was particularly suitable for this sort of deployment.

Whilst a typical Roman legion is thought to have been around 1,000-strong, it was actually organised according to task so the number of soldiers in any given legion varied. A legion was actually the sum of its detachments, meaning that up to 5,000 troops could be grouped together and still constitute a legion. What we can reasonably assume is that a British commander influenced by Roman doctrine would not have thought in terms of fixed sizes for units or rigid deployment plans. Instead he would have employed a flexible grouping designed to achieve his purpose. In a defensive posture, as we postulate for the Britons at the time of Badon Hill, the British commander would have planned primarily to hold his ground, but would have recognised also the requirement for a mobile force to strike effectively at the enemy when an opportunity arose.

Infantry

There is no record that details the organisation of post-Roman British infantry, but it is safe to surmise that they were an eclectic mix of British tribesmen and remnants drawn from former Roman auxiliaries. They might well have included warriors of Germanic descent prepared to fight against the newer Germanic arrivals. In a Roman legion, auxiliary infantry supplemented the heavily armoured legionary units in a variety of ways, including the provision of lighter and more mobile spearmen, slingers and archers. Whilst the exact numbers of men in a legion varied (as already described), the basic organisation was always the same. The smallest unit was the *contubernium* (tent group), made up of eight soldiers who shared a tent, a mule and eating equipment. These were organised into units called centuries under the command of a centurion. A century typically had eighty soldiers, rather than a hundred as might be assumed. The basic fighting unit was a cohort, comprising six centuries. A legion was composed of a number of cohorts, with the first cohort including extra personnel like clerks, engineers, and other specialists who did not usually fight. Auxiliary soldiers were also organised in cohorts and usually served under the command of Roman officers, though sometimes they fought under command of their own chiefs.

Post-Roman British infantry were most likely equipped and organised similarly to Roman auxiliary infantry or *pedites*. There may have been professional elements under the command of British warlords, but the bulk of an army would have been found from levies, part-time fighters who were liable to be mobilised in times of need. The basic weapon would have been a spear and certainly the full-time warriors would have carried a shield. Few, if any, would have been armed with swords, though they may have carried a long knife similar to the *seaxe*. Most would have been without armour and without helmets – that kind of equipment was the preserve of professional soldiers and the higher classes. Missile weapons may have included javelins for professional warriors and slings or bows for the levies. The sling was a favoured weapon among the Celtic tribes and even the youngest warriors were able to launch a stone with deadly accuracy and power.

Cavalry

In the early years of the Republic, the Roman cavalry was an elite force drawn from the aristocracy. However, this situation did not endure:

> *By the early first century, the relationship between cavalry service and membership in the elite had changed. Elite youths were no longer required to perform cavalry service, and many young men served, at most, a token year or two in the military. This lapse in military obligations is itself a marked change from the middle Republic. What is even more striking, substantial numbers of young Romans held political office in the first century without serving more than a year or two in the military, a practice that contravened the established custom of the middle Republic. At the same time foreign auxiliary cavalry completely replaced both the citizen cavalry contingents and those supplied by the Italian allies. By the end of the Republic, the link between a military service record and membership in the Roman elite had diminished greatly.*[6]

By the early fifth century, cavalry units were predominantly made up of foreign auxiliaries and had been for some considerable time. Dio records that 5,500 Sarmatian cavalry were posted to Britain by Marcus Aurelius in AD 175.

This force subsequently disappears from the records, except that one *ala* (cavalry regiment), the *Cuneus Sarmatarum*, is known to have been stationed at Ribchester, thus accounting for 500 of the Sarmatians. This *ala* appears to have remained at Ribchester until the end of Roman rule. Certainly, it is recorded there in the *Notitia Dignitatum*, a record generally considered to be up to date for the Western Empire in the 420s. Nothing is known about the other 5,000, but we can surmise that they were stationed around Britain.

Two fragments of a tombstone found at Chester in 1890 show a horseman wearing a cloak and a conical helmet. He is holding a dragon standard and is armed with a sword. Both man and horse are depicted as being clad in tight-fitting scale armour. This attire was characteristic of Sarmatian or Alanian heavy cavalry. The Alans were an Iranian nomadic group among the Sarmatians. The dragon standard depicted on the Chester stone was also characteristic of the Sarmatian military. It had a metal head and a cloth body designed like a windsock, which gave it a semblance of life in a breeze. It has been suggested that these standards served not only the traditional purpose of marking a unit's position in battle, but also that they indicated the wind direction for the Sarmatian archers. There are other records of auxiliary cavalry units serving Rome in Britain, particularly of units raised from the Frisii of Holland, one each at Papcastle, Housesteads and Binchester. Another unit of unknown origin was based at Brougham.[7]

British military groupings continued to employ cavalry after the Romans withdrew. We can be sure of this because the Anglo-Saxons referred to British cavalry as *horswealhas*. János Makkay, a Hungarian academic, proposed that descendants of Roman auxiliary cavalry forces, in particular the Sarmatians, provide the historical basis for King Arthur's armoured knights:

> *The closed society of Sarmatian* cataphractarii *in Britain was able to maintain its ethnic features during the Late Roman period and afterwards. One reason is that their troops, called* cuneus Sarmatorum, equitum Sarmatorum Bremetennacensium Gordianorum *were not part of any military organization in active service. Consequently, after the withdrawal of the Roman army, they continued to live on their accustomed sites (Chester, Ribchester, etc.). They were still called Sarmatians after 250 years. A semihistoric Arthur lived about A.D. 500. He was very probably*

a descendant of those Alan horsemen, a battle leader of the Romanized Celts and Britons against the Anglo-Saxons, who invaded Britain after the Roman army had withdrawn. Arthur and his military leaders could therefore manage to train the natives as armoured horseman after Iranian patterns against the attacks of Angles and Saxons fighting on feet until their victory at Badon Hill.[8]

This scenario has been explored in historical fiction and film. It is doubtful that Roman-era cavalry forces remained unchanged down the centuries. We similarly cannot envisage British cavalry at the time of Badon Hill as conforming to the exact organisation and tactics of the Roman *alae*. What we can follow are threads in some records, particularly the *Welsh Annals*, which allow for the possibility that a mounted force similar to Sarmatian cavalry was available to the Britons in the South West. There is evidence that a contingent of Alans settled in Armorica, Brittany, and retained a reputation for outstanding horsemanship. Bishop Gregory of Tours, a sixth-century Gallo-Roman historian, records them in his *Historia Francorum* as having fought in the latter part of the sixth century and there are records of them in the later Middle Ages. Accounts stress that they preferred to remain mounted at all times in contrast with all their neighbours, who dismounted in battle.[9] Of all the British tribes, the Dumnonii were the most involved in migrations to Brittany. Therefore, it is likely that Dumnonia in particular maintained a cavalry tradition based on the Roman model.

Arguments against such a capability for the Britons in the Badon era are often based on the perceived economic state of Britain and its lack of a centralised leadership at the time. It is true that maintaining such a force would have been expensive and only a prosperous society could have achieved it, but that is precisely why we can look to Dumnonia and her allies as having the necessary means. A cohesive and militarised British society was resisting Germanic expansion in the traditional homelands of the Dumnonii and Durotriges (the evidence already outlined for this will be elaborated upon in the next chapter). Moreover, the region maintained links to the Eastern Roman Empire, Africa and Gaul, indicating a long-standing tradition of trade. Artefacts from Cadbury, in particular, indicate that a wealthy society flourished there through the fifth century and beyond. Whilst much of Britain was undoubtedly fragmented, the South West was both rich and militarily powerful.

The Germanic military

The Old English word *dryht* was used to describe a Saxon warband, formed from a particular alliance or *sibb*, usually of blood relatives who banded together to form a fighting force in time of war. A *dryht* varied in size according to the clan from which it was drawn and comprised a mix of younger, inexperienced warriors, *geogùth*, and veterans, *dugùth*. In larger campaigns a number of war-bands came together as a political and military grouping known as the *Saetan* under command of an *éaldorman*. By the eighth century, the title *Éaldorman* was used to refer to the hereditary ruler of a *scíre*, from which the modern word shire is derived.

Once Anglo–Saxon kingdoms became more established, they were able to muster larger armies and the concept of the *Fyrd* or *Hére* emerged. Both words were used to describe an Anglo–Saxon military force, including a sea-borne one, usually raised from levies for times of war. Such a force was often a militia formed by the citizens of a *scíre* and led by their *éaldorman* with the support of his *ðegns* (thanes) as junior commanders. Of the underling tenant farmers who made up the *Fyrd*, some were free but others were held in bondage. Command of such an army was vested in their king, who was protected by his *héarthweru* (hearth-guards), who all had the status of *Gesith* (companion of the king), a term used to refer to all royal household members. If a king could not lead his troops in person he would appoint a general called the *Hérewísa* to command in his name.

Tacitus tells us how the Germanics were organised and equipped for battle. At the time of the Badon campaign, as far as can be judged, their way of war had changed little from his first-century description:

> *Only a very few use swords or lances. The spears that they carry - 'frameae' is the native word – have short and narrow heads, but are so sharp and easy to handle, that the same weapon serves a need for close or distant fighting. The horseman asks no more than his shield and spear, but the infantry have also javelins to shower, several per man, and they can hurl them to a great distance; for they are either naked or only lightly clad in their cloaks. There is nothing ostentatious in their turn out. Only the shields are picked out with carefully selected colours. Few have body armour; only*

here and there will you see a helmet of metal or hide. Their horses are not distinguished either for beauty or for speed, nor are they trained in Roman fashion to execute various turns. They ride them straight ahead or with a single swing to the right, keeping the wheeling line so perfect that no one drops behind the rest. On general survey, their strength is seen to lie rather in their infantry, and that is why they combine the two arms in battle. The men who they select from the whole force and station in the van are fleet of foot and fit admirably into cavalry action. The number of these chosen men is exactly fixed. A hundred are drawn from each district, and 'the hundred' is the name they bear at home.[10]

Tacitus may have misunderstood the complexity of the term 'hundred', or it may have evolved with time. In seventh-century England, the measure of a hundred district was its ability to support approximately 100 households under an *ěaldorman*, who was responsible for administration, justice, supplying military troops and leading them. The civil hundred was sometimes referred to as a 'small hundred' to distinguish it from the 'long hundred' or 'great hundred', which referred to 120 warriors, a standard-sized unit in battle. Sometimes several tribes, each under their own king, grouped together to form a nation, presided over by a high king. Tacitus is again an invaluable source regarding the Germanic attitude towards military leadership:

They choose their kings for their noble birth, their leaders for their valour. The power even of the kings is not absolute or arbitrary. As for the leaders, it is their example rather than their authority that wins them special admiration – for their energy, their distinction, or their presence in the van of fight ... On the field of battle it is a disgrace to the chief to be surpassed in valour by his companions, to the companions not to come up to the valour of their chief. As for leaving a battle alive after your chief has fallen, that means lifelong infamy and shame. To defend and protect him, to put down one's own acts of heroism to his credit – that is what they really mean by 'allegiance'. The chiefs fight for victory, the companions for their chief.[11]

These chiefs and their warriors were masters of the swift and savage raid and their immediate successes in Britain owed much to the surprise and ferocity of their attacks. In that respect, their activities in the earliest years of the post-Roman period were comparable to the later Viking raids. And like the later Danish armies that subjugated much of England and came close to conquering Wessex, these early Germanic warbands could be expected to acquit themselves well, particularly when under competent leadership. At the tactical level they had everything required for success in war, they simply had to direct their forces to best effect. At the time of Badon Hill, it is likely that they were forced for the first time in Britain to adopt a more strategic approach to their military operations because, as they encroached upon the South West, they faced a much stronger and better organised British resistance.

There is not much detail on record regarding the early Germanic warriors in Britain, but it seems that their equipment as described by Tacitus remained much the same. Recovered items from burial and sacrificial sites show that only the most important and richest possessed swords, helmets and armour at this time. Artefact finds reveal that earlier Saxons were buried in the main with spear and shield. Bows and arrows are also to be found, but there is little reference to the use of the bow in early pitched battles. It may have been more commonly used for hunting, or perhaps raiding or actions at sea. As late as 1066, the relatively poor performance by bowmen in battle has been ascribed to the short range of bows, which forced archers to adopt vulnerable positions, too close to enemy lines. The deadly longbow of Crecy and Agincourt fame was yet to make its mark on the battlefield. Very few *seaxes* have been recovered from burial sites in Britain, whereas they are commonly found on the continent. This reinforces the idea that the number of Germanic warriors present in Britain was relatively small rather than that they eschewed the use of the *seaxe*. Such weapons would have been hard to replace on an expedition and on a warrior's death would have been passed down to his kin rather than buried. Regarding personal protection, the helmets and mail armour recovered are largely Roman in origin up until the fourth century, suggesting that these items were mostly plundered. But from the fifth century onwards, there is evidence of Germanic manufacture.

Whilst Saxons did ride mounted in battle as described by Tacitus, it appears that this was rare. By preference, mounted troops rode to the place of battle and then dismounted to fight on foot. Certainly, the strength of the later *Fyrd* infantry lay in their discipline and cohesion in dismounted combat, as was the case for the Roman legions and other effective ancient armies. They fought in close order where maintaining the integrity of the shield-wall was critical, and was achieved through sheer collective physical strength. Shields were traditionally round in shape and made of linden, a comparatively light wood that is easily worked and fibrous. Its fibrosity afforded a degree of resistance to hacking and prodding by weapons. As shield-wall tactics developed, the size of shields appears to have increased to as much as 48 inches in diameter, necessitating that the shield was hung from the shoulder by a leather strap. However, in the Badon era, a 30- to 36-inch diameter shield would have been the norm. To form the shield-wall a warrior stood, leaning forward with his left shoulder to the fore and his shield interlocked with his neighbours'. The left leg was braced forward and the right trailed to the rear. As a group they braced to absorb the shock and pressure of an enemy charge from the front. Younger, less experienced warriors were placed in the centre of the wall and the strength of the entire mass was generated by the outermost warriors on each flank exerting inward pressure, body to body. This helped to prevent a potentially weaker combatant conceding his place and thus breaking the line. It also ensured that the experienced warriors guarded the more vulnerable flanks and reacted appropriately to emerging threats.

Once locked together in this manner, five men occupied a space about 2 metres in width, so a 'long hundred' three ranks deep would have presented a frontage of roughly 16 metres. This left little space for the front rank to employ their weapons, so their role in combat was largely a trial of strength as the shield-wall either pushed to drive back the enemy or held firm to resist being driven back. For the front rank, the short sword or *seaxe* was the most viable weapon, used to make short thrusts under the shield, hoping to find an opponent's exposed groin or midriff. Subsequent ranks of soldiers manipulated their spears over the shoulders or through the legs of their comrades to the front, the principal aim being to inflict wounds to the head and neck or the feet and lower legs of the soldiers in the opposing ranks. Wounds to the neck, torso and femoral artery would have caused immediate incapacitation. Well-drilled units would have been adept at quickly replacing the fallen in order to maintain the integrity of the shield-wall. It is hard to imagine a grimmer and more testing place for any warrior than to be in the shield-wall during combat.

A solid shield-wall was also capable of resisting a cavalry charge by bracing spears forwards and upwards, their butts in the ground, effectively presenting a wall of spikes. In support of the static shield-wall units, particularly when in a defensive posture, men armed with throwing spears, slings and bows could operate from the flanks, the rear and even in front of the infantry. All manner of projectiles would be hurled, depending on what was to hand, even rocks and lumps of wood.

Trials by modern re-enactment groups have revealed that more complex manoeuvres were possible. In defence, well-trained troops could divide and re-form, for example to create a temporary gap for skirmishing missile troops placed forwards to withdraw through. In attack, warriors could adjust the wall into a wedge formation whilst advancing, the aim being to then force right through the enemy ranks. Lighter, more mobile infantry might sometimes be packed inside the wedge ready to skirmish out and fight more openly as the enemy ranks split, to try and exploit any such loss of cohesion. Soldiers in the shield-wall ranks could un-brace at any time and widen their frontage into a skirmish line to fight more openly as necessary. When an unengaged unit was faced by a salvo of missile-fire, the shields would be raised so the troops could shelter under them.[12] An arrow wound to the eye or face, as rumoured to have been inflicted on King Harold at Hastings, was a prevalent injury among less experienced troops who were prone to look aloft hoping to dodge the incoming missiles.

Such tactics served Saxon armies well, but we must bear in mind that at the time of Badon the warbands assembled together were relatively small compared to the conscript armies of the *Fyrd*. They may have been accustomed to a more offensive and loose form of fighting, and been less well-schooled in the more refined tactics of coordinated shield-walls. Their preparation, organisation and size cannot be compared with that of a later *Fyrd*, and certainly not with the Roman legions that preceded them on Britain's battlefields. For example, the Roman invasion force in AD 43 arrived self-contained, ready to operate in a hostile environment with sophisticated combat service support:

The total effective strength of the units embarked for the invasion would have been about 40,000 men (all soldiers, tradesmen or otherwise in the combat zone are fighting soldiers); and the overall operational strength, including the specialists and others at Force Headquarters and at Base, would probably have been nearer 45,000.[13]

Any Germanic army in Britain would have been considered large, even at ten per cent of the strength quoted above. Alfred's Wessex army at its strongest was probably around 4,000, and more often his clashes with the Danes involved armies of 1,000 or so. Harold's English army at Hastings is usually estimated to have been only 3,000–4,000, mainly due to severe losses amongst the mobilised armies of Mercia and Northumbria at Fulford Gate. Also, his haste to march south to confront William after fighting at Stamford Bridge left no time for other forces to assemble. In Ælle's time, the immediate recruiting base was far smaller, consisting of those settlements established and consolidated in previous campaigns. The Germanic *modus operandi* at the time was to raid, capture and settle incrementally, the most realistic strategy for armies that lacked sufficient numbers to conquer kingdoms wholesale. An expeditionary force was made up almost exclusively of fighting troops prepared for a short campaign, reliant on their own success in war and on pillage for sustenance. If they lost a battle, the survivors were forced to return to their home settlements where their survival thereafter might depend on the actions of the neighbour they had just antagonised. To bypass an enemy stronghold in pursuit of a more distant objective would have carried the considerable risk of isolating a force in a region where it might soon find itself heavily outnumbered. Even if such a tactic were successful, and gained new territory, the occupiers would have found it difficult to bring the extra warriors and their families required to settle the land permanently. All of these factors dictated their preference for capturing coastal strips and using their maritime assets to bring in reinforcements unopposed.

Maritime capability

Based on archaeological finds, a typical fifth-century Germanic ship would have carried between thirty and fifty-five men. The vessels were best suited to coastal waters where navigation was more assured and shelter close at hand. Nonetheless, the Germanic ships and crews were more than capable of accomplishing lengthy voyages across open seas when necessary.[14] The ships relied on oars for propulsion but could make good headway under sail if conditions were favourable. The warriors themselves would row, seated on wooden chests that served both as bench and travelling receptacle for their personal possessions. Warriors afloat relied on their ship's individual master for their instructions and orders and such masters were considerably experienced in the science of navigation. They would have made use of tidal streams to hasten progress where such knowledge existed from previous voyages. Germanic ships, built for exploration and raiding, were suited to inland waterways due to their manoeuvrability and shallow draught. They were not designed for combat whilst afloat, unlike Roman warships that were built with a mind to maintain supremacy on the high seas and incorporated rams, boarding ramps and raised platforms for archers, for example. Once the Saxon Shore was no longer protected by Rome's vessels, the fifth-century Germanics who sailed to Britain were safer on their passage and therefore at their most vulnerable when making landfall and disembarking. For this reason they looked to maintain stealth, sometimes even taking deliberate risks to gain advantage from bad weather:

> *Captains and crews alike, to a man they teach or learn the art of brigandage; therefore let me urgently caution you to be ever on the alert. For the Saxon is the most ferocious of all foes. He comes on you without warning; when you expect his attack he makes away. Resistance only moves him to contempt; a rash opponent is soon down. If he pursues he overtakes; if he flies himself, he is never caught. Shipwrecks to him are no terror, but only so much training. His is no mere acquaintance with the perils of the sea; he knows them as he knows himself. A storm puts his enemies off their guard, preventing his preparations from being seen; the chance of taking the foe by surprise makes him gladly face every hazard of rough waters and broken rocks.*[15]

Regarding the scale of early maritime operations, the *Anglo-Saxon Chronicle* is significant only in that it omits any mention of large fleets. There are just five entries for the fifth and sixth centuries that note the use of ships, and all refer to the arrival of either three or five vessels, each time bearing a new leader and his men to Britain. The broad figures that can be deduced, ranging from around ninety to 250 warriors arriving at one time, are realistic for the likely size of expeditionary warbands. The movement of warriors' families to Britain from the European mainland would have been a lengthy process and a significant feat of seamanship, given the capacity of the boats. Michael E. Jones makes a thorough case for the relatively small scale of the Germanic invasions as a whole, describing in detail the limitations of their vessels and using this as one of the primary factors in his argument for small armies.[16] Some scholars disagree on this and feel the evidence for limited seafaring is overstated. However, the time taken for Germanic dominance to become established in Britain indicates that small fleets brought small armies ashore in a piecemeal fashion.

Relative strengths

Having assessed that warbands were small and that new alliances were developing out of necessity, it would be useful to consider the strength of the armies that clashed at Badon. But estimating the fighting strength of either force is fraught with difficulty due to the lack of any records. Godsal described the early Germanic armies as small, but his estimated figures are actually very large for the times. This was probably because his theories relied on armies capable of rather grand manoeuvres. He estimated the combined fighting strength of Kent, Sussex, Wessex and the Angles for a version of events that proposes that an assault on London was the second stage of the Germanic occupation of southern Britain:

> *The armies of those days were always small compared to modern ones, and were fought in close order. If there were 10,000 of the invaders and about double that number of the Britons, it is about what we should expect, but any estimate must be uncertain, and there may well have been many more, having regard to the enormous interests at stake.*[17]

Godsal does not reveal why we should expect such numbers to have been present, probably because there is no reliable way of making an estimate as he concludes. Nonetheless, an approximation could be reached by trying to determine the Germanic populations in Britain and from that the likely numbers of warriors available. For the Saxons, the basic unit of land was the hide, assessed as the area required to support one family. Wide variations existed because a hide could be anything from about 40 acres to 4 square miles, depending on the quality and utility of the land. Thus, the number of families in any given area was dictated by the nature of the land available to support its inhabitants.

Approximately a hundred hides made up a 'hundred', and a *villare* or *scíre* contained many hundreds. The Isle of Wight *villare* covers approximately 94,000 acres. Divide by forty and a figure of 2,350 Germanic families is obtained for the highest expected population density. Bede informs us that over 1,200 families were exterminated when Cædwalla seized the island in 686. The Domesday Book records approximately a hundred manors on the island. Ruth Waller, author of the 2006 paper *Archaeological Resource Assessment of the Isle of Wight: Early Medieval period,* informs us that 'most manorial settlements of the time probably consisted of the manor house and a few surrounding peasant dwellings, although one or two may have been associated with nucleated settlements'.[18]

On the basis of the above, Bede's figure looks to be about right for the total number of families that inhabited the Isle of Wight in 686. The density of settlement nearly 200 years before this would undoubtedly have been lower – somewhere around one third of Bede's figure seems reasonable. For an early Germanic population on a piece of ground the size of the Isle of Wight, we can therefore estimate 400 families at the very most. By crudely placing a shape of the Isle of Wight on the same scale map of Kent and Sussex it is possible to estimate the relative numbers of families there also. (When trying this at home with a pair of scissors and a map, one will be delighted to discover that the shape of the Isle of Wight is extremely fit for purpose.) Using Arnold's maps to delineate the settled Germanic areas at the end of the fifth century, this methodology reveals that Kent probably supported no more than 1,600 families and Sussex no more than 1,200.[19] Kent was not the leader of this enterprise and a good guess is that it supplied no more than 500 warriors. If we allow that each family in Ælle's Sussex had two warriors and then extract twenty per cent to guard the homeland, we are left with roughly 1,900. By this reasoned guesswork we can say that somewhere between 2,000–2,500 warriors marched westwards on the Badon campaign from Sussex and Kent combined.

Wielding the paper cut-out of the Isle of Wight across Devon, Somerset and Dorset is an amusing but fruitless exercise to determine the British strength, because the populations in these areas had been in place for much longer. A more sensible approach is to estimate how many troops were needed to defend a large hillfort or garrison, and whether they could be supported for any length of time. A British defensive plan would have to have considered the need for logistic support to any standing army. Water, grazing and productive land was plentiful in the South West. With good organisation, a large force could be sustained for some considerable time within their own territory. If confined to a fort, access to potable water would have been a concern, but each individual could have carried skins or urns and survived for some time, including by drinking beer or wine, which carried less risk of contamination. Water was available through springs, streams, wells and ponds in the low areas. Dew ponds could produce a limited amount of water in the higher hillforts. Cadbury had a well inside the fortifications near the main gate, which is marked on maps to this day.

Cadbury's outer rampart circumference is around 1,600 metres. Full coverage could have been gained if each man on the outer defences occupied roughly 1 metre, enough space to launch a sling, throw a javelin or wield a sword or spear against an enemy scaling the revetments. Inside the inner embankment were 62,000 square metres of living space, equal to 38 per man based on occupancy by 1,600 warriors. As a general rule, an attacking force in ancient times needed to outnumber the defenders by three-to-one to be successful, more if the enemy was behind fortifications. This is only a guide, but since a siege more often than not proved costly in manpower for the attacker, 1,600 warriors should easily have been sufficient to defend a hillfort such as Cadbury against an attacking force of 2,500.

Some months after making the above deduction, I read John Peddie's book, *Alfred: Warrior King*. In discussing the defence of the fortified burh at Wareham against the Danes, Peddie quotes Alfred's 'later calculations' and reveals that the king himself estimated that 2,180 yards of ramparts (1,990 metres) would have required a defending force of 1,600 men, based on four men occupying one pole of wall, a pole being an ancient measure equating to 5½ yards (5 metres).[20] We can therefore be fairly confident that a warrior per metre of rampart is a good measure of the requirement. As for the relative strengths of armies in the field, suffice it to say that the Romano-British forces in the South West significantly outnumbered the Germanics, but they also had an extensive frontier to defend. In seeking a decisive victory, a major consideration for both sides was how to bring superior numbers to bear at the right place and time.

Summary

It is evident that commanders on both sides had many factors to consider when preparing for war. The Germanics had to balance their urgent need to expand (and ambition to do so) with constraints on the numbers of warriors and other assets such as ships. Their primary consideration had to be to defend what they had already captured, but they also faced overcrowding and gaining new territory to address this was a priority. On the British side, there was a realisation that the South West could fall as easily as Kent and Sussex if a coordinated plan for defence was not put in place. The plan required military cooperation between factions who had previously been vying for their own disparate ends. Most of all, the British required strong leadership and the evidence from Gildas and others points towards successive war leaders called Ambrosius as the men who supplied it. Whilst neither side would have wanted to rush into an ill-prepared campaign, the pressure was clearly on the Germanics to attack, thus prompting the British to plan and execute a defensive posture. With that in mind, we must next determine how each side went about its military business in preparing for this escalation to conflict on a larger scale. The time for skirmishes had come to an end and the warlords were gathering larger armies. This required them to plan their operations effectively or risk losing considerably more in defeat than they had in the past.

Chapter Four

The British in the South West

The British have always coped without becoming a dictatorship
– Frederick Forsyth

In the early sixth century, the growing Germanic presence in south-east Britain was probably viewed by the post-Roman British as an unavoidable legacy of Rome's occupation and the turmoil that followed its ending. The peoples of Kent, Sussex, East Anglia and Norfolk were a mix of those natives who had long been cowed and others from home and abroad who had accepted or even embraced Roman rule. Resistance to the subsequent wave of Germanic immigration there seems to have crumbled relatively quickly, either through lack of organisation or will to resist. To the west the picture was different. As history tells us, there is often a point in war where one side draws a line in the sand and the fight becomes one of national survival. West of the Hampshire Avon, Rome had conquered the ancient British tribe they called the Durotriges in brutal fashion, but at the same time had forged agreements that allowed the neighbouring kingdom of Dumnonia, in the South West Peninsula, to coop-erate and prosper. In the wake of Rome's withdrawal, the former Durotrigan territories had been re-established by Romano-British groups, including the sophisticated Belgae, who between them built the Wansdyke and Bokerley defences. Such works are indicative of societies prepared to invest heavily to protect their lands, and there is no doubt that the military forces required for this task were also available and prepared. Centuries later these lands were at the very heart of the kingdom of Wessex. There is very little in the sources to tell us how this came about, so we must follow the few clues that are available.

The Ambrosius dynasty

Most of the region that we recognise today as Thomas Hardy's Wessex remained British for many years after Ceawlin's reign, a war leader described in the *Anglo-Saxon*

Chronicle as a king of Wessex. It is more accurate to say that he led the Gewisse, a people identified as having become established in the Thames Valley some time after the end of Roman rule. Ceawlin's rule was terminated somewhere towards the end of the sixth century. Dorset is sometimes described as having begun to fall to the West Saxons under Cynegils in c. 614, but this is an unsound assumption, as we shall see when analysing the battle fought in that year. The case for the existence in the fifth and sixth centuries of a strong British military ethos throughout the South West and a capability to match it is, by contrast, compelling. The political and social make-up of the area is less clear, in particular what links the former Durotrigan territory might have had with neighbouring Britons, especially with Dumnonia to its west. As a bulwark against Germanic aggression, the Wansdyke and Bokerley territories would have been important to Dumnonia and there is evidence that Ambrosius Aurelianus exercised widespread influence in these areas. An Ambrosius is sometimes also associated with fighting that took place further east, for instance at Danebury hillfort near Nether Wallop where the nearby place-name Amport is cited as evidence. Henry of Huntingdon recorded in the early twelfth century that Ambrosius personally killed Horsa at the Battle of Aylesford in Kent.[1] It must be borne in mind, though, that some accounts of Ambrosius, especially Geoffrey of Monmouth's, appear to conflate two individuals. The earlier Aurelius Ambrosius, or Ambrosius the Elder, was probably the father of the Ambrosius named by Gildas and a more likely candidate for a British leader who fought in Kent.

The idea that the British fought for at least two generations under the leadership of an 'Ambrosius dynasty' is entirely consistent with the time taken for the Germanics to settle and secure Kent and Sussex before progressing into Hampshire. Before the Germanics reached the Hampshire Avon, the British were already re-occupying Iron Age hillfort sites, most of which had been neglected for centuries because the Romans preferred to garrison their forces in the towns. Extensive military engineering works have been uncovered by archaeologists at Cadbury Castle hillfort, where enhancements to the Iron Age defensive dykes eventually enclosed 18 acres. The defences at Cadbury were strengthened in five stages, at least two of which occurred after the Roman occupation. This work culminated in the early sixth century, around the time that the Badon campaign was launched. Michelle Biehl is an archaeologist and author of the 1991 paper *A Short History of Arthurian Archaeology*. In it she lists works and artefacts that have been uncovered at Cadbury as part of a wider attempt to see if the existence of an historical King Arthur is possible and not refuted by physical evidence:

> *This refortification consisted of an unmortared stone wall, sixteen feet thick, with blocks of Roman masonry on top of it, in addition to a surrounding earth bank, an internal drystone wall, and a gate tower with two entrances (Alcock 1968). Area postholes suggested other buildings and a small amount of Tintagel-like sherds of class A, B, and some D pottery were also discovered ... the widely scattered small amounts found at Cadbury suggested a 'civilized settlement' (Alcock, Ashe 1971). Due to the amount of imported luxury goods, it was also surmised that the occupants of the fortified settlement were people of standing.*
>
> *There are the remains of many hillforts that were re-occupied during the post-Roman years but none were refortified on the same scale as Cadbury and none were anywhere as large as that eighteen acre site. The site was occupied at the right time, with the pottery sherds and other finds dating it at the late fifth century into the early sixth century.*[2]

Biehl's 'right time' relates to whether the site's association with Arthurian legend is plausible. We could instead state that it was 'the right time for the British defences to be prepared in anticipation of the Badon campaign'. Archaeologists have established that a large number of Iron Age hillforts were refortified and occupied anew, across the South West in particular, but also elsewhere in Britain. This is evidence that the Britons were preparing for a war in which hillforts were destined to play a key role as garrisons and strongholds. In his 1981 book, *In Search of the Dark Ages*, Michael Wood, the historian and television presenter, suggests that whilst it is tempting to conclude that these preparations were coordinated by military leaders, there is no evidence for this and the work could have been organised on a local basis.[3] Counter to this is the level of effort, the number of sites involved and the timing, all of which imply coordination. If there was no coordinated plan, then we need to explain why the steady progress of Germanic annexation of British territory stalled so abruptly, and for so long. Such an explanation is difficult, because small local communities trying to defend in isolation would have been soft targets indeed, effectively offering themselves to be destroyed piecemeal in the wake of incremental Germanic gains of territory. Moreover, Gildas provides the contemporary written evidence for coordination of the effort when he stresses the much-needed injection of leadership provided by Ambrosius.

Once we accept that there was organised coordination and cooperation between groups on the British side, we can begin to discern the strategy that lay behind it. Cadbury Castle has already been identified as important among a number of hillforts refortified at this point in history. Strategically, Cadbury was the fortress and garrison at the centre of all those and guarded the gateway to the South West Peninsula. It dominated the key routes that converged from the north and east on their way towards the difficult terrain of the Somerset marshes and on into Devon and Cornwall. Any military commander of British forces in the South West would have regarded Cadbury as 'vital ground', a military term for terrain that is of such significance that its loss will render the entire defence untenable. Yet reinforcing and holding Cadbury could not have prevented an aggressor from making territorial gains in much of the region to its east. It was too far removed from both the Hampshire Avon and the Upper Thames Valley to play any direct role in fighting as the Badon campaign took shape. To prevent Germanic incursions into the Somerset, Dorset and Wiltshire region, it was necessary for the British to defend across an entire front that linked the Severn Valley to the south coast. This defensive line was a dog-leg, based on the linear features of the Wansdyke and the Hampshire Avon, with the joint running through the environs of Pewsey and Marlborough in Wiltshire.

All of this points to the need for the various groups of Britons to have formed a regional alliance. If the sub-kingdoms to the east and north of Dumnonia had not allied themselves with Dumnonia, they would have been much weaker. Equally, it was in Dumnonia's interest to keep these territories British as a buffer zone against Germanic encroachment. From the evidence available, it seems likely that British military command of this alliance was vested in Ambrosius and his descendants, from somewhere in the latter half of the fifth century and into the sixth. These war leaders were not kings but seem to have been sworn to several kings of differing stature. Records of those British kings who united in the face of the threat are scarce and their stories, derived mostly from the *Welsh Annals*, are entangled in myth and cannot be regarded as accurate. Nonetheless, these annals do provide us with a number of names and some ideas of where and when they ruled.

The rulers of territories to the west of the immediate conflict zone had a vested interest in arresting Germanic expansion and may well have contributed to an alliance. A chieftain called Gwrwawr is recorded as having ruled in Dumnonia, and he was apparently succeeded by his son Tudvawl some time in the early 500s. Little else is known of these chieftains, but Tudvawl is recorded as the father of Custennyn, more commonly known as Constantine. Fact and fantasy begin to merge at this point, but Constantine is remembered not only as a chieftain of Dumnonia but also as High King of Britain. According to Geoffrey of Monmouth, he inherited this title from his cousin Arthur on Arthur's death in 542. There were three minor kingdoms to the west of the River Severn: Ergyng, Gwent and Glywysing. Ergyng was ruled in c. 510 and beyond by Cynfyn, who was succeeded by his son Gwrgan *Mawr* (the Great), a title bestowed on him for prowess in battle. Ergyng has been identified as the same kingdom as Gewisse in the Wye region, the origins of which will be discussed later. A character called Caradoc is thought to have ruled Ergyng and Gwent in the mid-sixth century and, according to Welsh legend, he was a contemporary of Arthur. This adds to the confusion because the name Cerdic, as applied by the *Anglo-Saxon Chronicle* to the West Saxon leader, is an anglicised version of Caradoc. In southern Gwent, a ruler called Honorius, or Ynyr, is recorded around the early sixth century. Ynyr is an alternative candidate for Ambrosius himself. Ruling Glywysing (West Gwent) at the same time there was Gwynllw or Gunlyu *Milwr* (the Warrior), who spent much of his early life in battle to earn his title. The names of leaders east of the Severn are even harder to find in the records. There is a legend that makes mention of a king called Einion in the Silchester area and there is a possible ruler called Elafius in Winchester in the 440s, but there are no recorded successors. The suggestion from the records is that there were numerous kingdoms, all of them small geographically but quick to war when required. In the face of a new threat from foreign peoples, it is entirely believable that they banded together to face it.

Commander's initial analysis

Ambrosius, or whoever else the military commander of such a diverse alliance might have been, was on the backfoot following the Germanic successes to the east, and he faced a daunting task. He had to unify his command and put together a robust plan of defence designed to counter a Germanic move that might materialise anywhere across the extensive frontier I have identified. He would necessarily have divided the ground into discrete areas of responsibility, each under the command of a regional leader, who might have been a king charged with operating in his own territory, or a subordinate leader considered sufficiently capable of the task. It helps our understanding if we consider the ground in the same way as the commander might have done, breaking it down initially into two areas, that which lay north of the Wansdyke (the Cotswolds and Upper Thames Valley), and the land to the south (Dorset and Wiltshire), which formed the buffer zone between the south coast Germanics and the borderlands of British Dumnonia.

As the fifth century drew to a close, Britons in Wales, the Cotswolds and the upper reaches of the Thames were all still some distance from the trouble that was brewing with the Germanics, who had spread their influence west as far as the Hampshire Avon. An equal threat to these regions was the opportunism of the Picts and Irish tribes, who had redoubled their raids since Rome's withdrawal from Britain. Other Germanic groups began to encroach on the Lower Thames region from the fens of today's Norfolk and East Anglia. There was no direct threat to Dumnonia's land border at this time. Between the Hampshire Avon and Dumnonia was a region that lent itself well to defence. It included much of the high chalk country with its network of hillforts. The defensive potential of this area, which today encompasses Dorset, southern Wiltshire and eastern Somerset, was supplemented by the large forest called Selwood. All that remains of Selwood today is a fragmented series of ancient woodland areas that straddle the Somerset/Wiltshire borders. The existence of the medieval woodland to the south and east of the remnants of Selwood suggests that up until the eighth century there was little open country between Selwood proper and the forests of southern Hampshire, which were in turn contiguous with the Wealden Forest. An attacking force would have had all of these natural defences to contend with before reaching the borders of Dumnonia.[4] Even then, the border regions of Dumnonia included a natural defensive line, a narrow frontage of high ground, again replete with ancient hillforts, between the Somerset Levels and the south coast.

From this we can assess that, through the Badon Hill era, the South West Peninsula and the Cotswolds remained relatively secure and the attention of British military commanders was focused predominantly on the Hampshire

Avon frontier. It would be understandable if the defences against piracy and raids from the sea were afforded a lower priority, but this threat had to be considered nonetheless, so a degree of coastal surveillance and protection was required. Likewise, the possibility of a threat materialising in the Lower Thames region could not be ignored. Amesbury, the fortress of Ambrosius, was a natural centre of gravity for a British commander faced by this situation, being on the Avon itself equidistant from the Thames Valley and the south coast. West of the Hampshire Avon, across Dorset and Wiltshire, the key terrain from a military perspective was the high chalk downland and its associated hillforts. For the alliance's territories to survive intact, including Amesbury as the probable powerbase of the commander, defence had to be aggressive right up to the Hampshire Avon. The British territories of Bokerley and Wansdyke identified in Chapter Two would have been fundamental to this posture and no part of them would have been abandoned lightly to the enemy.

Ambrosius would have borne foremost in his mind that the operational level objective for the Germanics was to capture good agricultural land and hold on to it. Overcrowding in their territories meant that the taking of plunder alone was no longer sufficient. With this known 'enemy intent' in his mind, he would have deduced that whilst they might engage in some level of raiding, including by way of diversion, their main offensive would materialise close to the frontier and would seek to gain considerable new ground. He could make an educated guess at a number of areas that met the conditions the Germanics required for their own ambitions. With an extensive frontier to consider overall, he could not afford to gamble by placing his forces on any single specific axis that he identified as likely for an offensive, but he would have tried to identify a number of likely axes on which to focus. He would have thought through in some detail which areas could be defended by the enemy once they had captured them. Through such a thought process, he was consciously placing himself in the mind of the Germanic commander in a manner we would define as manoeuvrist today. To illustrate the complexity of these considerations it is worth noting Map 4, which marks the dozens of hillfort sites available within 20 miles of Frankenbury, a fort overlooking the Avon from the east side, and one that was most probably held by Germanics as the Badon campaign loomed. It is clear that a number of these forts west of the river would have been integral to the plan for defence. Further archaeological evidence of refortification

▲ Hillfort

Map 4: Hillforts of the Hampshire Avon Frontier

may yet indicate which these were, but we can also make a considered military assessment based on the geography.

It was impossible to place a garrison on every hillfort or potential strong-point. Ambrosius needed to make clear choices, prioritising his effort to ensure that his defence was not spread too thinly whilst ensuring that he could bring decisive combat power to bear once the Germanic threat materialised. Any merger of enemy warbands into a more sizeable army would have been a clear indication of a coming offensive that he could not afford to miss. From these considerations, he would have decided to place considerable emphasis on the gathering of information about enemy movements by land and sea to gain early warning of an attack. Effective 360-degree surveillance was needed, because he simply could not afford to be taken by surprise, particularly by a force of any great strength. The need to meet a concerted offensive with a suitably strong defence meant he had to position carefully one or more strike-forces, in places from which they could close with the enemy quickly. Ideally, a strike-force would be able to deliver sufficient destructive capability to guarantee success in open battle against the largest army the Germanics could muster.

By this stage of his thought process Ambrosius had probably begun to for-mulate a plan similar to that of King Alfred's military restructuring of Wessex in the aftermath of the first Danish incursions, as recorded in the *Burghal Hidage*. This tenth-century document detailed the location and military man-power requirements of thirty-three forts, chosen to enable the forces of Wessex to mobilise quickly and occupy secure garrisons. The garrisons were placed to facilitate the denial of the principal river and road routes to any Danish army on the offensive and served as places of safety. Every citizen of Wessex could reach one in a single day's ride. The concept allowed for an invading army to penetrate the borders of Wessex, but ensured it could not capture important objectives easily nor secure key lines of communication to further the cam-paign. The resurrected hillforts of the sixth century served a similar purpose to the fortified towns of the *Burghal Hidage*. They were wartime garrisons and also places of refuge for civilians. They were part of a coordinated plan that ensured any invading army could be brought to battle on the defender's terms. The Germanic forces under Ælle's command had to secure one or more of these garrisons if they were to capture new ground and thereafter sustain themselves on it. They were effectively refused any option to simply occupy territory between the forts, because this would leave them isolated, vulnerable to counter-attack and lacking sustainable lines of communication.

The Germanic commander of the Badon campaign, probably Ælle of Sussex, knew that the success of any offensive designed to breach the Hampshire Avon frontier rested on the capture of a significant fortress. He chose a fort known as Badon Hill for his primary objective. For reasons already outlined, it is most probable that this fort was Badbury Rings, in today's Dorset. To some degree, Ælle's strategy played into British hands, not because he chose a particular hillfort but because he was unwittingly conforming to the British commander's plan. It was the British strategy overall that undid Ælle. The result would most likely have been the same regardless of any particular location for the decisive battle. To understand this fully, we must add more to our understanding of how the British side crafted their plans.

The British intent

Some required effects would have emerged from Ambrosius' initial deliberations. First, he needed to identify and track enemy force elements – in modern terminology the FIND effect. Once the enemy was on the offensive he required his forces to DISRUPT and DELAY the main Germanic force in order to buy time enough to manoeuvre his striking-forces for a decisive counter-attack. Finally, he would have been very clear in his mind that the main effort was to DESTROY the enemy force. The destruction of the enemy force was important because winning an engagement without inflicting serious and lasting damage would not have diminished the Germanic threat enough to allow British warriors to return to their lands and farms in sufficient security. A number of indecisive skirmishes had no doubt been fought up to this point but the overall situation along the Hampshire Avon frontier was precarious and prolonging the stalemate was certainly not in the British interest. Once Ambrosius judged that his forces were ready and capable of victory, he would have planned to ensure that the Germanic alliance would be rendered unfit to return and fight another day, not least because he could ill-afford to keep a large part of his own army deployed permanently.

With no obvious point of reference for the enemy incursion, it is difficult to transfer the particular effects identified above into an intent schematic related directly to a map or diagram of dispositions. In modern military planning, this situation is not unusual and the schematic presented is therefore a conceptual model, shaped only roughly to the geography. Figure 3 is a suggested intent schematic for the defence of the South West based on the considerations outlined to this point, the need to identify the enemy axis, gain some time to prepare, and then strike at the enemy decisively.

The effects designed to counter the enemy are spread across the full frontage of the area of operations and include the coastline. In this schematic, Ambrosius is seeking to destroy the enemy, having accepted that he would probably have to allow an initial incursion to some degree. Knowing he could not afford to deploy sufficient troops to each and every garrison or locality, he was prepared instead to temporarily trade territory for time to set the conditions for a decisive action. This required confidence in the fighting abilities of his troops and assurance that each of his force elements would play their part. In modern parlance, Mission Command is 'the exercise of authority and direction by the commander using

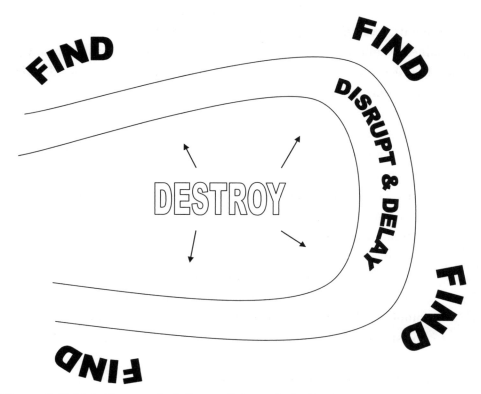

Figure 3: British Commander's Intent Schematic for Defence

mission orders to enable disciplined initiative within the commander's intent to empower agile and adaptive leaders in the conduct of unified land operations'.[5] Ambrosius was forced to adopt the tenets of Mission Command whether this came naturally to him or not, because he could not personally supervise all of the planning and execution over such a wide geographical area. Whether the subordinate commanders were disciplined, agile or adaptive is open to question, but we can guess that they were fierce and independent leaders in their own right. It is probable that broad direction from above was all they would accept. The British plan was manoeuvrist and mission-orientated by default.

The guiding concept set out in the intent schematic would have helped the commander to explain his plan, and thereafter develop it with the help of the subordinate commanders. The development of such a concept into a planned deployment would have required a good eye for the terrain and how best to make use of it. Central to the emerging concept of operations would be to 1) identify the type and strength of troops required for each effect, and 2) prioritise the locations to use. The British would have chosen their garrisons and strongpoints, treading a careful balance to ensure each one could hold against a sustained assault whilst avoiding the deployment of too many men in any one place. In order to arrive at the optimum solution, a multitude of considerations would have come into play. But the key factors were:

- accessibility and proximity of bases to useful military lines of communication (for rapid reinforcement and counter-attack as well as to deny the enemy their use)
- inter-visibility/cooperation between bases for mutual support
- coordination of patrols and other surveillance activity
- communications, particularly how to achieve early warning of enemy movement
- existing defensive works and ease of enhancement
- numbers of local defenders available at each site (levy troops)
- numbers of civilians requiring protection within the site
- logistics (including water and food supply for men and animals)

With these factors in mind, let us now look at each of the effects that the commander wanted to achieve in detail.

Finding the enemy

Ambrosius would have directed that observation posts or patrols be put in place all along the land frontier and on the cliffs and promontories of the coast. Small detachments were to keep watch and raise the alarm when necessary. Throughout history, accomplished military commanders have recognised the role of every soldier in the surveillance effort. The primary duty of a sentry has always been to provide localised early warning by reporting suspicious movement and activity. Surveillance duties might well have been undertaken by ageing warriors past their prime or youths unready for full combat duties. Covert operations such as reconnaissance patrols would have required a higher grade of soldier. The value of effective reconnaissance and surveillance, both overt and covert, has been recognised and noted in the very earliest records. In the *Iliad*, Homer informs us that reconnaissance was carried out by specialist units within the ancient Greek forces who operated in groups as small as two or three foot soldiers, or by larger groups of up to thirty horsemen.[6] Such teams were selected from the cavalry or the lightly armed troops called *psiloi* and were able to move fast and with stealth across all types of terrain.

Modern surveillance aids such as thermal imaging devices enable the detection of the enemy a long way off, even at night. In ancient times when the naked eye alone was the sensor, sentry duties were performed by larger groups. This was partly to ensure sufficient coverage but also in order that they had sufficient strength to fight a delaying action, the purpose of which was to buy time for the main army to make ready for battle. Homer refers to night pickets and guards posted outside the defensive walls in 'seven pickets of one hundred' to provide security for an army of a hundred thousand.[7] This duty was apparently given to the more junior soldiers. In the *Cyropaedia*, Xenophon tells how the duties were divided into watches to ensure that soldiers had sufficient rest to preserve their alertness and also to enable them to move and fight with the army the next day without being too fatigued.[8]

Given these details from the ninth century BC, it is reasonable to assume that specialist reconnaissance forces were available to the Dark Age British commander and there is contemporary evidence to support this. In AD 367, raids on Roman Britain reached crisis point when Nectarides, Count of the Saxon Shore, was killed by Germanic pirates, and Fullofaudes, commander of the northern garrisons, was ambushed and killed, probably by Picts. The subsequent collapse of the defence in the north of Britain led to a flood of 'barbarians' who rampaged south as far as the Midlands. The Emperor Valentinian sent three generals in quick succession to stabilise the situation, but none achieved success. Finally, in 368, Count Theodosius, a highly experienced officer of Spanish descent, was given command of a force consisting of some of Rome's finest auxiliary troops and elements of the Imperial Guard. His principal difficulty was locating the rebel bands, scattered as they were and reluctant to present themselves for pitched battle. Eventually, he hunted them down. His one change on restoring order in 369 was to abolish a frontier organisation known as the *Arcani*, who he blamed for revealing details of Roman troop movements to the enemy in return for bribes. The *Arcani* were British auxiliary troops tasked with living and operating deep in enemy territory in order to track and report the movements of the Picts and other tribes who posed a threat.[9] However untrustworthy the practitioners had proved to be, the concept of covert reconnaissance and the skills necessary to achieve it were clearly present among British tribes.

The British held a further trump card when it came to espionage. It is agreed by Dr Francis Pryor and other academics that substantial numbers of Britons remained in the areas lost to the Germanics, living out their lives under varying circumstances.[10] Spies and informants may well have been available, but deriving useful intelligence from them would have required some form of basic information and intelligence handling procedure. For instance, a report of thirty Saxon warriors moving through a particular village in the occupied territories might mean very little on its own. But if the informant were to provide detail, perhaps of the markings on their shields or some other indicator of their origin, such a report might be critical. A single piece of information like this might have been the key to determining that new enemy troops were moving into an area, suggesting that an operation was underway and triggering the move of forces ready to counter. Certainly, when a sizeable force arrived anew or concentrated together in the Germanic territories, it should not have gone unnoticed. The British might well have employed spies, who roved covertly through enemy territories, gathering information with their own eyes but also second-hand from any willing informants. Such activity would have been vital alongside the overt surveillance of the frontier itself. As anyone who enjoys a walk on the southern chalk downs will know, visibility is often obscured or denied altogether by mist, rain and low cloud. These conditions and the hours of darkness meant that twenty-four-hour visibility from the heights was impossible. A coordinated plan for overt and covert surveillance was required.

Disruption, delay and static defence

Hillforts formed the garrison hubs and strongpoints around which the British military activity revolved. Each defined sector or area of operations needed to muster a garrison force that could react to an enemy incursion or landing. Some garrisons would have been quite small, but they needed to be strong enough to harass the enemy and delay him. These tasks, if performed away from the walls, were best suited to mounted troops. Fast-moving, lightly equipped infantry could also have played a harassing role. Germanic forces would also have sought to capture and hold suitable locations for their own operating bases, without which they could not hope to hold and settle new territory. In order to ensure the protection of these bases, such as the hillforts close to the frontier, Ambrosius would have identified two possible courses of action, both of which contributed to his DISRUPT and DELAY effects. One method was to harass and ambush the enemy as they approached, the second to ensure that the forts were manned sufficiently to hold firm, denying the enemy any immediate success and inflicting casualties. The local environment would have been a major factor in deciding which course of action would be most effective for each locality. Harassment and raiding of the enemy whilst he was on the move would have been the tactic of choice in the forests. In more open terrain, the protection offered by the forts presented the best chance to delay and disrupt the Germanic forces, provided that in the overall plan there was sufficient power to strike against an enemy force that chose simply to bypass a garrison or strongpoint.

From a British perspective, the static defence of the garrisons and strongpoints would have been a task given to detachments of infantry. We cannot judge how effective the British troops would have been when fighting man-to-man in open battle against the Germanic tribes, but they would certainly have enjoyed some key advantages when defending prepared strongpoints. Wooden or stone revetments and palisade defences constructed to supplement the raised-earth embankments of the hillforts provided good protection against the bow or sling. The height advantage accorded to the defenders increased the potential range for the employment of thrown weapons and other missiles. The ancient tribes who built the hillforts had designed them to maximise the effect of slung stones, particularly in those areas with intricate patterns of earth banks near the entrance ramps and gates. Missiles could be rained down with accuracy and ferocity on attackers who were simultaneously exposed from several angles and channelled into selected killing areas. Palisade defences were an effective deterrent against even the most ferocious and capable of foes, because the only way to guarantee the success of an assault was to attack in overwhelming numbers. Even if the attackers were superior in number, those who reached the foot of the revetments unharmed still faced the considerable difficulties inherent in either scaling them or reducing them sufficient to make a breach. Such efforts required an acceptance of heavy casualties that Dark Age commanders usually sought to avoid, not through cowardice but for the very practical reason of ensuring the survival of their clan. The Germanics, suited to rapid and ferocious attack that quickly put an enemy to flight or broke his cohesion, relied predominantly on hand-to-hand combat. They did not possess the engineering or ballistic skills and equipment that had enabled the Romans to clear the Celts from the hillforts so effectively 500 years previously. A concerted effort to defend these strongpoints could repulse an enemy that did not possess overwhelming numbers or the technology to breach the defences.

Ambrosius would also have considered the requirement for depth in the overall defence to ensure that Germanic forces could not slip past forward positions to capture objectives deeper in British territory, a strategy the Danes later adopted against Alfred. Whatever the matrix of hillforts chosen for occupation, there remained much territory between the garrisons that needed to be considered in the overall plan of defence. Modern technology ensures that remote surveillance devices and weapons of considerable range and lethality can cover gaps between positions, but in ancient warfare large numbers of troops were required to achieve comprehensive coverage. Gaps between forts would have been monitored and patrolled by groups of warriors tasked to provide mobile surveillance and reconnaissance. Manpower constraints undoubtedly influenced the British plan. It was simply not possible to occupy every location that would have been identified as useful. For this reason, the commander would have considered how best to create an effective striking force to deal a decisive blow once the main body of the enemy force was located and brought to battle.

The striking force

An enduring principle of defence is 'offensive action'. This might appear counter-intuitive to the non-military reader but it means that a force in defence should not wait passively to be attacked. Rather, it should seek to surprise the enemy, hitting him hard and early in order to break up the cohesion of his attack. The DISRUPT and DELAY effects are an example of offensive spirit within a defensive posture. The next consideration for the commander is when, where and how he can go on the offensive to inflict maximum damage on the enemy – in other words how to accomplish the DESTROY effect:

> *A striking force must be assigned to conduct offensive action against the enemy and to exploit opportunities. To increase the chance of success, the striking force should surprise the enemy.*[11]

The size and disposition of the striking force will depend on the concept of operations, but the aim is to concentrate combat power at the point of strike. Doctrinally, a striking force is not the same as a reserve force because it will have a designated task, whereas a reserve remains uncommitted so it can react as ordered when required. The considerations for positioning a striking force and a reserve are similar, however, as both need to move quickly into action once called upon. In ancient times, cavalry was usually the best option for a striking force because it could remain at some distance from the fray but strike hard and cohesively once committed. Maximising the advantages of cavalry has long been a guiding principle of mounted warfare. Vegetius, a writer on warfare and military principles from the days of the Later Roman Empire, compiled many maxims from earlier Roman sources, including:

> *A general should know what part of his own cavalry is most proper to oppose any particular squadrons or troops of the enemy. For from some causes not to be accounted for some particular corps fight better against others, and those who have defeated superior enemies are often overcome by an inferior force.*[12]

Cavalry was particularly effective if it could achieve surprise against infantry who were unprepared or not trained to receive a cavalry charge. Immediately after breaking a body of infantry, a cavalry force could inflict horrific damage by riding down the fleeing or scattered individuals whose only hope of withstanding cavalry action was lost once they broke ranks. Ambrosius, understanding the way that the Germanics fought, would have known that, whilst they had the courage and capability to resist a cavalry charge, if launched with surprise such an action could unnerve and scatter the strongest of opponents, especially if it could inflict shock:

> *A force can be said to be shocked if it displays any or all of the following conditions: reduced participation in combat; flight, panic or surrender of significant numbers; or inappropriate responses to the opponent's actions ... The tactical effects of shock may be perceived as local panic or collapse. If exploited, they may lead to more general collapse, which may in turn lead to paralysis at the operational or strategic levels. There are three main causes of shock effects: surprise, shock action and destruction. Although these can be described separately, they tend to overlap in the complex environment of the battlefield. The greatest shock effect results from a combination of all three causes.*[13]

The striking force of cavalry was arguably the single most important force element in the British plan. If it could be brought to bear effectively, it had the potential to win any battle outright. If it could not reach the field of combat in time, or if it lost the element of surprise, the whole British strategy might fail. To maximise their effect, ideally the available cavalry forces would mass together and surprise the enemy. With a large frontage to cover, it is likely that the commander was forced to consider holding striking forces in more than one location, with the trade-off that achieving such concentration would be more time consuming.

Reserves

The concept of holding part of a military force in reserve to deal with unexpected developments has been understood and put into practice for millennia. Vegetius advocated that several bodies of reserves be kept in readiness:

> *The method of having bodies of reserves in rear of the army, composed of choice infantry and cavalry, commanded by the supernumerary lieutenant*

generals, counts and tribunes, is very judicious and of great consequence
towards the gaining of a battle. Some should be posted in rear of the wings
and some near the centre, to be ready to fly immediately to the assistance
of any part of the line which is hard pressed, to prevent its being pierced, to
supply the vacancies made therein during the action and thereby to keep up
the courage of their fellow soldiers and check the impetuosity of the enemy.
This was an invention of the Lacedaemonians, in which they were imitated
by the Carthaginians. The Romans have since observed it, and indeed no
better disposition can be found.[14]

For the British preparing to defend across an entire frontier, the principles were
similar but the considerations were different. At a tactical level, the hillforts
or other garrison areas could only sustain a limited number of troops. Anyone
inside the perimeter was likely to have had an immediate task in defence of
the ramparts and could not be spared to wait around like a dedicated reserve
for pitched battle. At the operational level, a number of reserves would ideally have been maintained to counter incursions. These would not necessarily
have been housed in any one garrison but would have roved between locations,
staying ready to react swiftly to any developing danger. Mounted troops would
have been chosen for their speed of reaction. It is unlikely that Ambrosius
would have wanted to maintain dedicated pockets of infantry reserves in the
open at the cost of manning every possible defended locality. Nonetheless,
some troops in the garrisons may have been assigned a dual role, prepared to
redeploy from their routine tasks in defence to counter an unexpected enemy
move.

  With the majority of foot troops committed to defence, the commander
would have needed excellent command and control in order to achieve sufficient flexibility to redeploy infantry who were not in contact in an effective
and timely manner. Therefore, in looking to create an effective reserve, the
commander probably decided to give this task to cavalry. As with the garrison
troops, he had to be careful of the risks involved in any decision to create a dual
role for the mounted troops by tasking them as both striking force and reserve.
What becomes very clear is that the identification of the enemy's main effort
was crucial, because the British could not afford to launch a strike or commit a
reserve to the wrong place or at the wrong time.

Concealment and deception

Ambrosius wanted to maximise his chances of dealing a decisive blow to his enemy. Keeping some of his forces hidden and concealing his strategy would have been an important consideration. Efforts to keep forces hidden until they engaged would extend also to deceiving the enemy about troop numbers and dispositions. It would have been difficult to conceal the fact that an area had been fortified and prepared for fighting, but it would have been possible nonetheless to deny the enemy information or deceive him regarding the strength of the defenders inside each location. Some observation posts on hilltops in the main defensive area would have been overt, their occupants ready to vacate if threatened. Other lookouts would have been camouflaged and concealed to ensure they were not neutralised or displaced by raids as a precursor to the enemy's main offensive.

Most important was to conceal the location of the striking forces and reserves. This was essential in order to ensure they had the best chance of achieving surprise once committed. The terrain across much of the South West would have lent itself to this, with suitable grazing sites screened by areas of forest or located in valleys and combes that could not be observed easily by the enemy. The commanders of these hidden forces would have ensured that a number of possible routes were reconnoitred to allow rapid movement to the anticipated locations for battle. The Britons would have enjoyed considerable advantage when seeking to move bodies of troops, because they were most familiar with the geography of their kingdoms.

Deception, the art of tricking one's enemy into believing that a course of action is being pursued whilst executing something entirely different, has turned the tide of battles and campaigns throughout history. The options available to the Dark Age British were limited in part by the sheer spread of their deployment, but innovation and imagination was no doubt employed by local commanders. One option would have been to construct dummy positions and decoys, to make troop numbers in the garrisons appear greater than they were.

Lines of communication

Inevitably, with the collapse of Roman rule in Britain, there was a general decline in the maintenance and building of engineering works. Nonetheless, for some time the quality of Rome's engineering ensured a legacy of relatively efficient roads, supplemented by the network of older trackways from the Bronze and Iron Ages. These land routes linked population centres, but also served as connections to the inland navigable waterways and coastal harbours that aided military movement by boat. These lines of communication, and particularly the hubs where they intersected, would have formed an integral part of the British plan for the long-term defence of the area. Ambrosius would have considered the requirement to move force elements around as the situation developed, to pass messages, and to move non-combatants to safety. Across southern Britain we can still discern the places where major routes converged in ancient times. In the Hampshire Avon frontier region, there were three strategic hubs at Winchester, Sarum and Badbury Rings.

The threat of a Germanic seaborne operation was also ever-present. From a British perspective beaches, harbours and estuaries would have required watching and defending in case of enemy landings. The coastline in the immediate area of interest extended from Christchurch to Weymouth. There were plenty of available landing sites west of Weymouth, but the distance from the frontier probably ruled out any major Germanic maritime excursions there. Navigable rivers accessible from the central south coast were relatively restricted compared to the Thames and other major rivers. It is unlikely that the Germanics would have considered rivers such as the Stour for substantial military operations against an alert and prepared enemy. Nonetheless, the British would have been alive to the potential for diversions or raids to manifest along such waterways and in their estuaries.

Pulling the plan together

When considering all of these factors from a British commander's perspective, we can identify three possible strategic lines of defence for a South West alliance of Britons confronting a Germanic threat from the east: the Hampshire Avon; a middle line running through Badbury Rings to Cadbury, much of which is also defined by the course of the River Stour; and a line in depth between Maiden Castle and Ham Hill. These opportunities meant that the defence did not have to be completely forward-leaning along the line of the Avon. Ambrosius would most likely have considered a scheme of manoeuvre that allowed the Germanics some freedom to advance in order to bring them into a situation of his choosing. Making the best use of the geographical features for the deployment of his forces depended on his assessment of how the Germanics would come at him, in particular determining their most likely choice for an operational objective.

Summary

Defensive preparations in the post-Roman period, exemplified by the archaeological evidence at Cadbury, did not happen at random. The hypothetical British strategy outlined in this chapter was prescient of the much-lauded *Burghal Hidage* organised by Alfred three-and-a-half centuries later, which provided security across a similar stretch of territory by then called Wessex. We can be sure that there was an effective British military command structure in place by the late fifth century to coordinate the campaign that was to culminate at Badon Hill.

The British commander Ambrosius was likely to have crafted a defensive plan based around a number of strongholds and the ability to move forces between them swiftly when required. The defence of hillforts undoubtedly formed the backbone of the plan, that much is obvious from a map study alone but is confirmed by the archaeological evidence of refortification. Cadbury Castle is easily identified as an important location but it is equally possible to identify Castle Ditches and Badbury Rings as two of the strongest outposts with strategic importance in the frontier zone. These forward garrisons were the immediate guardians of the lines of communication that allowed access to the British heartlands. A number of lesser garrisons would have been spread between such strongholds and along the vulnerable areas of coast. To supplement this network, reconnaissance patrols would have probed for information across the frontier, whilst small outposts kept watch. We can be equally sure that sited somewhere carefully was the jewel in the British crown: a striking force of cavalry equipped and trained similarly to the *alae* that had first arrived to Britain in Roman times. This force had the destructive power to break an opposing army at one stroke. All that was required to achieve such a feat was that the right circumstances presented to allow the British cavalry to time their strike and launch it to maximum effect.

It is true that the British seem to have been in disarray during the initial Germanic aggression in Kent and Sussex, as they lost defended locations rather too easily. It is also possible to identify the reasons for this. The Germanic threat in Kent had arisen from within, from the Jutes already settled there. In Sussex, the British had been disorganised and ill-prepared to resist the landings on the coast and the determined savagery of Ælle and his warbands. Germanic attacks prior to Badon had often been prosecuted with relatively small forces that made best use of surprise, speed in the assault and a level of aggression that had unhinged the cohesiveness of the British. The difference in the Badon campaign was that larger armies were about to be unleashed. Whilst the shield-wall clashes on the battlefield would continue to determine tactical outcomes, the relative skills of the opposing commanders in using their forces effectively would decide the campaign. West of the Hampshire Avon, British war leaders, most likely under the command of what we can call an Ambrosius dynasty, had the collective potential to bring a formidable army into the field. The challenge for the command structure was to ensure that this army could achieve myriad tasks and still bring sufficient combat power to bear in one place when the opportunity was right. We know that somehow this feat of arms was achieved at Badon Hill, bringing to an end the earliest period of Germanic advances across southern Britain.

The Badon campaign cannot be placed precisely in time but a considered assessment of the military postures through this period has been presented, a period that forced the Britons to recognise that their separate territories had either to come together in the face of the Germanic threat or perish by it. The Germanics also realised that the days of the warbands were drawing to a close. Larger armies were needed if lasting gains were to be made. In this chapter we have determined the likely British campaign plan for defence. Next, we must look at the considerations for an offensive from a Germanic perspective.

Chapter Five

The Badon Campaign

*War – the ordinary man's most convenient means of escaping from the
ordinary.*
                                                    – Philip Caputo

Germanic options

There were two identifiable courses of action open to the Germanics
once they consolidated their territories to the east of the Hampshire
Avon. They could try to expand their influence northwards up
the Avon and Itchen Valleys, or they could continue to make gains close to
the coast by crossing the Avon into the Bokerley/Wansdyke territories. For a
while there was little pressure to act, but population growth alone would have
necessitated further efforts to expand at some point. Another strong influence on the Germanic leaders was the very nature of the warriors they led. A
desire for battle was ever-present within the clans and this impulse stood to
reignite the war with the Britons:

> *Many noble youths, if the land of their birth is stagnating in a protracted*
> *peace, deliberately seek out other tribes, where some war is afoot. The*
> *Germans have no taste for peace; renown is easier won among perils, and*
> *you cannot maintain a large body of companions except by violence and*
> *war. The companions are prodigal in their demands on the generosity of*
> *their chiefs. It is always 'give me that war-horse' or 'give me that bloody*
> *and vicious spear'. As for meals with their plentiful, if homely, fare, they*
> *count simply as pay. Such open-handedness must have war and plunder to*
> *feed it.*[1]

The giving of prizes to reward success in battle was important to the Saxon elite.
War and plunder were the incentives for the warriors of the Angles, Saxons and
Jutes, who were encroaching onto British territory at this time. Achieving glory

was a priority and preferably led to riches, including the acquisition of agricultural land. The onus was on kings and war leaders to deliver these if they wished to retain their power and influence. Germanic commanders trying to manage such expectations would nevertheless have paid heed to the growing military strength of the Britons and would have recognised around this time a need to achieve greater cohesiveness in their own military operations. The war leaders of a number of factions would likely have met to consider possible alliances and objectives for a joint campaign. Foremost in their discussions would have been the question of strategy, and the debate would have been influenced by their knowledge of the British dispositions as well as the amount and quality of land they might reasonably aspire to capture.

One option for the Germanic forces at this stage would have been to make use of their seafaring capabilities to progress along the Channel coastline. However, it is important to be realistic about what they could achieve by this means beyond opportunistic raiding. Haywood argued that the capabilities of the pre-Viking Germanic seafarers had been greatly underestimated by previous writers, referring to the individual capabilities of the boats and crews rather than their collective ability as a fleet.[2] Haywood concentrated his study deliberately on the Roman-era Germanic tribes who were settled between the Rhine and the Jutland peninsula, groups who had a history of seafaring devoted to warfare and piracy. The Germanic tribes who first arrived in Kent and Sussex were predominantly from these regions. It can be safely assumed that they were capable sailors, but wholesale migration of their peoples across the seas was a new phenomenon and looks to have taken place incrementally. Of the eight *Anglo-Saxon Chronicle* entries from 477 to 514, four describe landings and specify the number of ships (three, five, two and three respectively) that arrived in Britain. These figures suggest that around sixty to 150 warriors arrived at any one time. Thus, from the *Chronicle* we can deduce little about the total number of ships available to any one group on their home shores. There is nothing to suggest that Germanic fleets of the time matched those of the Danes, who came to menace Britain centuries later. Thirty-five shiploads is quoted for the Danish raiding army of 840, and in 877 it is recorded that 120 ships were lost in a great storm off Swanage as the Danes attempted to sail a fleet from Wareham to Exeter.

It therefore seems unlikely that Ælle, or any other Germanic leader of the time, was able to project an army of thousands into a new region by sea. That leaves the possibility that, once settled in the South East, the new arrivals established mutually beneficial alliances to raise a sizeable land army. Potential interested parties included some of the Germanic groups already settled in Roman times. There is evidence of a Saxon presence in the Salisbury region well before 552. This casts even more doubt upon the early *Anglo-Saxon Chronicle* entries, which record the capture of Sarum in 552 as part of a series of victories achieved by the West Saxons. That said, the allegiance of any of the longer established Germanic groups is hard to judge. There was plenty of warring between Germanic factions as they competed for space in Britain. Some Germanic populations had lived amongst and interbred with the Romano-British for generations and may well have been minded to resist the new influx rather than support it.

At the start of the sixth century, any northward expansion out of Sussex and Hampshire would have been ambitious from a Germanic perspective. It would have taken warriors away from the coastal areas that were still being settled and needed defending. The established enclaves could be reinforced and resupplied by sea, but extending the lines of logistic support for new operations inland would have to wait. Campaigning northwards would have created extensive land borders for the newly captured areas, leaving too much frontage exposed to attack. Establishing effective lines of communication would have been complicated by the dense forest barriers. Given these constraints on Sussex and its allies, a westward expansion was by far the more likely course for them. It is most likely that they tried to continue their 'land grabs' along the south coast, an already established and successful *modus operandi* which was the strategy of least risk and most gain. This played both to their maritime strengths and their territorial ambitions on land. West of the Hampshire Avon lay Poole Harbour, the second largest natural harbour in the world. Capturing it would have been particularly tempting, but before assuming that such action became part of a strategy, it is worth looking at the broader Germanic considerations for planning a renewed offensive.

Offensive operations

The primary aim of Germanic military operations in Britain in the early fifth century was to capture territory. The manoeuvrist doctrine of today does not concern itself much with the taking of ground per se. Instead, the defeat of the enemy is the primary focus:

> *Offensive operations are the decisive activity during major combat operations. Their principal purpose is to defeat an enemy by shattering his cohesion and destroying his will to fight* ... *The selective physical destruction of enemy forces in conjunction with other means of attack* ... *and the denial of his freedom of action will exert significant psychological pressure and lead* [the enemy] *to the belief that he is defeated.*[3]

Previous Germanic advances along the south coast had been successful due to swift and aggressive actions against Britons who were slow to react or unable to organise effective resistance. This situation had changed. Ambrosius had prepared the Britons effectively for the coming war across a wide area. Using the modern terminology from the extract above, the Germanic commander should have been looking for the most productive selective physical destruction of enemy forces that could be achieved. His campaign objectives needed to be realistic and he could not have expected to defeat Ambrosius outright. In determining where to attack, he needed to identify key terrain. Key terrain in this instance was a feature or an area which, if lost, would cause a significant part of the British defence to collapse. In looking to bring this about, the Germanic commander would have actively sought to discover all he could about the British dispositions. Effective reconnaissance and information-gathering was required to identify any enemy weaknesses. Raids and covert patrols would have been launched all along the frontier to assess the British defences.

Having gathered information in this way, the Germanic commander would have known he was about to invade an area characterised by strong and coordinated defences. We can surmise that he was broadly aware of how the British had deployed and that he would have perceived the highly mobile British cavalry as a particular threat. As he planned his offensive, it would have become obvious that an element of surprise was going to be crucial if the initial assault was to succeed. He could not allow the British time to mass against his force and significantly outnumber it in an open battle. A substantial Germanic force gathering near the Hampshire Avon could not have gone unnoticed by British spies and informants, so achieving outright surprise would have been impossible. The Germanics might have considered trying deception measures, like a feint or a demonstration, in order to draw attention away from the main attack.[4] However, such ruses required the diversion of manpower away from the main force.

The Germanic Army had to gain a foothold in a new area and ensure that any attempt to recapture that territory would be costly for the British. The chosen objective needed to be relatively close to the existing Germanic holdings in order to ensure protected lines of communication for resupply, reinforcement and an orderly retreat if things went awry. The Germanic commander would have known that he was about to goad the British and a question for him was how far dare he push his luck in so doing. This had to be weighed against the amount of new territory he could realistically aspire to capture and hold. It is safe to surmise that the Germanic commander would have considered his forces able to outmatch the British in the initial assault. He knew he would be unable to achieve numerical superiority for any length of time, but local superiority could be gained through surprise and speed. Ideally from his perspective the British, spread relatively thinly in order to defend across a large area, would be unable to concentrate their efforts in one locality fast enough to counter such a move. For this reason, the Germanic commander would have leaned towards a plan based on speed of execution for a limited offensive, followed by rapid transition to an effective defence. That was the only way he could gain territory and hold it. The choice of objective was the Germanic commander's to make, and with it came the initiative at the outset of the campaign.

Whether he knew it or not, the Dark Age Germanic commander contemplating a strategy to extend his borders beyond early Sussex and Hampshire was in a similar position to that which the Roman commander Vespasian had faced some 450 years earlier. Aulus Plautius had landed in AD 43 at Richborough, Kent, with a total force of about 40,000. The region encompassing today's Sussex and Hampshire was quickly pacified before the Second Legion Augusta was unleashed on the South West. Led by Vespasian, who was later to become emperor, the legion first captured the Isle of Wight and thereafter over twenty hillforts fell, despite having been bastions for one of the fiercest Celtic tribes, the Durotriges. Rather than come to terms like some British tribes, the Durotriges fought hard. But Roman superiority in martial affairs overmatched them. Roman records show that some hillforts were laid siege to and the inhabitants starved out. It is recorded that some Celtic populations were massacred to the last man, woman and child. Some tribes were more accepting and cooperative. The Dumnonii, for example, entered into an agreement with the Roman occupiers. The relatively small sizes of the Roman garrisons recorded in the South West testify that an enduring cooperation existed in this area. That cooperation was based on mutual benefit and, for the Celts perhaps, an instinct for survival following the brutal demonstration of Roman military power against the Durotriges. The Romans wanted a share in the rich mineral wealth of the region and, from a military perspective, they also needed to secure their western flank before pushing north. Vespasian was reluctant to commit manpower to large garrisons unless strictly necessary. He had organised and deliberately implemented a pact with the Dumnonii just as surely as his strategy had required the outright destruction of the Durotriges.

In the earliest stages of Vespasian's campaign in Dorset, his land forces crossed the Hampshire Avon and linked-up with his maritime fleet, which had landed at Hamworthy, a peninsula of land jutting into Poole Harbour that enabled an effective defence of the initial landing sites (see Map 5). He proceeded to secure a logistical base at Lake Farm just a short march to the north of the harbour. Once ready, he committed his forces to attack the complex of hillforts occupied by the Durotriges. The first objective was modern-day Badbury Rings and, once it was secured, Roman engineers commenced the construction of military roads that still emanate from it to this day. Vespasian's subsequent campaign in Dorset was clinical. His primary axis was north-west up the Stour Valley, securing further hillforts at Spetisbury, Hod Hill and Hambledon Hill. This achieved three campaign goals. It split the Durotriges territory in half-making coordinated resistance difficult. It seized vital high ground that could be defended and held. And it secured what would be the Romans' northern flank in the next phase. This next phase saw a second axis of advance opened westwards, which allowed the Second Legion Augusta to strike at Maiden Castle, which John Peddie calls the 'strategically and politically important stronghold' of the Durotriges.[5] It soon fell to the might of Rome and the Celtic tribe was finished as a military power.

It is not unusual in military history to discover that certain battlefields have been involved in numerous conflicts across many centuries, usually due to their proximity to major routes or other important strategic features in the landscape.

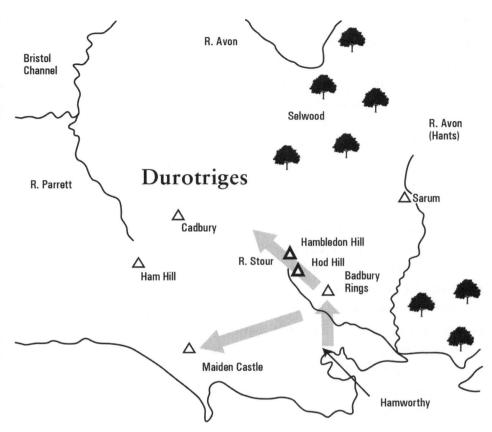

Map 5: Vespasian in Dorset

Megiddo in the north of Israel was a battle site in the fifteenth century BC, in 609 BC and again in AD 1918, whilst Edirne (Adrianople) in Turkey witnessed fifteen battles in nine different centuries between AD 313 and 1913. It is very likely that the region encompassing the hillfort at Badbury Rings and the harbour at Poole was viewed by the Dark Age Germanics in much the same way as it had been by the Romans. It was a gateway to the South West, a defendable foothold to take and hold at all costs in the opening phase of the Badon campaign.

The Germanic combat estimate

A strategy to conquer the South West similar to that devised and executed by Vespasian would have appealed equally to Ælle. It would have forced the Britons to withdraw either north or west. Any that went west were effectively cut off in the South West Peninsula, and could be held in check there due to the relatively short border between the Bristol and English Channels. That would have complicated the options available to Dumnonia and any remnant allies for a counter-offensive, because their forces were isolated from each other. Yet the newly formed Germanic alliance had neither the numbers nor the necessary logistic support that Vespasian had enjoyed. Realistically, the Germanic gains would have to be made by continuing the piecemeal capture of territory, so campaign planning would likely have focused on achieving the initial, more limited goals.

When deciding which piece of territory to target, Ælle would have considered what he knew of the enemy strengths and dispositions to assess the likely British reactions to any incursion. The total strength of the British force can only be guessed at today, and the same was probably true then from his perspective. His most pressing concern was the British deployment around and within the immediate objectives that he considered it possible to capture. It is likely that he knew the British dispositions in outline but not in detail. His assessment would have included the British territories to the north, such as Silchester, and he probably had intelligence regarding the degree of cooperation that existed between the British kingdoms. It is certainly safe to say that Ælle would have been aware of any opposing commander whose remit was as wide-ranging as Gildas describes for Ambrosius.

Sources of information would have included recent sightings and reported engagements from warbands in the frontier zone, together with reports from any other informants such as traders and other travellers. There was a flourishing trade between Britain, North Africa and the Byzantine Empire in the fifth and sixth centuries, which continued despite the conflict. The seafaring Germanics may well have had access to information from merchants who moved freely within the British realms. Covert reconnaissance would have been attempted and, in all likelihood, raids would have been launched in order to gain information as well as to indulge warriors seeking their traditional pursuits of pillage and general mayhem. From all of this we can assess that Ælle had a reasonable idea of the strengths and dispositions of the British, particularly in the defended localities close to the frontier.

The Germanic requirement to secure territory brought with it a number of implied tasks. There was the need to secure and protect lines of communication to the new area of operations, as well as to plan for its consolidation and settlement once sufficient territory had been secured. The nature of the terrain dictated how far from the frontier the expeditionary force could reasonably expect to operate. It was harder to maintain security of routes through extensive forest or marshland, for example. A major constraint was the number of troops available for the new campaign given the number required to remain behind and defend existing territory. The county boundary first established between Dorset and Hampshire suggests that the coastal region around today's Christchurch Harbour and Bournemouth Bay, originally in Hampshire, was settled early by Germanics as already illustrated in Map 3. The Britons at the time may well have felt that they had yielded little beyond land characterised by heath and sandy soils, a small harbour at Christchurch and the abandoned iron industry at Hengistbury. The camp at Dudsbury on the River Stour probably defined the limit of Germanic exploitation at this time. From Ælle's perspective, this extant incursion across the line of the Hampshire Avon provided a possible base from which he could strike deeper into the valuable territory upriver along the Stour.

Another possible start point for the campaign was further north, at Charford, identified by Major as the 'point of attack' for a Saxon offensive in 519. Major based this on the *Anglo-Saxon Chronicle*, which has the West Saxon leaders Cerdic and Cynric advancing along the south coast, reaching Charford in 508 and fighting a battle there in 519, which established their rule. This scenario was debunked to a degree in Chapter One and is explored again briefly with the same result in Chapter Seven. It seems that the *Chronicle* authors were deliberately bringing Charford on the Hampshire Avon into the story of Wessex right around the time that Badon was contested. In so doing, they might have been harking back to Ælle's activities, attributing them somewhat mischievously to Cerdic and Cynric and neatly avoiding any mention of Badon because it was a heavy Saxon defeat.

In considering another alternative axis for an offensive to the north, vulnerable Winchester was probably absorbed by the Germanics in the earliest stages of their breakout from the south-east pocket. Thus, it also offered an opportunity as a base from which to strike northwards against *Caer Celemion* with its Silchester powerbase. But that would have been a higher risk option when one considers the problem of consolidating any gains. It follows that, immediately prior to Badon, the Germanic leadership most likely made a key decision to try and expand their territories westwards along the Channel Coast. At the operational level, the capture of at least one of the British strongpoints west of the Avon was necessary to ensure that the newly gained territory could be consolidated and defended.

Preliminary actions

The new Germanic kingdoms of Kent and Sussex were relatively secure at this time as far as we can tell and any remaining British populations within them might well have been subdued and compliant. However, assessing the strength of the military force available to them either separately or as allies is very difficult because, unlike for later battles and campaigns, there is no mention in the written records of numbers of men or ships involved. The Jutish leader of Kent, which the sources imply was King Oisc at this time, would presumably have had some say in how to conduct a military venture that he contributed troops to. He would probably have known and approved of the plan for the offensive and would only have allowed his forces to take part in what he considered to be a worthy venture. It is possible that he was under some pressure, perhaps from his sons' impatience to prove themselves and also because his own territory was threatened by the new arrivals to Britain. Ælle's initial advances along the south coast appear to have been eastwards towards Kent territory. Oisc would have been cognisant of the growth of Ælle's Sussex as South Saxon boats continued to arrive from the continent. That growth was a potential threat to Kent. Oisc would have been wary of a possible war with his new neighbours – better to keep them close as allies. As already estimated, the Kent force probably consisted of no more than 500 warriors if one accepts that they were junior partners in Ælle's venture.

The Kent detachment probably marched on foot to a rendezvous point with the warriors from Sussex. A fit warband could have covered 15 to 20 miles a day with ease. It is also possible that they moved by sea to landing sites in Hampshire. But a single sea move of 500 men would have required around fifteen ships, a sizeable flotilla for a relatively short journey. Whatever the means of travel to the forests of Hampshire, the Jutes of Kent would at some point have been met by guides and taken to an assembly area to marry-up with the army of Sussex.

The Germanic force would have mustered as covertly as possible, but it is likely that some elements of the British surveillance package picked up on 2,000 or more warriors concentrating and preparing for action. Ambrosius would have received the first sporadic reports of such a gathering and tried to decide what the sum of his information amounted to. It is difficult to maintain forces constantly at the highest readiness and therefore likely that he instigated a scalable system of alert. He would certainly have increased his forces' readiness a notch at this time. This would have involved moving extra troops into the frontier zone for surveillance, some of which would have bolstered existing operations through covert patrolling with the specific aim of observing the Germanic preparations. Extra overt observation posts on hilltops would also have been established with orders to watch for incursions. Larger outposts would already have their orders in respect to any harassing attacks they would be expected to mount in order to delay and disrupt the enemy's preparatory moves. Troops newly mobilised would have begun to occupy their designated garrisons. A contingency plan to move civilians out of threatened areas might also have been activated.

With the build-up of his substantial army detected, the Germanic commander would have considered deception measures to try and maintain some element of surprise. He might have considered a feint against one objective to try and disguise his real intent, but this would have dispersed his combat power. It is hard to see how the Germanic alliance could have achieved strategic surprise given the number of troops mobilised and the assessed readiness of the British. At the tactical level, though, it was possible to keep an element of surprise in the battle-plan, for example, a sudden advance and attack in strength to overwhelm one part of the British defences quickly.

Even from today's maps, Castle Ditches and Badbury Rings stand out as the most prominent fortresses challenging any Germanic encroachment westwards. Castle Ditches certainly played a part in the fighting that eventually began to reduce British holdings in Dorset. A report of excavations at the site in 1960 states that 'a few Mesolithic artefacts were found and there was post Romano-British activity on and within the rampart'.[6] More recently a Saxon burial site at Breamore on the banks of the Avon, 4 miles east of Whitsbury, has revealed 'a profusion of spears and shield bosses', the dates of which 'could extend from the late fifth to the early seventh century'.[7] Other non-military artefacts from this cemetery suggest the presence of Saxons of high status, but no swords were found. When the Saxons did begin to press into Dorset, it seems that they avoided initially the high chalk area of the Bokerley territory. North of Bokerley they expanded in increments along the line of the Roman road that ran from Old Salisbury to the Mendip lead mines and south-west up the valleys of the Rivers Nadder and Ebble towards Shaftesbury. The best assessment that can be made for the early sixth century is that Castle Ditches remained in British hands, with the limit of Saxon exploitation very close to it until some considerable time later. Eagles identified a similar pattern from archaeological evidence:

> It is argued that Bokerley Dyke formed a part of the eastern border of the Civitas Durotrigum. From a fifth-century nucleus round Old Sarum, to the east, sixth-century 'Anglo-Saxon' culture, and probably presence, spread westwards across the Dyke, to reach as far as Seaxpenn ('the Saxons' hill') and Combs Ditch, an area which may have coincided with a pagus centred upon Badbury Rings. However, to the west of Teffont ('the funta on the boundary'), immediately north of the Dyke, it is only in the seventh century that Anglo-Saxons are first evident, as is the case in the remainder of Dorset. Saxon acquisition of this former Romano-British civitas was, therefore, piecemeal and long-drawn-out.[8]

The easternmost parts of the Bokerley territory provide the most credible objectives that a Germanic commander would have aspired to capture at the time of the Badon campaign. Nonetheless, prominent authors have often dismissed the region as away from the Germanic axis of advance as assessed by them. Ashe, who has written several books on the factual basis behind the Arthurian legends, considered the historical case for Badbury Rings as Badon Hill but found it wanting. He claimed that the site is too far away from the strong early Saxon populations and 'not in the path of any plausible offensive'.[9] His standing as a renowned authority on Arthur has ensured that this view has been perpetuated, but on examination it fails to convince. Badbury Rings was very much in the path of Ælle's most plausible axis for his offensive.

There has been only limited archaeological investigation at Badbury Rings, but a geophysical survey and accompanying excavation in 2000 confirmed the presence of a Romano–Celtic temple immediately to the south-west of the hill-fort. This temple and its accompanying ancient tribal centre were attested to by Papworth's investigations of the area in the mid-1990s, which concluded that buildings on the site continued to be used until the end of the Roman period.[10] There is no reason to suppose that they were abandoned after that point. 'The Rings' is a 7-hectare multivallate Iron Age hillfort with defences consisting of three concentric circular ditches and embankments. Unlike the majority of hillforts in the region, it is not situated on particularly high or steep ground. It is approached on all sides by relatively gentle slopes and thus the site was not naturally defensible without the banks and ditches. The amount of human endeavour devoted to its construction can only point to its particular importance in the Iron Age as a regional centre and communications hub. It is likely that the site was prepared strongly by the fifth century British for the same reason. To capture it would have required a siege, like Ælle's earlier effort at *Andredes-ceaster* (Pevensey) in 491, where all of the Britons in the fort were killed according to the *Anglo-Saxon Chronicle*.[11]

At Pevensey, the South Saxons had prevailed but a later account written by Henry of Huntingdon in the early-twelfth century suggests it was far from easy for them. Although his sources are unknown his record is vivid:

Ella was joined by auxiliaries from his own country, with whose assistance he laid siege to Andredecester, a strongly-fortified town. The Britons swarmed together like wasps, assailing the besiegers by daily ambuscades and nocturnal sallies. There was neither day nor night in which some new alarm did not harass the minds of the Saxons; but the more they were provoked, the more vigorously they pressed the siege. Whenever they advanced to the assault of the town, the Britons from without falling on their rear with their archers and slingers drew the Pagans away from the walls to resist their own attack, which the Britons, lighter of foot, avoided by taking refuge in the woods; and when they turned again to assault the town, again the Britons hung on their rear. The Saxons were for some time harassed by these manoeuvres, till, having lost a great number of men, they divided their army into two bodies, one of which carried on the siege, while the other repelled the attacks from without. After this the Britons were so reduced by continual famine that they were unable any longer to withstand the force of the besiegers, so that they all fell by the edge of the sword, with their women and children, not one escaping alive.

The foreigners were so enraged at the loss they had sustained that they totally destroyed the city, and it was never afterwards rebuilt, so that its desolate site is all that is now pointed out to travellers.[12]

If Henry of Huntingdon's account is accurate it is clear that Ælle would not have taken a decision to undertake another difficult siege lightly. The fort at Pevensey is some way inland today, but given the higher sea levels in the fifth century, it has been described for those times as 'easily besieged, lying at the end of a small, low-lying peninsula'.[13] Is Huntingdon's account in any way accurate, then? Perhaps it is exaggerated and Ælle took Pevensey with relative ease, which might have encouraged him when he looked westwards at the hillforts across the Avon. When one considers the strategic situation at the time, together with the discernible military activity along the Hampshire Avon frontier, it is difficult to argue against Badbury Rings as a possible objective for Ælle and, thus, as the site of Badon Hill. Badbury Rings as Badon Hill is not a new suggestion by any means. In his 1883 papers, *Origines Celticae*, Dr Edwin Guest argued the case, noting that the 'elevated site, its great strength and evident importance, and its name, all alike favour the hypothesis'.[14] The Rings is the highest feature for some distance around, but as noted already, the ground surrounding the embankments slopes away gently. Unlike at many other hillfort sites, there are no natural steep slopes or other obstacles to enhance the fort's defensive properties in the immediate vicinity. On the one hand that would have allowed a besieging army an easy approach. On the other, it would have left the besiegers more exposed than at Pevensey, for example, where they had gained some protection because the narrow peninsula restricted the British options for manoeuvre and counter-attack.

The seeds of Germanic failure

The Germanic commander who lost the battle at Badon Hill would not have launched a costly assault on a strongly defended position without due care and consideration. Exactly why his forces failed to capture their objective will never be known, but a major error of judgement cannot be ruled out. Was the campaign based on a flawed plan to begin with, or did the execution of a sound plan go horribly wrong? We can only speculate about how well he managed his information in the planning stages and whether he was able to turn it into useful intelligence. As a bare minimum, he would have considered the strength of the British forces ready to oppose him immediately, and the likely strength and time into action of reinforcements. He would have formed his own ideas regarding the battlefield strengths and weaknesses of his enemy based on his experience of fighting in Sussex and Hampshire. He should have considered what he knew of the current situation alongside that knowledge gained from earlier campaigns. That might have given him pause had he paid more heed to the renewed military cohesiveness amongst the Britons, but it is entirely possible he simply underestimated his opponents.

Underestimating one's opponent has often led armies to ignominious defeat. On 6 May 53 BC, a Roman campaign against the Parthians led by Triumvir Marcus Licinius Crassus ended in disaster at the battle of Carrhae. In planning his campaign, Crassus boasted that he would conquer the East as far as Bactria and India, describing earlier victories by his contemporaries Lucullus and Pompey as 'child's play'. He misjudged Parthia's strong national identity and the resulting determination of its people to protect their independence. Despite advice from knowledgeable allies, he engaged in battle with little idea of what the Parthians had prepared against him. Basing his views on earlier Roman conquests, he was convinced that he could dominate under any circumstances. But when it came to battle the Parthians, despite being heavily outnumbered by the Romans, employed horse archers armed with powerful compound bows to devastating effect. Of the Roman force of nearly 5,500, there were only 500 survivors, all of whom were taken captive by the Parthians.

If the Germanic commander at Badon was similarly focused on his own ambitions and what he thought his own forces were capable of, rather than on the enemy, then one can see the beginnings of his downfall. Ælle needed land for his people and the prestige of continued success in war, both of which added unwelcome pressures to his considerations. Also, compared to a warband, this larger Germanic army was more difficult to sustain on campaign. Therefore, rapid success was required to avoid returning home with little to show. Perhaps due to overconfidence or pressure to succeed, there was no voice of caution to warn of the potential difficulties ahead. Ultimately, the decision to launch the Badon campaign, which led to a siege at Badon Hill, was made. The failings of Crassus were documented by the Roman historians Plutarch and Dio Cassius, but all we know for certain about Badon is that the campaign failed. It is possible nonetheless to consider the commander's state of mind and whether his decision-making was flawed and sowed the seeds of that failure.

Sometimes a decision-maker becomes so focused on the desired outcome of his plan that associated risks are considered but each one is assessed to be manageable. He fails to appreciate that the sum total of the risk involved is likely to scupper the plan. Once events are in motion decision paralysis can set in even as the situation worsens and the consequences of pursuing the flawed strategy become clear. In warfare, even as a bad situation develops a commander often has various chances to reverse his fortunes before it is too late. Yet, because the catastrophe is not imminently upon him he presses forward, ignoring the signs in the same way as he ignored the cumulative sum of the risks. By the time he realises he will fail it is too late to adjust. At this point commanders have been known to start blaming their subordinates, adding to the stress, because once the commander loses credibility those under him lose faith in his enterprise.

Pech and Durden constructed a model of similar behaviour that is reproduced at Figure 4. They also cite Hitler's ill-advised persistence in trying to capture Stalingrad as an example of a leader prone to this mindset:

> … *he must have known that the Russian armies had improved greatly in leadership, training, and material since previous major battles. Hitler's Chief of Staff, General Kurt Zeitzler, pleaded with him day after day to permit a withdrawal of troops, but Hitler, having no concept of fluid defence tactics, was not able to admit that the Sixth Army was being sacrificed to an unsound plan.*[15]

In planning and executing the Badon campaign, it is possible that the Germanic commander was subject to some or all of the weaknesses described above. The Germanic allies could not have been wholly ignorant of the strengths of the British alliance, but they attacked nonetheless.

The decision-making process resulting in failure is influenced by …

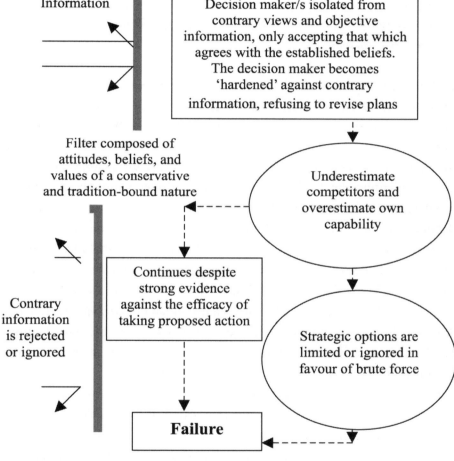

Figure 4: Negative influences on decision–making[16]

The legend of King Arthur

It is difficult to theorise about Badon Hill without also deciding where one stands regarding King Arthur. Gildas provides us with the name of the battle site, helps to bracket the date and confirms it was a siege but it is Nennius who first brings Arthur into the equation. A significant amount of research and effort has been focused onto identifying the sites for the entire list of twelve battles that Nennius attributes to Arthur, but Michael Wood perhaps delivers the most realistic and balanced verdict:

> *In the end, as with all the fictions in Nennius' list a case can be made to support almost any identification, but all evaporate on close inspection. All we can say is that they are not the battles of a fifth century leader fighting the Anglo-Saxons.*[17]

With little to go on bar myths and legends, people who attempt to identify a single person as the historical Arthur usually conclude that he was a war leader based either in Wales or in northern Britain. Blake and Scott, founders of the Centre for Arthurian Studies, have devoted years of research to the subject and they concur with Wood. They make a good case for a number of the locations on Nennius' list to be in Wales, but they also conclude that their Welsh-based Arthur never fought the Saxons and that most of the locations, including Badon, may not be associated with him at all.[18] There are numerous arguments of varying strength for an 'Arthur of the North'. These include a Cumbrian king, *Arthur ic Uibar* (Arthur son of Uther); *Arthuis*, who ruled over a kingdom around *Ebrauc* (York); a king of *Elmet* (West Yorkshire), also called *Arthuis*; and a Scottish prince, *Artur*, the son of King Aidan of *Dalriada*. Arguments to promote all of these often quote place-names in support, the most famous of which is Arthur's Seat in Holyrood Park, Edinburgh. Most of the locations on Nennius' list can be argued to be in northern Britain.

Despite all of the above, the siege of Badon Hill appears to be the genesis of the Arthur legend. The reason for this may well have more to do with the decisive presence of armoured cavalry on the battlefield than anything else. In an age where the Roman legions were long gone and few warriors wore helmets or body armour, the spectacle of Sarmatian-style cavalry, with horses and men alike clad in scale armour, would have been uniquely impressive and remained long in the minds of any who saw them in action on the battlefields of Britain. If such a force turned the battle at Badon to the Britons' advantage, the feat would have entered the collective memory of a folk destined to continue wars against Germanic invaders down the generations. The commander of the cavalry force at Badon Hill is almost certainly the earliest inspiration for the legendary Arthur. More than that we cannot say, except to conclude that some of the Arthurian legends may be based on the real deeds of historical characters, now lost from any reliable records. Unfortunately, credible scenarios for the early battles in Dark Age Britain seem to get lost or disregarded in the frenzy of speculation about Arthur. To put it simply, Arthur gets in the way of the scholarship.

Alternative locations for Badon

Regarding the site of the battle, there have been other long-standing contenders besides Badbury Rings. Several suggested sites are in the Thames region based on the hypothesis that it was fought as the Germanic *foederati* there revolted and the resultant fighting spilled out of the Thames basin. A variant of this hypothesis is that Ælle marched north from Sussex to gather part of his force in the Thames Valley, before attacking the Britons in the region. Both theories are inclined to mention the 'Goring Gap' as strategically important, because it was able to facilitate the movement of armies. Goring lies on the east bank of the Thames, roughly 6 miles south of Wallingford, an Anglo–Saxon name meaning 'ford of the wealhas' (foreigners). The gap is found in the chalk hills near Goring where the Thames enters the hilly region around Pangbourne and Reading. Goring is also the point at which the ancient Ridgeway track crosses the Thames, so it is easy to see why military scholars afford it such significance.

Liddington Castle is a popular suggested location for Badon based on the idea that a Germanic threat emanated from the Thames Valley region. Its candidacy as the battle site relies also on the name of the nearby village of Badbury. One difficulty with this scenario is envisaging how the defeat of a Germanic army in the Thames region led to the noticeable loss of South Saxon influence along the Channel Coast. It only has credence if Ælle and his warriors were part of that army, or were defeated elsewhere at the same time, a highly unlikely coincidence. For this reason those who argue for a Thames Valley location invariably propose that a Germanic alliance under Ælle was trying to inflict a strategic defeat on the British and gain control of much of southern Britain at one stroke. If such was the case then many locations come into play. With this, as with any other scenario, one has to decide what the early Germanic war leaders were realistically capable of achieving through force of arms. All of the evidence for the early growth of Kent, Sussex and the Anglian kingdoms to the north of the Thames indicates incremental growth through the fifth and well into the sixth century. The same applies to Middlesex, whose army is sometimes described as having marched through the Goring Gap and into the upper Thames Valley to fight at Badon. Liddington is some considerable way to the west of their identifiable lands and it is uncertain how well-established Middlesex was at this stage, if at all.

The hillfort at Liddington is also rather small at about 120 metres in diameter internally. Unlike the larger forts, it is difficult to see how it could support a force of any size for any time. Its occupiers would have been poorly provisioned for water in particular, reduced to carrying it up from streams in the valleys below or using dew ponds. All in all, it represents a poor choice for a defensive garrison as part of the British matrix we have identified. That said, the fort does occupy a strategically important spot, with far-reaching views in all directions. It would have been an excellent military outpost for observation and early warning.

A Thames Valley/Ridgeway location for Badon Hill implies that the army of Sussex moved a long distance in pursuit of a strategic goal. Godsal was an early proponent of such actions. He and others like him influenced the debate for some considerable time, not least because they took the *Anglo-Saxon Chronicle* to be an accurate record of events. In *The Storming of London*, Godsal added many embellishments to a Thames Valley scenario derived from the *Chronicle*. In his build-up to the climax of a campaign led by Ælle, he presented an amalgamation of deployments:

> *We have a complex state of affairs to deal with. Beginning at the west, we have Cerdic pressing up the Itchen Valley; and later on Bieda and Maegla, and also the West Saxons, landing on the shores of the Solent; the South Saxons pressing westward; Aelle in the Thames Valley somewhere between Windsor and Reading, fighting going on in the Chiltern Hills and the north of Middlesex, and parties landing on the shores of Essex. The objectives of the period are first Winchester and then Silchester. Then the securing possession of the Thames Valley by clearing the Chilterns, and the construction of the Henley-Wallingford dyke. Then the beyond.*[19]

Godsal was convinced that London had fallen to Ælle early on, arguing that the supreme leader of the Germanic armies would have struck first for the heart of his enemy's kingdom. A gradual reduction of British power that took centuries was replaced in his book by one sweeping campaign. Godsal suggested that Ælle commanded in person the two key parts of this campaign, first the 'storming of London' and then a series of victories in the Thames Valley and surrounding areas. He proposed that the second phase was launched from London in 495 in order to ensure an unopposed landing for Cerdic, who planned to link up with Ælle. He also proposed that Silchester, trapped between the two armies, was surrounded, starved and collapsed without a fight. The story has all the elements of grand strategy but little if any of it is credible. In order for Godsal to fit everything in, the grand campaign in the Thames Valley had to take place simultaneously with the fighting that secured Kent and Sussex for the Germanics. Badon hardly merited a mention. Godsal suggested that it was seventy years later (c. 565) once the Britons regained their strength. He never addressed how this scenario fitted with the contemporary account by Gildas.

Further to the west, Bath is another longstanding contender for the site of Badon Hill. Nennius, writing in the ninth century, implies in his *Historia Brittonum* that Bath and Badon are the same place. Add Geoffrey of Monmouth's *History of the Kings of Britain* to the evidence and it is easy to see why Bath has become a favoured location for Badon:

> *The Saxons, having now no provisions to sustain them, and being just ready to starve with hunger, begged for leave to go out; in consideration whereof they offered to leave all their gold and silver behind them, and return back to Germany with nothing but their empty ships. They promised also that they would pay him tribute from Germany, and leave hostages with him. Arthur, after consultation about it, granted their petition; allowing them only leave to depart, and retaining all their treasures, as also hostages for payment of the tribute. But as they were under sail on their return home, they repented of their bargain, and tacked about again towards Britain, and went on shore at Totness. No sooner were they landed, than they made an utter devastation of the country as far as the Severn Sea, and put all the peasants to the sword. From thence they pursued their furious march to the town of Bath, and laid siege to it.*[20]

Geoffrey describes his sources thus: 'just as if written, they were proclaimed by many people joyfully and from memory.'[21] The truth is that whilst he drew inspiration from authors such as Gildas, Nennius and Bede, much of Geoffrey's work originates from ancient Celtic mythology. He is far from trustworthy as a source. A landing at Totnes and the degree of havoc wrought on the advance to Bath is fanciful to say the least. Bath was not a realistic choice of objective for Sussex and its allies, and Geoffrey's campaign, as described, looks nothing like a realistic plan to capture a viable and defendable territory. Before he could even contemplate such an expedition, Ælle had first to break the deadlock along the south coast.

The arguments for Bath as Badon Hill present a similar set of problems as those for a Thames Valley location, but are magnified further. Ceawlin's protracted struggles in the later sixth century show how difficult and lengthy the process was to secure the region between the headwaters of the Thames and the Severn Estuary, assuming he achieved as much as the *Chronicle* suggests. Aside from the obvious association of the place-name, Bath is usually mooted as the site because of its strategic importance. Once again, though, the supposition is that Germanic armies at this time were capable of mounting expeditionary campaigns to subjugate, consolidate and settle very large areas of territory. Bath, 42 miles as the crow flies from Charford on the Hampshire Avon, is simply too distant from the south coast Germanic territories which, at the time of Badon, were secured by relatively small armies. The newly emerging kingdoms of the east coast were even further from Bath.

John Morris was the first professional historian to undertake a comprehensive assessment of the scattered evidence concerning the history of Britain from AD 350 to 650. In his 1973 book, *The Age of Arthur*, he accepted Bath as the site of Badon largely on the basis that a number of writers had suggested it previously. He nonetheless proposed a version of the campaign in which a large infantry-based army led by Ælle set out deliberately to ravage the countryside that the Britons relied upon to support their cavalry-centric forces. He then constructed an unlikely argument whereby a British cavalry force was besieged, probably on Solsbury Hill, but was able to hold-out for some time before launching a mounted counter-attack.[22] This theory has very little credibility from a military perspective. A highly mobile cavalry force is unlikely to have allowed itself to be trapped on a hilltop by lumbering infantry. However, when such a luminary as Morris says that Bath/Solsbury Hill 'best fits both Gildas' choice of words and the nature of the campaign', then the idea gains credence.

The archaeological evidence that does exist dates the Germanic settlement of the Bath region to the middle/late sixth century, a period that broadly concurs with the dates in the *Anglo-Saxon Chronicle*. The argument for Bath as Badon therefore supposes that the Germanics were defeated there and driven back, which delayed their eventual settlement of the region. This argument ignores the difficulties pertaining to time, distance and military strength required for the Germanic army to advance to Bath in the first place. An alternative idea, often mooted, is that the Bath region was invaded from the sea via the Bristol Channel. One has to question why a Germanic force would have attempted this. Passage around the South West Peninsula has always been notoriously hazardous for small vessels. The Romans called the whole Cornwall region *Belerion*, or sea of storms. The scale of effort and risk involved in a maritime invasion of the Bath region launched from south-east Britain is inconsistent with the military capabilities of the Germanic groups at the time. It is very unlikely that their commanders would have considered this course of action when direct expansion by land was possible from their own borders.

The texts that have rooted Bath in history as Badon have largely originated due to speculative early sources being taken at face value, particularly in Victorian times. As a final example of how some early authors were prone to be liberal with their interpretations (and to avoid picking on Godsal too much) it is worth citing Daniel Henry Haigh, a noted Victorian scholar of Anglo-Saxon history and literature. In his 1861 tome, *The Conquest of Britain by the Saxons*, he is so fixated on Bath as the location for Badon that he is forced to reject the much more solid case for Ælle's earlier siege to have been at Pevensey:

> *Andredes-ceaster has been identified with Pevensey, and Pevensey is almost certainly Anderida, one of the fortresses of the Saxon shore; but as Ælle had been resident for more than twelve years in Britain, and had made advances into the interior during the time, it does not seem likely that he would have left the fortresses of the coast of Sussex so long unoccupied. We must, therefore, look for it inland, and within, or on the borders of, the great forest of Andred. In the Parliamentary Gazetteer it is said,*

that Silchester was destroyed by Ælle on his way to Bath. I do not know on what authority this statement is made, but it is exactly in accordance with my own conclusions, that the siege of Andredes-ceaster immediately preceded that of Bath, and that Ælle was present at the latter.[23]

Summary

There is nothing in the primary sources that helps us to directly find a location for Badon Hill. We can therefore draw only broad conclusions from them and supplement those with military judgement. Given the approximate date of Badon, it is very likely that a British alliance was confronted by Germanics from a number of groups who coalesced under Ælle of Sussex, somewhere close to an established Hampshire Avon frontier zone. Clashes intensified as a result of mounting pressure on the settlers to expand their territories. Map 6 illustrates the assessed situation immediately prior to the battle of Badon Hill.

Ælle eventually made a singular attempt to break the deadlock by launching a coordinated offensive across the Hampshire Avon. The reasons why this venture went so badly wrong are unlikely to be found in comparing the numerical strengths of the opposing forces that clashed. The result of the campaigning is far more likely to have been influenced by a British strategy that the Germanics were unprepared for. Ælle is unlikely to have been lured into any specific trap laid for him, but perhaps through boldness he placed his forces in a situation that he had not anticipated. Had he ensured that his army met the Britons in open battle, his Germanic alliance might have prevailed. Instead, he was drawn into a siege, the duration of which allowed the British to concentrate combat power and counter-attack decisively.

Badbury Rings is the foremost candidate for Badon Hill given all of the evidence we can find for the situation that prevailed in the late fifth/early sixth century. The hillfort there stands out as an important communications hub for ancient routes and a key garrison for the British defenders of the South West. Equally, for a Sussex-led Germanic alliance it offered a tempting objective within easy reach of the frontier. The Germanics stood to gain not only a necessary foothold across the Hampshire Avon, but also Poole Harbour and its surrounds, a region of particular military and economic value.

Map 6: The Badon Campaign

Chapter Six

The Siege of Badon Hill

I think there are in Valhalla
more than six hundred and forty doors;
out of a single door at a time
will tramp nine hundred and sixty men,
champions advancing on the monster.

from Gylfaginning – *The Deluding of Gylfi*

Descriptions of the battle at Badon Hill provided by authors down the centuries are all speculative. Many seize upon a sentence in the *Historia Brittonum* that credits the British victory to a singular effort made by Arthur.[1] Nennius composed the *Historia* in the ninth century and it is credible that he recorded the battle in the way he did because his sources referred to a single decisive action on the battlefield. More than that we cannot say. In attempting to draw a realistic picture one must look for the likely tactics employed by both sides and suggest why the Britons prevailed, having already reached a generalised view that Ælle, or whoever it was that led the Germanics, made some key mistakes in the planning and execution of the campaign. Gildas' description of the battle as a siege is useful because it narrows the options available at the tactical level for both sides. Simply put, one side must defend a perimeter and the other must breach it. From the strategic picture defined in previous chapters it is clear that the Germanics were on the offensive. The probability is therefore that they were the besiegers. Gildas also points to the singular leadership of Ambrosius. The inference from this is that the Britons were well-organised and this allows us to assess how a well-ordered defensive network coped when a static point within it was attacked.

Badbury Rings was a key part of the defensive strategy of the Britons along the Hampshire Avon frontier. If there is archaeological proof of a battle to be found there, it is likely to be scattered far and wide. A routed army cut down individually and in groups as they fled would have left little in the way of enduring evidence. Discarded weapons and equipment would have been taken from the dead and wounded in the hours that followed. It is highly unlikely that any mercy was shown to those caught, wounded or otherwise. Badbury Rings was definitely re-occupied by the Romano-British. In 2004, above the layers of expected Iron Age finds, archaeologists discovered 'an unexpected floor of rammed chalk and scattered on its surface were scraps of occupation evidence. Fragments of worn late Roman pottery, a spiral bronze ring, a few nails, a worn 4th century coin and patches of charcoal perhaps remains of cooking fires.'[2] The best that might be hoped for from any future dig are clear signs that the site was refortified like Cadbury and others during the period in question. In the absence of that we can only speculate on an event for which almost no detail at all is available from any reliable record. We do know beyond doubt that this battle was a major victory for the British and thus we need some explanation of how the Germanic Army was destroyed or routed. It is impossible to determine exactly how the battle unfolded, so the approach taken here is to draw together our knowledge of the opposing sides and to make assumptions based on similar events from military history. In this way the speculation is at least as informed as it can be. The generic scenario presented is that a besieged British outpost held-out long enough for a relief force to arrive and break the siege decisively. The 'three days and three nights' derived from the *Welsh Annals* is used as a duration for the actions, being reasonable enough in the context of the times and distances assessed for the scenario.[3]

Launching the offensive

Given the considerations for the Germanic commander already discussed, we can assume that there was an attempt to achieve surprise. This probably involved some preliminary movement of his forces by night. Nautical twilight, when the horizon at sea is still visible, would have provided sufficient light for an army to organise itself and begin to slip away from all but the closest of observers. After twilight had faded, the weather, terrain, moon-state and amount of ambient light from the stars would have determined the degree of darkness in which movement had to be accomplished. Let us place the battle in autumn, with harvests already gathered and the maximum number of warriors free to go on campaign. In late September, nautical twilight in Hampshire would have been around 7 p.m. with sunrise shortly before 6 a.m., allowing nearly eleven hours for night operations. Any deceptions designed to confuse observers, such as a deliberate move in a different direction, would have been made in the hours before sunset, otherwise they would have been ineffective. Only under cover of darkness would the army have had a chance to move obscured from view and thus keep secret the intended objective. Using Frankenbury hillfort as a possible assembly area, a march south of 7 miles along the fringes of Germanic-held territory would have brought the attacking force to one possible crossing point of the Avon. Today there is a small bridge to the west of the tiny village of Ellingham, 2 miles north of Ringwood. The name Ellingham can be derived from the Old English words meaning 'the village of Ælle's people'. It is tempting to think that this name goes all the way back to the time of Badon, but there is nothing recorded to substantiate such a claim. Nonetheless, a river crossing made here would have been a realistic choice for an incursion across the frontier and a subsequent advance direct towards Badbury Rings.

Assuming a large force moved by night, guides would have been used at the head of each column of marching warriors. More than one route was likely used to prevent the army from stringing out over too great a distance. In such a manner, 2 to 3 miles an hour could have been covered, so before midnight the troops could have been fording the Avon. Suitable crossing points would already have been known or identified and tested as part of the reconnaissance operations. Weather would have been a factor, but a relatively benign autumn would have offered a good chance of the rivers not being swollen by rains. Beyond the Avon, a further march of 12 miles would have brought the Germanic army through Ringwood Forest and to the lower slopes of King Down, a mile or so east of Badbury Rings. An approach from this direction would have been hidden from the fort itself by intervening high ground.

The above scenario represents a march of 17 miles, perhaps close to the upper limit for one night with a large force involved, but certainly possible with carefully chosen routes and guides to lead the way. Even if deception failed, any British scouts able to observe and track the force would have been unable to pass information back to their local commanders quickly enough to enable an effective counter-move. By the time the news that a significant Germanic offensive had been launched reached the ears of a British regional commander, it is safe to assume that the Germanic force was already poised for an assault on Badbury. Of course, it is also possible that the Germanics concentrated their forces more overtly, allowing for a much shorter and more rapid advance. Whatever the mechanics of the preliminary moves, it has to be assumed that the British were not caught unaware and the Germanics did not immediately breach the fort's defences. Thus, the Germanics were forced either to commit to a siege or to give up on their proposed objective. Gildas tells us that they chose to lay siege.

The first thing that would have struck the Germanic warriors as they approached Badbury Rings would have been the huge scale of the earthworks. The larger hillforts remain impressive today, even with the earthen embankments eroded by time. Ælle's men would have been looking at dykes up to 6 metres in height, topped by wooden ramparts adding a further couple of metres or more, with outer ditches serving to augment the overall effect of the elevations. When the fort was first constructed in the Iron Age, there were two entrances, one east and one west. The west entrance was altered later and is the most complex in design, with the gateway in the innermost embankment protected by a bulged extension of the second rampart and then again by the smaller outer rampart (see Figures 5 and 6). It is unlikely that the gateway on the eastern side that faced the enemy threat was rebuilt in the Dark Ages. Therefore, at the time of the Badon campaign we can picture the site as a considerable structure of earth banks topped by timber defences, with a single entrance track threading through the western embankments. Any warrior tasked to breach these defences lugging a share of the weight of a wooden ladder or climbing pole would have felt immediately vulnerable. Those due to climb such items in the van of the assault would have realised that death or serious injury was assured. Yet these ancient warriors were more than capable of maintaining their courage in such situations. The adrenaline rush of the immediate assault would have helped to propel them to the first ditch and, hence, into the particular hell of siege warfare.

Accounts of sieges through the ages have illustrated the concentrated intensity of the fighting. From the earliest records of warfare to many centuries after Badon one can read of the desperate courage that manifests when barricades must be overcome in battle. At the storming of Badajoz in 1812, over forty assaults were made on breaches in the walls, with troops repeatedly clambering over piles of rubble and mounds of dead, wounded and dying comrades.

Many of the bodies were burning and the wounded crawled and writhed in pitiful heaps, calling out for relief where none was available. Two thousand of Wellington's best troops were wounded and killed in the approaches to the breaches. At another section of wall below the main castle defences, Picton's 3rd Division had crossed intervening flooded ditches and, despite great losses through drowning and from missiles and gunfire from the ramparts, a force was made ready with ladders at the foot of the walls. Despite the certainty of death the ladders were scaled. Those ladders that were not pushed away causing the climbers to fall to their deaths were leant against walls defended from the ramparts above by French muskets, bayonets and pikes. Logs, rocks and all manner of objects were hurled down at the British troops on the ladders, who nonetheless kept on climbing relentlessly, desperate to attain a foothold on the ramparts that might lead to possible survival. Many who fell were impaled on their comrades' bayonets. Over an hour of this one-sided slaughter had passed when Colonel Ridge, of the 5th Regiment, placed a ladder where a section of wall was lower and an embrasure afforded better protection. Ridge was first up the ladder, exhorting his men to follow. The ladder was crowded so quickly that the French could not push against its weight and dislodge it. Ridge held his sword above him for protection as did his men their muskets, tipped with bayonets. Incredibly, Ridge gained the ramparts alive and his men swarmed after him. In so doing, they captured the castle direct, a feature that was to have been the strongest bastion and last place of resistance for the French. Colonel Ridge was shot and killed as dark descended whilst leading his men through the castle into the town. Badajoz fell to Wellington's forces just a few hours later that same night.

The Germanics would have approached the ditches at Badon with a considered plan of attack. It was common in ancient sieges to launch multiple attacks on different parts of the defences, just as the assaults on breached walls were combined with escalade attacks at Badajoz some 1,300 years later. Therefore, at some point, the Germanic Army would have broken out from its linear marching formation and adopted a tactical formation prior to launching the assault. Figure 5a shows a scale representation of a force of just under 2,500 attackers spread out to the east of Badbury Rings. Figure 5b represents a subsequent deployment with the Germanic Army engaged in the siege, with echelons behind the assault troops to reinforce any breach and other units tasked to

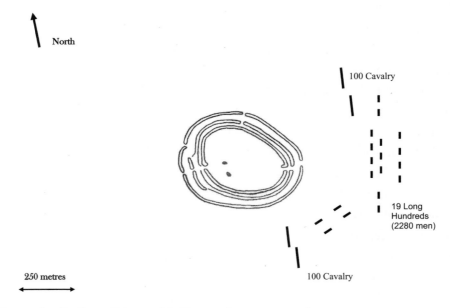

Figure 5a: Badbury Rings with Germanic army to scale

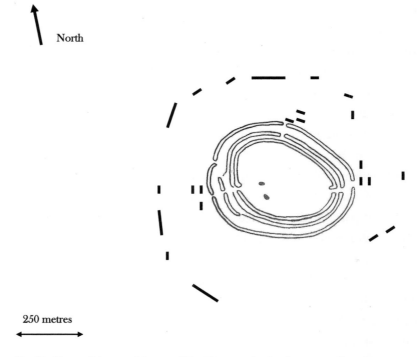

Figure 5b: Badbury Rings with possible Germanic deployment for siege

protect the operation from outside interference. When viewed to scale in this way, the severity of the task facing the Germanics becomes more apparent and it seems that three or four points of attack would have been the maximum possible (Figure 5b shows three).

The type of attack used in each area would have varied according to the nature of defences. Getting close to entrance gates was especially difficult. The complex series of earth banks and ditches at the main entrance to Badbury Rings is typical of Iron Age fort design that maximised the vulnerability of an attacking force to missile-fire, specifically from sling-launched pebbles. Attackers who successfully breached one rampart found themselves channelled by the earthworks into killing areas, where missiles could be launched at them from several directions from the next set of defences. To breach a wooden gate or barrier in an entrance gap through a dyke would require battering it through with kinetic force or burning it to the ground. Any such action would have to take place whilst the assaulting troops withstood a barrage of slung stones and other missiles.

Creating a breach in earth and timber defences with missile-fire would have required a number of accurate hits with a trebuchet (stone-thrower) or similar heavy siege engine. Traction trebuchets were invented by the Chinese and employed as early as the fourth century BC. However, there is no recorded use of them in European conflicts until the ninth century AD. For the Germanic Army besieging Badon, creating breaches in the revetments and palisades from a distance was out of the question. Even a crude battering ram attack against the gate would have required a relatively complex assault. In order to protect the battering ram crews and allow them enough freedom to operate, suppressive missile-fire would have to have been maintained to prevent the defenders from bringing their own weapons to bear. A protection force would have been required, deployed alongside the troops manning the battering ram with the sole task of shielding themselves and the troops carrying the ram from incoming projectiles. With these measures in place, a force could have attempted to break directly through a chosen barrier such as an entrance gate.

Similar measures would have been employed to protect teams trying to set the wooden palisade defences alight. Incendiaries based on mixtures including sulphur, petroleum and bitumen are recorded as having been put to military use as early as the ninth century BC. Greek fire, possibly an early form of gunpowder, did not appear on battlefields until the seventh century. Thus, for the Germanic forces at Badon, generating sufficient heat and flame to allow large timbers to catch would not have been easy. Defenders would certainly have planned to counter any basic fire-setting and would have designated some personnel as water or soil carriers, tasked with dousing any flames. Badbury Rings has seasonal ponds within its inner enclosure (the two largest are the eye-like shapes in Figures 5 and 6), so a water supply was probably available.

The difficulties inherent in creating a breach in a hillfort were such that scaling the walls or entering by stealth were the only viable options. Had Ælle's men entered the fort by trickery and slaughtered the inhabitants, the battle would surely have been recorded differently. The only credible assessment for this siege is that the Germanics tried to scale the walls. Detachments of attackers would have been assigned to specific sections of the defences. Supporting missile-fire would have been employed to cover the assaults and any sector of the defences noted as being weaker or providing greater cover and concealment from the ramparts would have been chosen as a point of attack. Such desperate scrambling probably occupied the Germanics for much of the first day, with attacking sub-units rotated to the rear as they became exhausted or suffered casualties.

Ælle would have been directing operations. Germanic war leaders gained and maintained their status largely through prowess in combat, but a siege is more complex than a clash of shield-walls. He would have needed time away from the immediate battle at the ramparts to stand back, assess progress and direct new initiatives as he saw fit. As the day wore on he would have cast more than one glance at the surrounding countryside, aware of the danger of a British counter-attack. He would certainly have had part of his force ready to protect his rear against interference from the outside, a clear requirement learned at *Andredes-ceaster* if not before. Other troops would have been engaged in support roles such as evacuating wounded, supplying water from local sources and gathering spent projectiles to ensure the maximum supply of ammunition.

British information and intelligence – triggering the strike

We can perhaps credit the Germanics with having achieved a degree of operational surprise, bringing the bulk of their army into combat at a time and place of their choosing. Nonetheless, it seems that was not enough to win a swift victory, even at the tactical level. The defenders at Badbury were prepared, which implies they had some forewarning of the impending assault. The distraction of immediately organising the defence, combined with the distances between British locations in the defensive matrix, suggests that any further warning up the chain of command would have taken time. Even if scouts were able to travel swiftly with some assessment of the number of attackers, the first thought for anyone in the British chain of command would have been whether their information was credible. What size was the Germanic force at Badbury? Was the attack a ruse? At the top of the chain, Ambrosius would have considered carefully before initiating any reaction and the quality of the information would have been of paramount importance.

Even if the British leader had doubts, it is inconceivable that he would have taken no action at all on hearing that such an important fort was under attack. Messages would have been dispatched to his nearby reserves and striking forces, bringing them to immediate readiness and some at least would have moved closer to Badbury. A mounted reconnaissance element of trusted warriors would have been dispatched to observe the action at the fort and maintain communications in order to build the intelligence picture. However, it would have been late in the day before such actions were achieved. Even if there was an immediate decision to move the striking force, it is unlikely that they were ready to join battle on the first day. We must presume that the British defenders of Badon Hill had to maintain their fortress intact for that first night at least.

As more information came in and the picture became clearer, Ambrosius would have moved his headquarters towards Badbury and ordered at least part of his striking force to make haste there. By way of example, cavalry at Tisbury, 18 miles to the north, could have ridden to Badbury and been ready for action within four hours. To ensure the defence remained cohesive a reserve cavalry unit, perhaps held near Cadbury, might also have been ordered to move to a more forward location. Crucial nodes in the defensive matrix would have been maintained at this stage, but once Ambrosius was sure that the Germanic Army was at Badbury, he would have mobilised whatever he could in that direction. Thus, by dawn on the second day, at least one part of the available striking force was preparing, unobserved by the Germanics, in a suitable assembly area near Badbury. Ambrosius, by now at the scene himself, would have wasted no time in taking his subordinate commanders forward to view the ongoing siege and to deliberate over the best course of action. The timing of a strike was critical. It is likely that once he was able to set his eyes upon the Germanic Army he would have been sure he was observing the enemy force *in toto*, rather than one part of it engaged in a feint. He had to assess and decide on certain risks. If the defenders inside Badbury Rings continued to hold he could delay his strike whilst he summoned more combat power. But if he delayed too long, the fort might fall. If the fort fell, then the Germanic Army would gain protection within its ramparts and the particular advantage that cavalry gave the Britons in the open would be negated, making an effective counter-attack far more difficult.

Reflections on Day One – stalemate

The Germanics would have withdrawn their forces from the immediate fight around the walls of Badon and made camp in a defensive posture after the first day of fighting. Ælle would have summoned his chiefs and elders to consult and to plan. It was not in the Germanic nature to abandon lightly a task such as this siege, albeit that the first day of fighting would have taken its toll. There would have been a number of casualties but probably not enough to force a withdrawal or change of plan. Based on the points of attack estimated in Figure 5b, and assuming rotation of units, a high percentage of the Germanic force would have been involved in the fierce combat close to the walls of the fort at some point. Given that the Germanics failed to breach the defences, most of the wounds inflicted would have been from slingshot, the most readily available missile weapon. Arrows, together with spears, axes and swords at closer range, would also have taken their toll. If we estimate that seventy-five per cent of the force was exposed to British weaponry at some point (1,860), then three per cent killed (fifty-six) and ten per cent wounded sufficiently to have required extraction (186) is a reasonable assumption. Of those wounds, a rough estimate is fifty per cent slingshot (ninety-three), thirty per cent other missiles, including arrows (fifty-six), ten per cent javelin/spear/ sword (eighteen) and the remainder from a variety of injuries including broken limbs, dislocations and so on (eighteen). A modern study of mortality rates for similar weaponry derived from the records of Ancient Greece deduced that death resulted in forty-two per cent of cases for arrow wounds, sixty-seven per cent for slingshot wounds, eighty per cent for spear wounds and 100 per cent for sword injuries.[4] The Ancient Greeks steadily improved their trauma management and medical care over time and were able to keep deaths as low as possible. There is no evidence that the Germanics of the sixth century had made similar advances in medicine, but using the figures from this study we can assess that of the 186 wounded, around 100 would have been incapacitated. Many of those most likely died some time later. A reasonable estimate therefore is that the Germanics lost 150 men on the first day and a further eighty were unfit to rejoin the battle.

Casualties are always expected in war, but perhaps the most worrying fact for the Germanic leadership was that its forces had failed to breach the British defences. The commanders would have assessed that British reinforcements were on the move towards Badbury and discussions would have centred on what strategy to pursue on the second day. On the positive side they had pro-jected a substantial army into an area of prime territory, and British resistance at that point comprised a smaller force than theirs. The Germanics would no doubt have been confident of their ability to match the British in open battle, but their opponents were entrenched and resisting fiercely at the Rings. They had not yet presented themselves for open battle and, thus, the Germanics at this juncture had been unable to initiate a decisive action. As their leaders discussed this, the negative aspects of their situation might have loomed larger than the positives. Surprise had been lost and reducing the hillfort was prov-ing more difficult than anticipated. Some obvious implications arose. First, there was little point in wandering off in search of another objective only to have Day One repeat itself. Second, one way to bring the army of the Britons to open battle was to continue to threaten this objective. The Germanics had not strayed too far from the frontier zone and were in a position to maintain supplies and continue to prosecute the operation. It is reasonable to assess, therefore, that they decided to try once more to make progress with the siege. In that event it is likely that they made some adjustments to their deployment in order to be better-prepared for a counter-attack. They might well have lifted the siege for a time in order to prepare more effective siege equipment.

Preparing for the second day

Possible equipment available to the Germanics beyond that already discussed includes siege mantlets that had been in use for over a millennium. Such mantlets are depicted on ancient Assyrian sculptures and the idea must surely

have spread to Europe by the fifth century. A mantlet was a relatively por-
table screen, manhandled into place. It was a wooden frame, covered in ani-
mal hide or slats of wood, large enough to shield small groups of warriors
from missile-fire. This allowed them to work unhindered by their shields, for
example to return fire from behind cover where otherwise none was available.
Manufacturing more ladders would also have been part of the second day's
work. Initiating heavier engineering works seems an unlikely option for the
Germanics. They were renowned for overcoming opponents with speed and
fury rather than for such undertakings. Mining under walls to make them collapse, a tactic associated with medieval sieges, was out of the question here.
Any substantial digging of the hard chalk around Badbury would have been
difficult, so to undermine the embankments would have been very time-con-
suming and probably ineffective. Earth and timber does not collapse like stone
structures do when foundations are weakened.

Half a millennium previously, Roman soldiers had constructed large earth
ramps all the way up to the ramparts and then advanced up them to defeat the
Celtic defenders of these very same Dorset hillforts. The ditches at Badbury
Rings are still markedly deep today despite centuries of erosion and, at the
time of Badon there might have been as much as 40 feet difference in height
from the base of the ditches to the top of the palisades. Building a siege-ramp
in the Roman style would have been extremely intensive in terms of manpower
and time, even if the Germanics were minded to try it. Limited digging of
cavities at the base of the wooden defences in order to set more substantial
fires might have been tried, but those digging and setting the fires would have
required considerable protection. We can conclude that the most likely method
employed for the continued Germanic attack was escalade, perhaps combined
with an attempt to batter through or burn down the lowest palisades or the
gates.

If Day One was a costly but unsuccessful attempt to overwhelm the British
defences as we suspect, then it is unlikely that Ælle would have allowed Day
Two to be an exact repeat of the failure. The British had clearly prepared their
defences well. In accordance with their strategy as defined in the schematic at
Figure 3, they had thus far achieved the DELAY and DISRUPT effects, buy-
ing time for Ambrosius and frustrating Ælle's attempts to establish a foothold
in British territory. A dilemma for Ælle was that an escalade assault is most

effective when the sheer number of troops committed to the walls simply over-whelms the defenders. However, in allocating his forces to their tasks he had to ensure that a sufficient protection force continued to watch the backs of the assaulting troops. Light cavalry would have been ideal to provide a screen and maybe some surveillance pickets to watch for the British approach. It was not necessary for the Germanics to put a ring of steel around the whole fort, but to protect numerous points of attack was a challenge.

For these reasons, adjustments to the Germanic plan probably concentrated their force more towards one sector of the defences they felt could most likely be overcome, as illustrated in Figure 6. This would have also allowed those units tasked with protecting the force to form-up more closely and effectively for battle in the open. As details of this plan filtered down to the Germanic troops, there may well have been a surge in morale. Their leaders appeared to know what to do. Warriors were not to be smashed pointlessly against the British fortress walls. There was time for some rest as well as for preparation of equipment and care for the wounded. If there were misgivings lower down the command chain it is unlikely they were voiced at this stage.

New plans and old lessons

Early on Day Two, the scene around Badbury Rings may have reflected bur-geoning industry rather than frantic combat. The attackers would have been busy in their camps and in the woods nearby, cutting, hauling and assembling timber for siege ladders and other items. On the ramparts the defenders would have slept where they fought. As it became apparent to them that combat was not to resume immediately, they would have looked to their own preparations for the next phase of fighting. Some of their number had been killed and the bodies would have been carried by comrades to a designated area and maybe even burned there to prevent the spread of disease. The wounded would have been tended to as far as was possible, and those fit to continue given tasks according to their degree of incapacity. All possible repairs and improvements would have been made across any sections of the palisades that required atten-tion. Ambrosius may well have viewed this activity from a vantage point such as that offered by the Bronze Age burial mound a mile to the west of the fort. The junior commanders of his immediately available cavalry would have been alongside him and most likely a small group of other trusted subordinates and staff. He would have realised from the observed activity that the siege was to be intensified as soon as the Germanics were ready. He could not have judged easily the state of the defenders, and this would have concerned him. He needed to assess how long they could hold against a renewed attack. If the fort fell and the Germanics were allowed to organise within its walls, then his key advantages of surprise and shock action in a counter-attack would be lost.

Exchanging information with those defending the fort would have been difficult but by no means impossible. For example, a small group of agile mounted troops tasked solely to pass messages could have ridden quickly to the outer walls. These were over 1,600 metres in circumference, too much for the Germanics to surround effectively. Dialogue might have sufficed, or written messages could have been thrown or launched by missile. In such a manner, Ambrosius could have delivered a few key questions and some direction to the commander of the defenders. By way of reply, something as simple as smoke signals would have been enough to answer yes or no, acknowledge instructions, or indicate that all was reasonably well. If the fort could continue to hold, more British units would have time to make their appointed rendezvous in order to join the fray. Cavalry and detachments of infantry would have been summoned, not just from those held in reserve but also from nearby sites such as Spetisbury Rings and Woolsbarrow Fort. Ambrosius would have been looking to commit as much combat power to the strike as possible.

A military commander with even the most rudimentary education in his trade would have been aware of some lessons from history. A member of the Ambrosius dynasty would certainly have been educated in such matters as well as being able to draw on his own and his immediate predecessors' experiences of combat. Which historic battles formed part of their education can only be guessed at, but like many situations in war this one at Badbury was already echoing the past. Just one year after the heroic action at Thermopylae, even the famed and fearsome Spartan warriors had been part of an army that refused to give battle. It was the summer of 479 BC and during their second invasion of Greek territory the Persians had been forced to adopt a defensive posture. Retreating to Boeotia, they constructed a fortified camp near the town of Plataea. The Greeks outnumbered the Persians sufficient to consider attacking them at the first opportunity and that had been their intent. However, on seeing that the fortified camp was surrounded by terrain ideally suited to cavalry, the Greeks halted their advance and refused to countenance such an attack. Combat was only provoked when the Persians abandoned this camp to pursue the Greeks who had eventually been forced to withdraw after their supply lines were cut. The Spartans were as instrumental as ever in the open fighting that followed and the pursuing Persian force was defeated, initiating the collapse of their entire army, including those who remained in the defences at Plataea. It is not the end result that is pertinent to the Badon situation, but the refusal of the Greeks to initiate a siege whilst vulnerable to cavalry should be noted.

The most likely explanation for the severity of the Germanic defeat at Badon is that they had no time to adjust their posture and react to a severe danger that materialised while their force was off-balance. The Badon campaign was not just another Germanic raid, but a concerted effort to push back the frontier permanently. Ælle simply had to succeed, and certainly the campaign could not be allowed to stumble at the first objective. It is easy to comprehend how such an attitude led to a fixation on capturing the hillfort. Recent experiences of the fighting in Britain may have bred an air of confidence among the Germanics, not without some foundation given the relative ease with which they had conquered territory to this point. The potential size of the gathering British force may not have been known to them. We can presume they knew they would be outnumbered at some point, but perhaps they assessed that there was sufficient time to capture Badon before that force arrived. The bigger the force that mustered against them, the more they needed to be inside those walls. With the benefit of hindsight we can say that at some earlier point they should have made a decision either to withdraw or to re-align and prepare for open battle. The most dangerous circumstances for the Germanics were those that allowed their forces to be engaged effectively whilst in a degree of disarray.

From a British perspective enough territory had been ceded to the invaders already. This latest incursion had breached a significant boundary and the aim was not only to beat it back but to defeat the aggressors decisively. Ambrosius recognised that his best chance to achieve this was to maximise the damage he could inflict through the effective employment of his cavalry. Many examples of devastating cavalry charges exist dating back to the most ancient of times. Long after Badon, and particularly as the age of gunpowder dawned, there were those who thought the days of cavalry as an effective force on the battlefield were numbered. They were very wrong. It is worth noting here the damage that could be wrought by cavalry even in the age of gunpowder. Such an example serves to emphasise just how devastating an effective charge at Badon Hill might have been.

On 16 May 1811, the British General William Beresford deployed his army on the low hills around the village of La Albuera, 12 miles south-east of Badajoz, to face the French under Marshal Soult. The battle is remembered for some of the most desperate and bloody fighting of the whole Peninsular Campaign, and not least for a single cavalry charge. At the height of the battle at La Albuera, Lieutenant Colonel John Colborne's brigade had just taken part in one of the fiercest exchanges of musket-fire ever recorded. It was the French who first began to give ground in the face of murderous short-range volleys of fire. Colborne's regiments pursued their advantage, advancing with bayonets fixed, in order to drive off the French force commanded by General Girard that had earlier appeared by surprise because of a masterly flanking manoeuvre. As the British advanced, a sudden and very fierce squall of rain and hail obscured visibility and rendered muskets useless due to the wet. The French cavalry division commander on the left flank, General Latour-Maubourg, saw his chance and committed 590 men of the 1st Vistula Uhlans to the charge. These Polish lancers were immediately followed by a further 305 cavalrymen of the French 2nd Hussars. Charging uphill, they smashed into three British battalions at once, the 3rd Regiment of Foot (the Buffs), the II/48th Northamptonshire Regiment and the II/66th Berkshires. Only the fourth regiment of Colborne's brigade, the 31st (Huntingdonshire) Regiment of Foot, was able to complete the drill for such an occasion and form square to defend itself. The other three regiments were scattered and their unfortunate members were mercilessly hacked down by sabre or skewered on the lances of the mounted troops:

I was knocked down by a horseman with his lance, which luckily did me no serious injury. In getting up I received a lance in my hip, and shortly after another in my knee, which slightly grazed me. I then rose, when a lancer hurried me to the rear, striking me on the side of the head with his lance ... He left me, and soon another came up, who would have killed me had not a French officer came up ... – Captain Gordon [an officer in Colborne's brigade][5]

Captain Gordon was unusually lucky to survive the attentions of five lancers. Out of the 1,966 men comprising Colborne's brigade, 1,413 were casualties (total British losses in the battle were 4,159). The Buffs started the battle with 728 men, 643 of whom became casualties. Most of this damage was inflicted in this one cavalry charge. Polish casualties from this action by the Uhlans, nicknamed the 'Devil's Poles' by the Spaniards, were light and they went on to mount at least one more successful charge in the same battle. According to Marshal Soult's after-action report, only 130 Uhlans were lost through the entire day's fighting.

At Badon, there were probably lulls in the fighting as commanders gathered and tactics and formations adjusted once the initial attempts to overrun the fort had stalled. The battlefield may have been relatively quiet as the Germanics prepared for a more effective attack and the British concentrated their forces some distance away. The fates of both armies might have been uncertain through a second night or longer. As the siege wore on, Ambrosius observing the Germanic dispositions would have continued to deliberate how his counter strike could best achieve surprise and maximum effect. He knew that the opportunity he sought to break the Germanic force completely would be lost if he dallied too long and allowed the Germanic Army any chance to consolidate.

Day Three – Counter-strike: the charge of 'Arthur's Cavalry'

It is quite possible that some of the British cavalrymen gathering in the Tarrant Valley, a little way to the west of Badbury, were of Sarmatian descent:

> The closed society of Sarmatian cataphractarii in Britain was able to maintain its ethnic features during the Late Roman period and afterwards. One reason is that their troops, called cuneus Sarmatorum, equitum Sarmatorum Bremetennacensium Gordianorum were not part of any military organization in active service. Consequently, after the withdrawal of the Roman army, they continued to live on their accustomed sites (Chester, Ribchester, etc.). They were still called Sarmatians after 250 years.[6]

The 5,500 Sarmatian cavalry troops brought to Britain by Marcus Aurelius in AD 175 had no homeland to return to. Since the seventh century BC, the

Sarmatians, a loose federation of nomadic tribes, had roamed Asia's measure-less steppes from China to the plains of Hungary. In the first century AD, a Sarmatian dynasty arose in the Bosporan region and remained there until dis-placed by the Goths in the early third century. The Sarmatians then resumed their nomadic lifestyle and fought as mercenaries for whoever would pay them, including the Goths. Traditional Sarmatian battle tactics included the use of horse archers, who rode close to the enemy lines and rained arrows down upon them. Archers were unarmoured but, like their counterparts in the heavier divisions, were extremely skilled riders who could manoeuvre their mounts with dexterity even as they used both hands to fire their bows. The effect of this tactic was to disturb enemy formations and soften them up for the main attack. This came in the form of a charge by *equites cataphractarii*, heavy lancers who were fully protected by helmets, lamellar cuirasses and other scale armour. Their Latin name translates as 'horsemen clothed fully in scale armour'. The lance used was traditionally the two-handed heavy kontos-type. The tradi-tional mounts of the Sarmatians were relatively small and the horses were clad in tightly fitting scale armour, except for those that bore the archers.

Given a day or more to act, the British could have assembled a formida-ble cavalry strike-force in close proximity to Badbury Rings. An estimated three detachments drawn together from across the frontier zone could have amounted to 600 lancers. In modern times the characteristics of tanks have been described as a 'holy trinity' of firepower, mobility and protection, each accorded a level of priority according to the design of tank. In the sixth century, a large force of armoured lancers had similar attributes in that it was mobile, protected and armed with fearsome weaponry. In addition to the cavalry, British infantry detachments were no doubt marching to the scene where they would have been assigned tasks without delay. One task would have been to form a screen between the Tarrant Valley and Badbury Rings. The orders for those troops would have been clear: to prevent the enemy's outposts and patrols from discovering the presence of the gathering cavalry force. As the Germanic Army renewed its escalade attack, Ambrosius would have been monitoring the readiness of his striking force. We can assume he decided to lead it in person. Once preparations were complete, these armoured horsemen would move closer to the Rings and finally form-up ready to charge, concealed to the last possible moment in the valley to the south of the modern village of Tarrant Rushton.

In positioning his forces anew for the attack against the fort, Ælle may have targeted a distinct area of the palisade defences identified as the weakest, based on the results of earlier assaults. With some units tasked to guard the attacking troops in this sector, the Germanic deployment had become a complex mix of attack and defence. The force protection troops in particular would have tried to choose their ground carefully – placing a shield-wall on a slope looking down on an enemy advance was always preferred, but the slopes immediately around the Rings were relatively gentle and open, providing little natural protection. Germanic cavalry numbers were probably small in proportion to the overall strength of the army. We must assume that some Germanic cavalry were present at Badon, but we know from the Roman historian Tacitus that the Germanic strength was usually 'seen to lie rather in their infantry', having noted also that 'they combine the two arms (infantry and cavalry) in battle'.[7] This is an interesting observation in itself. There are numerous accounts telling us that, in later times, mounted Anglo-Saxons invariably preferred to leave their horses to the rear and fight on foot. Such was the case at the battles of Stamford Bridge and Hastings in 1066 when the English cavalry, including Harold and his Royal Huscarls, fought dismounted as part of the infantry lines. It seems that at some point, in Britain at least, the combined arms concept fell out of favour. Whatever the favoured doctrine at the time of Badon, it is safe to assume that in a siege any mounted action would have been away from the walls where cavalry could properly manoeuvre.

Figure 6 shows an assessed disposition that reflects Ælle's plan to attack the weakest sector of the hillfort in strength whilst preparing also to resist a counter-attack. Reducing numbers of men and the additional requirements for protecting the force led inevitably to a less than ideal deployment for the Germanic troops. In Figure 6, an effects schematic has been overlaid to show what Ælle was trying to achieve. It was not easy, hence we can query why he did not lift the siege and array for open battle. The most likely answer is that the British striking force achieved sufficient surprise and speed of attack to thwart any such redeployment.

From this point forward, it is useful to consider in more detail the account provided by Nennius:

> *The twelfth was a most severe contest, when Arthur penetrated to the hill of Badon. In this engagement, nine hundred and forty fell by his hand alone, no one but the Lord affording him assistance.*[8]

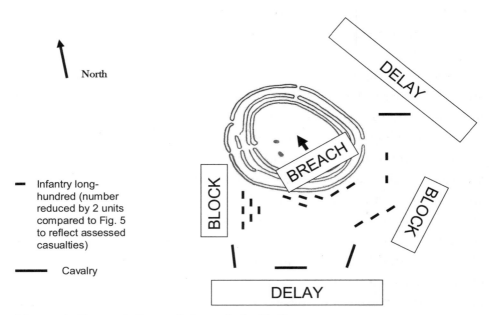

Figure 6: Germanic Intent Schematic for Badbury

The extract above was translated in 1819 by the Reverend W. Gunn from a Latin manuscript discovered in the Vatican library, which was originally edited in the tenth century by Mark the Hermit. Thus, we are reading a potentially altered version, but the emphasis is clearly on the singular leadership of Arthur and the number of casualties inflicted. Alternative translations usually quote 960 casualties, and some use the words 'fell in a single charge', the translator presumably deciding that 'by his hand alone' is too much of an exaggeration. Whatever the exact wording, Nennius describes a decisive action that resulted in many casualties and secured a British victory. It is interesting that the more widely accepted figure of 960 amounts to eight Saxon 'long hundreds' of 120 warriors each. Nennius possibly used this figure because he was privy to accounts that recalled the destruction of eight such units.

Nennius' use of the term 'penetrate' implies a British incursion into Germanic territory or a Germanic-held position. Based on this, a number of authors have proposed the Germanic forces were under siege not the British. This cannot be ruled out but it would have been very difficult for a British force to destroy an army enjoying the advantage of high ground or fortifications and ready to receive a charge. At Hastings, the English shield-wall repelled the Norman cavalry repeatedly. Harold's force was worn down, not swept away. Another alternative sometimes postulated for Badon is that a charge was mounted from within a besieged location by sallying out, through gates or otherwise. However, it is unlikely that the British allowed a cavalry force suited to open battle to become trapped inside a fort. Besides that, surprise, momentum and the concentrated effect of any charge would have been lost as the mounted troops exited the defences. An infantry charge, no matter how well-led, is also unlikely to have resulted in such a rout. Using the written sources alone, a probable explanation of how the situation developed at Badon Hill is arrived at if one combines the deliberate use of the word siege by Gildas with the implications of the Nennius account. The most likely scenario is that a British charge was launched against a besieging Germanic force. Eight 'long hundreds' routed or destroyed leaves little doubt that victory for the British followed quickly on from this action.

We know that cavalry forces were important elements of the British military at this time. The idea that they were direct descendants of Sarmatians who arrived in Roman times, or at least were equipped and trained in a similar way, is not new. In trying to explain the possible effect of a well-coordinated cavalry strike, even on a well-drilled and capable Germanic force, the most relevant historical example serendipitously leads us directly back to the Sarmatians, executing an action only a century or so before Badon. During the Gothic revolt in Thrace in AD 378, on the morning of 9 August, the Eastern Emperor of Rome, Valens, marched from the city of Adrianople at the head of some 20,000 troops. His aim was to find and destroy a Gothic army commanded by Fritigern, which threatened the town of Nike. Valens had recently received a warning from his cousin Gratian, the Western Emperor, not to underestimate the Alanic horsemen of the foe. This was because Gratian's army had recently been surprised by Gothic cavalry and had taken heavy losses in the engagement. As the army of Valens approached, it became clear to him that the Goths had formed a laager of their wagons, creating temporary fortifications all around themselves. Fritigern engaged in a ruse to buy time, pretending he wanted to negotiate. The reason for this is not known but it is possible he knew that the Gothic allied cavalry led by Alatheus and Saphrax were heading his way. In any event, in the scorching heat of mid-afternoon, the Roman forces launched their assault on the Gothic defences. What happened next may well have foreshadowed the events at Badon Hill:

> ... *in the meantime the cavalry of the Goths had returned with Alatheus and Saphrax, and with them a battalion of Alans; these descending from the mountains like a thunderbolt, spread confusion and slaughter among all whom in their rapid charge they came across.*[9]

The Roman cavalry on the right flank were swept away by the ferocity of the charge, leaving infantry units exposed on their flanks and from behind. At the same time, the Goths surged out from behind their makeshift defences and massed their infantry into an attack on the Roman centre. There was a long and bloody struggle between the opposing infantry before the Romans were defeated. One third of their strength is estimated to have been killed and the remainder routed. Just how decisive the Gothic cavalry action was in achieving this has been debated for centuries, given the intense fighting that continued afterwards until the day was settled. What is not in doubt is that the sudden arrival of the cavalry had an effect out of proportion to its numbers. The Roman forces had insufficient time and space to deploy effectively to meet the combined assaults mounted by the Goths. The Roman force had been deployed in order to besiege the Goths and, as a result, they found themselves trapped and unable to manoeuvre effectively between the fortifications, the Gothic infantry, and the highly mobile cavalry which beset them from different directions. The cavalry charge at Adrianople may not have secured victory outright, but it undoubtedly set the conditions for that victory.

Summary

The Germanic force that assembled to give battle at Badon included many hardened veterans of the campaigns against the Britons. Ælle of Sussex, who had proved to be a bold and ambitious war leader, probably commanded it. Given these observations we must look for some reason why the Sussex-led alliance was defeated. The scant clues point to a situation whereby these seasoned Germanic warriors were caught off-balance, perhaps only momentarily. But it was sufficient for the Britons to deliver a decisive blow that most probably came via a cavalry charge. Such a situation could have occurred at any location where the Anglo-Saxons sought to seize new territory, but in all likelihood it happened in the vicinity of the Hampshire Avon, and Badbury Rings was one of the most likely immediate objectives for a Germanic force seeking to break the deadlock along this frontier.

As the battle developed it seems that the British were able to take advantage of the situation that arose because they had planned effectively to DELAY, DISRUPT and ultimately strike back effectively against a Germanic offensive action. By contrast, the Germanic plan failed because it did not anticipate such levels of British preparedness and organisation. An additional factor may well have been that the Germanic command was overconfident. Ælle's venture at Badon appears to have foundered at least in part due to the sort of failure in the decision-making process that has occurred often in the history of warfare. The rout of his army, precipitated by the armoured horsemen of the Britons, would later become the stuff of legend.

The siege of Badon Hill marked the beginning of a protracted struggle for dominance in south-west Britain. Ælle and his warriors had failed in the first Anglo-Saxon attempt to establish a bridgehead into the territories that would later become the heart of Wessex. The power of the South Saxons waned as a result. The *Anglo-Saxon Chronicle* relates nothing of this. What it does do is hint that some decades after Badon, the struggle for Wessex resumed in earnest under new leaders. It was time for the Gewisse to seize their chance.

Chapter Seven

Cerdic to Ceawlin – The Early Gewisse

Men rise from one ambition to another: first, they seek to secure them-selves against attack, and then they attack others. – Niccolo Machiavelli

Aftermath of Badon

It is reasonable to conclude that the defeat of the Germanic Army at Badon accounts for the disappearance of South Saxon influence and a slowing down of Germanic expansion in southern Britain in the early sixth century. It is not possible to discern any settlement by Germanic groups to the west of the Hampshire Avon for many decades after Badon. The broad timeframe for this lull in expansion and associated suspension of major hostilities in the Avon frontier region coincides with a period of reverse migrations of Germanic set-tlers back to continental Europe. This reversal of fortune is attested to by more than one contemporary source, as Sir Frank Stenton notes in his influential work *Anglo-Saxon England*, first published in 1943:

> *There is also a general agreement between Procopius and the monk of Fulda as to the period in which these migrations took place. Theudebert, king of the Franks, to whose relations with Justinian Procopius owed whatever he knew of the affairs of Britain, reigned from 534 until 548. He is known to have boasted to Justinian of the number of peoples under his rule, and he was undoubtedly the Frankish king who, according to Procopius, used the migrations from Britain into Frankish territory as proof of his lord-ship over the island. The Thuringian war of Theuderich can be precisely dated to the year 531, some thirty years after the barbarian penetration of Britain had been checked by the battle of Mons Badonicus.*[1]

This passage links Badon to the reverse migrations somewhat tentatively, pre-sumably because Stenton's 'thirty years after' is based on his own assessment of a date for the battle. It is likely that the reverberations of the failed campaign had a more immediate effect, with some Germanic groups abandoning Britain for the continent in the immediate aftermath. Others may have left as overcrowding gradually worsened in the south coast territories that Ælle had failed to expand. Whatever the relative movements of populations, it is clear that the ramifications of the battle persisted for some time. At some point, though, the Germanic forces in southern Britain recovered and the fights for territory erupted once more. The *Anglo-Saxon Chronicle*, whilst omitting any mention of Badon, provides a narrative of the military actions that we can safely describe as post-Badon. The *Chronicle* describes for this era a series of battles in which the Germanics appear finally to break the stalemate in the South East, precipitating a significant advance northwards. According to the chroniclers, this action led to the capture of huge amounts of British territory, chiefly by Ceawlin of Wessex. It is vital that we examine this version of Ceawlin's campaigning in some detail because most academics harbour doubts over its authenticity. Ceawlin is fêted by Bede as the second Germanic leader after Ælle to hold *imperium* over other Germanic groups, thus marking him as a military leader of considerable note.[2] Sadly, Bede provides no other detail on Ceawlin. However, in addition to the *Anglo-Saxon Chronicle* we also have Æthelweard's *Chronicon* to examine for accounts of Ceawlin and his deeds. Æthelweard was likely an éaldorman of the western provinces (probably the whole of Wessex).[3] His *Chronicon*, which was written c. 975 to 983, is a Latin translation of a lost version of the *Anglo-Saxon Chronicle*. It contains material that is absent from Old English versions and is sometimes quite revealing, as we shall see.

Initially under the mentorship of his father Cynric, and later with his brother Cuthwulf and other relatives, Ceawlin is recorded as having reigned over a fairly extensive kingdom that included much territory in the Thames Valley. The territorial gains attributed to Cynric and Ceawlin in particular present us with a step-change in the rate of Germanic expansion. The military achievements of the West Saxons, as per the records, would certainly have required armies of thousands, at least as large as our estimate of the force mustered at Badon. Even if we accept that a fledgling West Saxon kingdom raised such an army, on close examination the heroics attributed to Cynric and his descendants challenge the imagination and are no longer taken at face value by serious historians. It is likely that their very names were chosen by the scribes in order to obfuscate events. The problem that faced the chroniclers was that the antecedents of the Wessex kings were not pureblood Saxons. Instead, it seems they had their origins among the Romano-British as much as the Germanics. The name Cynric can be derived from a contemporary British king called *Cunorix*. His father's name, Cerdic, is the same as the British *Ceredig*. Ceawlin translates to *Collen* in the British version. There is much to debate regarding the provenance of the West Saxon line of kings, but to do this carries a risk of diversion, away from the aim of this book which is to seek a cogent military chain of events and locations. For now, when following the deeds of Cerdic and his descendants, we should merely acknowledge that the ninth/tenth-century Wessex chroniclers probably dissembled, in part to promote a grander history for early Wessex and possibly also to hide the fact that Cerdic was not of Saxon blood.

Cynric and Ceawlin

The *Anglo-Saxon Chronicle* records that the West Saxons first made landfall at *Cerdices ora* (Cerdic's shore) in AD 495 or 514, depending on which entry is accepted. Cerdic's shore is variously proposed as somewhere on the south coast (usually near Southampton Water, with Calshot as a favourite), along the banks of the River Severn by some who wish to place Cerdic in battles against their 'historical Arthur', and at Great Yarmouth.[4] Cerdic and Cynric apparently went on to soundly beat the Britons in 508 (Netley), 519 (*Cerdices ford*), 527 (*Cerdices leah*) and 530 (Isle of Wight). The first Germanics to settle on the Isle of Wight were Jutes, not Saxons. This is recorded by Bede and is commensurate with archaeological finds.[5] There are several other anomalies that render the *Chronicle* highly unreliable for this period.[6] The chroniclers seem to have placed the earliest activities of their West Saxon kings in Hampshire, because that matched their scenario of an invasion via the south coast. The confusion arising from repetition in this sequence of events has been covered already. What we need to note at this point is the story pushed strongly by the Wessex scribes, that Cerdic and Cynric's kingdom was established in 519 as a result of their victory at *Cerdices ford*. Æthelweard says that *Cerdices ford* is 'on the river Avon', which is why it is usually assumed to be Charford.[7] Perhaps of greater interest are the words Æthelweard chose to transfer to his *Genealogy of King Alfred*, relating the events of 500 – 'In the sixth year from their arrival they encircled that western part of Britain now known as Wessex.'[8] An alternative translation says that 'they sailed round the western part of Britain which is now called Wessex'.[9] It is nowhere claimed that Cerdic and Cynric seized territory in what 'is now called Wessex', only that they were on the borders of it. It is a very clear admission that 'Wessex territory' at this time remained firmly in British hands. Cerdic and Cynric, despite claims they conquered Hampshire and Wight, were apparently strong enough only after a twenty-two-year gap to mount further challenges to the Britons, their expansion out of the Hampshire region beginning in earnest in 552. All of this obfuscation was necessary, because the scribes needed to get their heroes active in the Thames region rather than stalled at the Hampshire Avon, for reasons that will become clear. Thus, the 'official' record tells us that they campaigned northwards, up to the year of Ceawlin's accession:

> *552. Here Cynric fought against the Britons at the place which is named Salisbury* [Searo byrg], *and put the Britons to flight.*
>
> *556. Here Cynric and Ceawlin fought against the Britons at Bera's stronghold* [Beran byrg, now Barbury].
>
> *560. Here Ceawlin succeeded to the kingdom in Wessex.*[10]

Cynric and Ceawlin's campaigning as recorded in the *Chronicle* appears to have resulted in the conquest of a swathe of territory from the central south coast to the Thames Valley region, as far as the northern reaches of the Icknield Way. In order to achieve this from a start-point at Charford, they would have had to subdue the British kingdoms of *Caer Gwinntguic* and *Caer Celemion* (Winchester and Silchester), whilst ensuring their western flanks were secure from interference by the Britons beyond the Avon. We are asked to believe either that they conquered everything in their path or that they captured just enough territory to secure a corridor through their foes' territories, which gave them access into the Thames Valley region.

Searo byrg, now called Old Sarum, seems to have been chosen almost as a way-station on this route, a bridging objective between Charford and *Beran byrg*. It is a particularly large and impressive Iron Age hillfort whose defensive banks and ditches enclose 29 acres or so of the hilltop. In Roman times, it was named *Sorviodunum* and a small settlement was then in place, half a mile to its south-west in the bottom of the Avon Valley, where Stratford-sub-Castle is today. The archaeology of the fort shows it was resurrected for military use in the post-Roman period. The embankments at Sarum are particularly high and steep and it could hardly have been bettered in the Salisbury district for its defensive properties. It also provided exceptional fields of view across the Avon Valley and out along the four Roman roads that converged at the site.

An assault on Sarum would have presented significant difficulties for Cynric, not only because of the physical defences at the site but also because of the likely strength of his enemies in its area of influence. The status of Winchester, 22 miles to the east, is unknown, but if it had fallen to West Saxons so early the feat would surely have been lauded in the *Chronicle*. Possibly, then, it was still held by Britons. More significant, perhaps, is that Amesbury, the stronghold of Ambrosius, is only 7½ miles to the north of Sarum. Cynric would have had to defeat the people there too, descendants of the Britons who had held the South West so strongly in the Badon era. Further, there is no archaeological evidence for early Saxon settlement on the hill at Sarum. Finds have been restricted to a bronze brooch and a few silver pennies from the reigns of Athelstan (925-940) and Edgar the Peaceable (959-975). Other local finds suggest a 'richer than average' sixth-century Saxon community in the Salisbury area that probably represented the power behind a wider Wiltshire Saxon populace in the Avon Valley. It is not possible to distinguish how this community was founded.[11] One explanation could be that the area was settled earlier, by a Germanic mercenary group invited by the Britons, just like those identified in Kent and the Thames Valley. Another is that the sixth-century Germanics there were descended from the Belgae, whose Germanic origins have already been noted.

From a military scholar's perspective, a victory at Sarum for Cynric of Wessex in 552 seems highly unlikely. It does, however, serve a primary aim of the *Chronicle* authors, to promote the idea of the earliest West Saxons as particularly powerful. To reinforce their message the royal lineage linking Cynric back to Woden is accentuated in the *Chronicle* text for 552. The descendant Wessex kings from Cerdic to Alfred and beyond are also described at length in the text for 495. Having established Cynric's credentials, the next problem for the chroniclers was to get Ceawlin active in the Thames Valley. Their solution was that Cynric pressed on to secure *Beran byrg* (Barbury Castle) four years later, by which time Ceawlin was rising to prominence. Barbury Castle is an Iron Age hillfort located on the part of the Ridgeway track that follows the northern edge of the Marlborough Downs. The hillfort is 5 miles south of Swindon and from it, today, one can still enjoy exceptional views to the north across the M4 motorway, encompassing the modern urban sprawl but also the picturesque Vale of the White Horse and much of the upper Thames Valley region. The fort occupies about 10 acres and has entrances on its eastern and western edges. It is the most elaborate of the Ridgeway hillforts, comprising bivallate defences and a defensive outwork that screens the eastern entrance.

The course of the Wansdyke runs well to the south, so Barbury is assessed to be outside of the fifth-century Wansdyke territory, whereas in the Iron Age it almost certainly sat on the northern border of the Durotriges territory. Its strategic importance in the fifth century is therefore difficult to assess because it seems to have ended up as part of the Belgae territory delineated by Rome. There is insufficient evidence to suggest whether the Belgae or any other group persisted there in post-Roman times. Evidence has been found of post-Roman re-occupation of a hillfort at Oldbury, about 7 miles to the south-west of Barbury. Oldbury is part of the Wansdyke boundary and was most probably part of the British defensive matrix in the Badon Hill era. The same cannot so easily be claimed for Barbury, and it is possible that it had long since ceased to be an important part of any border chain of forts. Nevertheless, Barbury's dominating location on the Ridgeway and overall size and complexity made it an obvious choice for scribes wanting to fabricate a worthy conquest by Cynric. Neatly enough for them, it also introduced Ceawlin as a West Saxon presence in the Thames region. Whatever his origins, Ceawlin is identified as having inherited a kingdom that was Thames-centric. In the *Anglo-Saxon Chronicle* version this was made possible by the victory at Barbury. Subsequent campaigning along the Icknield Way would have potentially brought his army into conflict with *Calchwynedd*, a British kingdom of uncertain size and strength in the Chiltern Hills.

The march of the West Saxons from the south coast to Barbury presents a problem for archaeologists, scholars of the texts, and military historians. From 552 onwards, however, the *Chronicle* begins to reflect a more believable sequence of events. Ceawlin's military activity does genuinely seem to have been focused on battle sites in the Thames region. In order to make sense of this, we must return to the question of the provenance of the West Saxon leaders and the *Chronicle*'s assertion that they were warlords who came to Britain by sea. Scholars such as Sir Charles Oman, writing over a century ago, have long since disassociated themselves from this version of events. More recently, Yorke writes that:

> *We can no longer speak as confidently of the origins of Wessex as historians once felt able to do, but the area which has the best claim to have been the original homeland of the West Saxons is the upper Thames valley …*
>
> *Critical analysis of the accounts of the origins of Wessex suggest that Cerdic the founder of the West Saxon dynasty was establishing his position in the 530s, probably in the upper Thames valley.*[12]

The rise to prominence of the group that the *Chronicle* refers to as the West Saxons becomes more credible once one accepts that Alfred's scribes were manipulating the history of a people in the Thames Valley area called the Gewisse. It has been suggested that the name Gewisse originated from Gwent, which in the modern Welsh language can be either Gwennwys or Gwenhwys. Tellingly, the *Chronicle* names *Gewis* as an ancestor of Cerdic without any elaboration. There is a distinct possibility that the Gewisse had roots in southern Wales, but what little is written of them is in prose tales and myths and should be treated with caution. Notwithstanding this, it is indisputable that the British names Ceredig, Cunorix and Collen are close matches for Cerdic, Cynric and Ceawlin.

Ceredig was apparently born near the Firth of Forth in Scotland, son of Cunedda Wledig, who ruled over a kingdom called Manau Gododdin. Ceredig moved to northern Wales in the early fifth century in order to help in the fight against Irish invaders and was rewarded with lands that bordered Gwynedd, Powys and Dyfed, his new kingdom being named Ceredigion. There is no apparent link from Ceredig to Cunorix, but evidence of a chieftain named Cunorix exists in the form of the Wroxeter Stone. August Hunt, an American expert in Celtic and Germanic history, argued the case that the story of the West Saxon king Cynric has its basis in the history of the Briton, Cunorix:

> *The Wroxeter Stone is a memorial to a chieftain named Cunorix son of Maquicoline. R. P. Wright and K.H. Jackson date this stone 'somewhere roughly about 460-75 or so.' Maquicoline is a composite name meaning*

Son [Maqui-] of Coline. *The resemblance here of Cunorix and Coline to the* Anglo-Saxon Chronicle's *Cynric and his son Ceawlin is obvious. Some scholars would doubtless say this is coincidence, and that the discrepancy in dates for Cynric and Ceawlin and Cunorix and (Maqui)coline are too great to allow for an identification. I would say that an argument based on the very uncertain* Chronicle *dates is hazardous at best and that if there is indeed a relationship between the pairs Ceawlin-Cynric and Coline-Cunorix, then the date of the memorial stone must be favored over that of the document.*

There is also the problem of Cynric being the father of Ceawlin in the Anglo-Saxon tradition, while on the Wroxeter Stone it is (Maqui) coline who is the father of Cunorix. But such a confusion could easily have occurred simply by reading part of a genealogy list backwards.[13]

Whether the Gewisse originated in Wales or elsewhere in Britain is moot for the purposes of tracing Ceawlin's activity. By his time we are sure that they were in the Thames region. Finds of both Celtic and Germanic artefacts attest to their presence in the early sixth century. The point to note is that the earlier leaders of the Gewisse probably provided the *Chronicle* authors with some historical inspiration for their version of Cerdic and his descendants. This helps also to explain what happened to the mix of auxiliaries and mercenaries of Germanic origin who settled in the Thames Valley in the Roman era. Quite simply, they interbred with the Romano-British and the resulting populations gradually became more Germanic in their ways. As C.J. Arnold, a widely regarded authority on Anglo-Saxon history, puts it:

Attitudes about the fate of the British during and after the period of [Germanic] *migration have changed considerably over the last one hundred years. At one time the view was propounded that many were annihilated, as Bede suggested, but more recently there has been a gradual acceptance that they were present but invisible.*[14]

Arnold qualifies this by going on to suggest that previous assumptions regarding the annihilation or 'ethnic cleansing' of the British based on archaeological records are unsound. For example, one rejected assumption was that everything new in the fifth and sixth centuries must be the result of Germanic domination, rather than trade or the gradual sharing and adoption of common practices and goods by neighbouring ethnic communities. The modern and somewhat more enlightened theory is that groups co-existed and then merged. This provides good reasons to accept that mixed ethnic groups with proven martial backgrounds emerged in the upper Thames region at this time. Once their homelands were threatened by the turmoil that followed the collapse of Roman rule, it is only natural that they would have used their military forces to defend themselves locally. If successful in this, it follows that some groups who were militarily strong enough chose to exploit opportunities that arose beyond their bounds.

From this perspective, the military anomalies that arise out of the *Chronicle* begin to resolve. First, the 527 battle attributed jointly to Cerdic and Cynric at *Cerdices leah* (Cerdic's wood) is often sought without success in the south coast region, to match with the *Chronicle* account of the West Saxon landings there. Yet, as far back as 1883, Dr Edwin Guest suggested that the site actually lay on the northern banks of the River Thame, a major tributary of the Thames:

> Cerdices Leah, *or the Leah of Cerdic, appears to have consisted of Bernwood Forest and other woodlands to the north of it; and in Chearsley, the name of a village which lies on the eastern border of this district, we probably have a corruption of the old Anglo-Saxon name Cerdices Leah.*[15]

This site is entirely in keeping with Cerdic having fought to either defend or increase the size of a Thames Valley territory. Reporting this accurately in the *Anglo-Saxon Chronicle* would have been counter to the scribes' direction from above to make sure they antedated much of the territory claimed by Wessex in later years.[16] The sixth-century claims on Hampshire and the Isle of Wight are a case in point. It is now accepted that Jutes were the dominant settlers of these two regions through this period.

Consolidating the Thames Valley Gewisse kingdom

The Gewisse, in the latter part of the sixth century, were able to carve out a substantial territory in the Thames Valley region. From a military perspective, the course of the Thames and other rivers, together with lines of communication such as the Ridgeway and the Icknield Way would have assumed considerable importance in such operations. The annexation of territory in Ceawlin's era as described in the *Chronicle* is a credible scenario for Gewisse expansion, describing as it does the extension of established territories north-eastwards towards Bedford. Such a campaign is compatible with the actions of a kingdom that already had a presence in the Thames Valley and was able to take advantage of its military might in turbulent times. Thus, from the 556 record of a battle at Barbury, we can discern a period in which the manufactured history of the early West Saxons begins to meld with the modern idea that the Wessex dynasty originated among the Gewisse. A battle at Barbury might well have been a clash between Thames Valley groups and the Britons of the south west, a border clash in line with the picture of localised fighting that we have assessed as accurate for the times. Thereafter, both Ceawlin and his brother Cuthwulf (Cutha for short) become very active militarily. The establishment of extensive new territories in the Thames region is credited to Cuthwulf, although he seems to have paid for his efforts with his life:

> *568. Here Ceawlin and Cutha fought against Æthelberht and drove him into Kent; and they killed two ealdormen, Oslaf and Cnebba, on Wibba's Mount* [Wibbandun].

> *571. Here Cuthwulf fought against the Britons at Bedcanford and took 4 settlements: Limbury and Aylesbury, Benson and Eynsham; and in the same year he passed away.*[17]

Both of these entries warrant a detailed analysis. The 571 entry will be dealt with first because it puts the 568 entry in a previously unconsidered context. Into the twentieth century, *Bedcanford* was widely accepted to be Bedford. Some recent researchers disagree but no alternative is proffered and etymologists are essentially arguing over a misplaced letter 'c'. The other four translations are undisputed, but there has been much debate as to the significance of the four towns listed. Michael Swanton, translator and editor of the 1996 version of *The Anglo-Saxon Chronicles*, which is the source of the extracts above, describes them in a note as 'an odd collection of places seized'.[18] The usual assumptions include that they were important centres of power or were remembered as the sites of battles. Peter Marren, for example, describes them in his 2009 book *Battles of the Dark Ages* as 'seemingly insignificant', but suggests they may have been 'the fortified settlements of local magnates who were now overthrown once and for all'.[19] The truth is arguably much simpler. When viewed on the map it becomes clear that the four towns, together with Bedford, define a particular area of influence commensurate with an expanding Gewisse kingdom, between the Rivers Thames and Great Ouse. The geographical limits of this area can be described readily. From Eynsham the boundary follows the Thames south-east to Benson, from where it next follows the northern edge of the Chilterns and the Ridgeway to Aylesbury before continuing on this line to Limbury, now a suburb of Luton. Finally, the boundary turns due north about 16 miles to Bedford on the Great Ouse River which meanders back towards Brackley, 18 miles north-east of Eynsham.

It is entirely possible that the four towns are listed in this way primarily to indicate to the reader the overall extent of the territory captured. Cuthwulf's expanded kingdom had definable natural boundaries, the Thames and the Chiltern Hills in the south and the Great Ouse in the north. What is more, this kingdom contained some of the earliest sites with evidence of Germanic settlement, as we would expect. In their 2011 paper *Anglo-Saxon Oxfordshire*, archaeologists Sally Crawford and Anne Dodd noted that:

> *The places that seem to have been developing earliest, interestingly, are associated with the Thames, at the sites of the Benedictine abbeys at Abingdon and Eynsham, and the minster at Bampton.*[20]

There is also surviving evidence in today's landscape of man-made constructions that supplement natural features. North of Eynsham there are intermittent lengths of ancient dyke known, like many similar features elsewhere, as Grim's Ditch. Its course follows a line between Eynsham and Charlbury. Just south of Benson and running west to east towards Nettlebed is another Grim's Ditch, and sections of it are still present in several places close to or on the Ridgeway in the Chiltern Hills. In places, these dykes clearly filled gaps between natural features that served as territorial boundaries. These linear earthworks most likely originated in earlier times, but as with the Iron Age hillforts, they may have assumed a renewed importance to the Gewisse or their neighbours as defensive works or boundaries. The identification of Chearsley on the River

Thame as a likely site for *Cerdices leah* adds weight to the overall argument that Cerdic's descendants were active in expanding up to these very bounds. Map 7 provides a logical representation of the assessed Gewisse kingdom in c. 571. Ceawlin's absence from the 571 record of campaigning in the Oxford-Bedford area is worthy of note. He seems to have gone with his sons, Cuthwine and Cutha, to fight elsewhere or alongside a people other than 'his own', a choice of words by the *Chronicle* authors that we will return to in good time.[21] We are told that Ceawlin was co-leader at the 568 battle at *Wibbandun*, three years before Cuthwulf consolidated his hold over the Thames Valley territory with his victory at *Bedcanford*. If the site of *Wibbandun* can be identified, then it helps us to place in context the campaigns of both Cuthwulf and Ceawlin.

Wibbandun

The battle site for *Wibbandun* has never been identified with any certainty. The battle there provides the first record in the *Anglo-Saxon Chronicle* of internecine conflict between Germanic factions in Britain. But there is no explanation of how the situation arose. A traditional interpretation is that Ceawlin was distracted temporarily and had to engage in a separate war with Kent before he was able to turn his attention back to his campaigns against the British in the Thames region. Yet, if in 568 he was with Cuthwulf making steady progress on an offensive north-eastwards from Barbury, it is difficult to see why he would divert and threaten Kent. He was clearly not defending Gewisse interests separately from Cuthwulf because both are present at *Wibbandun*. There were compelling reasons for them to have concentrated their energies in the Thames Valley, not least that they had yet to establish supremacy. Equally, there was every reason not to have engaged in a potentially costly fight with Kent. Popular suggestions for the site of *Wibbandun* have been Wimbledon (based on the place-name alone and now largely discredited) and Whitmoor Common near Worplesdon. The latter site is now favoured, but the arguments for both are questionable and the lack of credibility regarding such an action by Ceawlin and Cuthwulf appears to have been overlooked. Both of these locations lie many miles outside of the Gewisse territory, way off their Oxford-Bedford campaign trail.

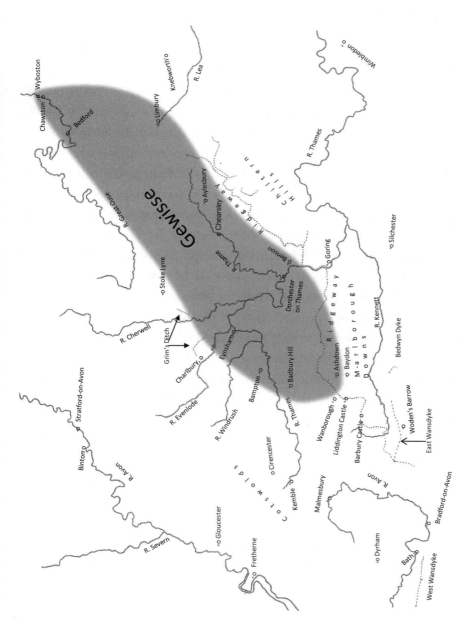

Map 7: Assessed Gewisse territory c. AD 571

To accept Wimbledon, or the now more popular Worplesdon, as valid for the site of this battle, one must first believe that the army of a fledgling Gewisse kingdom was capable of campaigning well outside its borders. To reach the borders of Kent required the Gewisse to cross a considerable swathe of territory to the south and east, away from the homeland that it had fought so hard to establish in the first place. The brothers in command of this army would have needed a very good reason to undertake such a venture. The logic behind this move is unsound from the start and becomes even more so when one is asked to believe that having achieved a victory in which he drove Æthelberht into Kent, Ceawlin turned away to the west without any apparent attempt to build on this success, for example by occupying territory in Kent or on its borders. An alternative scenario to support a Surrey location must presume that the king of Kent was threatening Gewisse interests by campaigning to the south-west of London. The Gewisse were confined to north of the Thames and archaeological evidence indicates that the British were holding out in the London area at this time. Kent's interests have been shown to be more inclined towards the east coast and Anglian territories. There is no good reason why the army of Kent would have met anyone other than the British in the Surrey region.

It seems clear that we must look for a more logical site for *Wibbandun* than Wimbledon or Worplesdon, and the first pointer to it is the known relationship between the powerful Jutes of Kent and the Anglians. There is evidence that the kings of Kent, known as the Oiscings after Oisc himself, were overlords of the Anglians. Sir Charles Oman assessed that:

> *The strength of the Oiscings in early days must have depended, not on the exact amount of territory occupied by their own Jutish war-band, but on their personal influence as generals of the combined Teutonic invaders of South Britain. It is thus alone that we can account for the fact that Æthelberht (560 – 617) was reckoned by Bede to have held the* imperium *of all Britain south of Humber, and was certainly granted homage and tribute by his immediate Saxon neighbours, and even by remoter Anglian dynasts farther to the north.*[22]

Æthelberht's dominance, from Kent to the Humber according to Bede, extended across those Anglian territories south of the Wash. It was this region that came under threat from the Gewisse as they looked to establish a defensible boundary on the Great Ouse River in the easternmost part of their territory. Rather than probing the borders of Kent, it is far more likely that Ceawlin clashed with Æthelberht here. *Wibbandun* is often written as *Wibba's Dun*. As such it is close phonetically to Wyboston, a small village 8 miles north-east of Bedford on the west bank of the Great Ouse. Based on the assessed Gewisse territory at this time this site is a strong contender for the battle. Previously unconsidered, it has more evidence attached to it than the obvious similarities of name.

The date, 568, sits well within the context of Ceawlin and Cuthwulf campaigning together in the years before Cuthwulf was left to consolidate the region via a victory at Bedford. The brothers most likely clashed with Æthelberht and his Anglian clients because the Gewisse expansion threatened Æthelberht's east coast hegemony. Supporting evidence for this idea is found when one looks at the named participants in the fight. Cnebba, named as slain in this battle, has been associated with Knebworth, which lies 20 miles to the south of Wyboston. Cnebba was a noble and maybe even a king of the *Iclingas*, the ruling elite who later became kings of the Mercians, beginning with Creoda in 584. Cnebba's likely geographical area of influence adds weight to the theory that he may have died at Wyboston, defending his interests along the Great Ouse. Further supplementary evidence is to be found just half-a-mile south of Wyboston, where there is a village called Chawston. The origin of the place-name is not listed anywhere. It has probably been lost over time, but Chawston is easily derived from the Old English *Ceawston* or *Ceawlinston*.[23]

Wyboston is the most likely site of *Wibbandun*. A defeat there for Æthelberht would have damaged his overlord status and diminished his influence over the Anglians. The idea that he was driven or 'pursued' into Kent (depending on which *Chronicle* translation is preferred) should not be taken literally. Similar phraseology is often to be found in the *Chronicle* when one king bests another. A defeat suffered as part of an expedition to help his Anglian clients would have caused Æthelberht to withdraw into Kent to recover, and that is most likely what happened. Another consequence of the battle, the slaying of Cnebba at the hands of Ceawlin and Cuthwulf, probably sowed the earliest seeds of the enmity between the Mercian Angles and the Gewisse. This feud was to last for generations and reverberate through many of the events that shaped early Wessex.

Westward from the Thames – The Battle of Dyrham

Implicit in the result of such a battle on the Ouse is that the Gewisse were freed from Anglian interference for the moment. This would have enabled Ceawlin to take his warbands westwards to further his own ambitions, leaving the consolidation of the newly won Gewisse territory in Cuthwulf's hands, just as the 571 *Chronicle* account describes. Significant clues as to how this situation progressed are in subsequent *Chronicle* entries, beginning with a decisive victory credited to Ceawlin and his son Cuthwine in 577:

> *577. Here Cuthwine and Ceawlin fought against the Britons, and they killed 3 kings, Coinmail and Condidan and Farinmail, in the place which is called Dyrham; and took 3 cities: Gloucester and Cirencester, and Bath.*[24]

Once again, a sizeable piece of territory was apparently annexed in one fell swoop. There are three cities seized and three kings slain, which makes the entry sound more like a piece of prose from the sagas than a record of fact. Furthermore, the British kings named have never been identified as historical figures. In a 1983 article, *The Settlement of England in Bede and the Chronicle,* Professor Patrick Sims-Williams suggested that all three kings in the 577 entry might have been Welsh rulers named out of context. According to Sims-Williams, Condidan is possibly derived from the Welsh Cynddylan, a Welsh ruler in the Wroxeter region who was killed in the mid-seventh century.[25]

The dubious nature of this particular entry causes many to doubt that any such battle took place at Dyrham. That judgement may be hasty. In the context of an established Gewisse presence expanding westwards, a battle at Dyrham makes sense. It is also impossible to ignore the growth of the Hwicce, a federation of smaller groups with 'mingled Anglian and Saxon stock' in the Gloucester-Bath-Cirencester area.[26] It seems that British power was lost or diluted in the Cotswold region in the late sixth century. The *Chronicle* authors might well be giving us a suitably heroic version of how that happened. The presence of Anglians in the mix suggests that a leader was able to unite disparate Germanic factions. This, together with evidence that the Hwicce grouping encompassed Britons as well goes a long way towards explaining why Ceawlin is described in the *Chronicle* as fighting away from 'his own' in 584. It might seem like too much of a leap of imagination to propose that Ceawlin accepted Anglians into his expeditionary army having defeated them at *Wibbandun*, but such pacts between victors and vanquished are recorded elsewhere in Anglo-Saxon history. Ceawlin's fame and status as *Bretwalda* might have accrued from his prowess in leading a campaign which established the Hwicce settlements in the Cotswolds. Alternatively, he may simply have joined forces with existing Hwicce there. In either case, the spread of Gewisse influence under Ceawlin seems to have reached its zenith around 577.

The *Chronicle* account emphasises a swift and costly defeat for the British at Dyrham, but this is open to debate. We are likely seeing towns listed as a convenient way of describing the expanding boundaries of early Wessex, just like in the entry for 571. The additional naming of the defeated kings serves to emphasise the achievements of Ceawlin. The problem with mapping any Gewisse expansion westwards, based on the 577 entry, is that the scale of the immediate conquest as described does not sit comfortably with the archaeological evidence available. Artefact finds suggest that, whilst a Germanic presence in the form of the Hwicce people emerged around Cirencester quite soon after 577, it was not until later that their influence spread to encompass Bath and Gloucester.

A kingdom beset on all sides – the battles at *Fethan leag* and *Woddes beorge*

Although probably less impressive in reality than the substantial campaigns described in the *Anglo-Saxon Chronicle*, the early efforts of the Gewisse in establishing a kingdom were notable. They were probably established as a community in Roman times when the prevailing security situation meant that defending their own borders was unnecessary. Instead they fought as proxies elsewhere, probably against the northern tribes and thus played their part in ensuring security across Roman Britain. Once the Romans left they were suddenly far more exposed to threats, from their British neighbours and increasingly from the new continental Germanic arrivals. They certainly did not inherit military advantages from their surrounding geography, and were soon beset on all sides by enemies. It becomes increasingly clear from the written records, together with a cursory study of the terrain, that this was never a secure kingdom. The trials of the Gewisse leaders were many as they fought successive enemies in battles aimed more at survival than conquest. The fragility of Ceawlin's position in particular becomes apparent in the *Chronicle* entry for 584:

> *584. Here Ceawlin and Cutha fought against the Britons at the place which is named Battle Wood* [Fethan leag], *and Cutha was killed; and Ceawlin took many towns and countless war-loot, and in anger he turned back to his own [territory].*[27]

Anger is a somewhat surprising state of mind for one who gained such wealth. The Reverend James Ingram's 1823 translation of the *Chronicle* says that Ceawlin 'retreated to his own people', omitting any mention of his state of mind.[28] Ceawlin's anger might be explained if he was grieving over Cutha's death, or resented being forced away from his independent ventures because the Gewisse territory was under pressure. To assess the most likely chain of events it would help if we could locate the lost battle site of *Fethan leag*.

The third sentence in the *Chronicle* text for 584 is almost certainly an exaggeration. If Ceawlin had taken many towns then at least some would be named, as they were in previous accounts. Such information would help in the search for *Fethan leag*, because the site would surely be in proximity to the towns. We are also left to ponder the enigma of the final sentence of this entry, whichever version is preferred: who were Ceawlin's own people and where was his own territory? One clue to the answer lies in his earlier split with Cuthwulf. Ceawlin was clearly a war leader who exercised power over one faction among several that were spread across the Gewisse and Hwicce territories. His final downfall in battle was to take place back in the Vale of the White Horse region at *Woddes beorge*, midway between Hwicce lands and the Gewisse heartlands occupied by his original kinfolk. It is not clear whether Ceawlin was still on the offensive at this final battle. *Fethan leag*, on the other hand, is clearly portrayed as part of an ongoing offensive campaign. One possibility is that the towns cited as captured are not named in order to avoid repeating the names of towns claimed for Wessex earlier, in the 577 *Chronicle* entry. If so then *Fethan leag* could have been another battle that formed part of the struggle to control the Gloucester-Bath-Cirencester area.

Researchers usually favour their choice from three main contenders for the site of *Fethan leag*, Faddiley in Cheshire, Fretherne near Gloucester and Stoke Lyne in Oxfordshire. Faddiley was preferred by Godsal. He presented it as the northernmost battle fought by Ceawlin in a campaign that enabled him to establish a powerbase at Wednesbury near West Bromwich. Godsal also proposed that Ceawlin was able to achieve such far-reaching success through an alliance with the Angles and that the breakdown of this arrangement contributed to his final defeat at Wednesbury (Godsal's candidate for *Woddes beorge*) in 592.[29] Godsal's underlying assumption is that through this period the British were conquered by way of a series of large scale campaigns led by powerful *Bretwaldas*, including Ceawlin. This viewpoint was based on his somewhat misguided interpretation of Bede's works and the *Anglo-Saxon Chronicle*. Faddiley is too far north to be a battle site for the Gewisse under Ceawlin.

Fretherne, the only place in Britain of that name, lies at the neck of a promontory of land formed by a huge meander of the River Severn about 7 miles south-west of Gloucester. The idea that it was the site of Ceawlin's *Fethan leag* dates back to at least 1731, and a number of later *Chronicle* translators accepted it as the definitive site.[30] The road through Fretherne leads on through Arlingham to the Severn and terminates on the east bank at an ancient crossing site opposite Newnham:

> *Newnham is thought to have been settled because of the relative ease of crossing the river there. The commanding site, close to the water's edge but above the flood level, was clearly a contributory cause. The crossing at Newnham was presumably in use in the first century A.D.*[31]

The Severn is the obvious natural western boundary for a coherent kingdom or territory in the Gloucester-Bath-Cirencester region. Marren draws attention to what he calls the 'strategic triangle' in this area but, whilst this promontory is very clear on his map and obviously a key feature on the western border of this triangle, he fails to mention Fretherne as a possible battle site.[32] This is surprising because from the geography alone, it is easy to understand how Ceawlin might have faced British enemies somewhere on this promontory and at Fretherne in particular. Above the village and dominating the narrowest part of the promontory (just under 1¼ miles from bank to bank at this point) is

Barrow Hill. It would have been an obvious site to choose to defend, either for a force wanting to deny Ceawlin access to the river through fear of his invading territory on the far bank, or for Ceawlin himself to have chosen to block against a force intruding from that far side of the river.

The third established proposal for *Fethan leag* is that it is a lost name from the environs of Stoke Lyne, Oxfordshire.[33] Stoke Lyne lies 5 miles south of Brackley where the headwaters of the Great Ouse rise. If the battle occurred at this site, it would reinforce the significance of this particular river as a northern boundary for the Gewisse. Ceawlin may have fought in this location in the context of a defence of a Thames Valley kingdom. However, this scenario is difficult to square with the wording in the *Anglo-Saxon Chronicle*, because in a defensive battle at Stoke Lyne, Ceawlin would presumably have already returned to his own territory or people – the Gewisse (see Map 7).

The argument for Stoke Lyne holds together if the Gewisse were fighting for their very existence in the Thames Valley region. In such a situation, Ceawlin's forces are less likely to have been fighting as far west as the River Severn. On the other hand, the River Severn location clearly has all the ingredients for a battle between the Germanic occupiers of Marren's 'strategic triangle' and the *Walas* (Welsh) to their west. The time and the situation, viewed in the light of a continuation of the Dyrham campaign westwards, are right for a battle led by Ceawlin. The emergence of the Hwicce in the Gloucester region suggests that they could have been involved in a battle at Fretherne as they consolidated their boundaries. Ceawlin either leading or fighting alongside the Hwicce provides the most reasonable explanation of his subsequent return to his own territory/people. On balance, Fretherne has more to recommend it than Stoke Lyne in that it offers at least a partial explanation to the riddle of Ceawlin's allegiances and makes more sense of the *Chronicle*'s hint at large territorial gains. The presence of a large army of Britons at Stoke Lyne at this time is also harder to infer than the gathering of such a force at Fretherne, where there was a clear threat to uniquely British territory.

Cutha's demise and Ceawlin's withdrawal in 584 are indications that the Gewisse as a whole were under pressure. It seems that Ceawlin, having reached the pinnacle of his power at *Fethan leag*, was forced to return to help the Gewisse in their increasingly desperate struggle to survive:

592. Here there was great slaughter at Woden's Barrow [Woddes beorge], *and Ceawlin was driven out.*[34]

If *Fethan leag* really did represent the peak of Ceawlin's achievements in war then *Woddes beorge* was surely the nadir. In Ingram's earlier translation, the events of 592 as portrayed present a paradox in describing 'a great slaughter of Britons' in the same sentence that makes clear that Ceawlin was driven from his kingdom.[35] The A, B and C versions of the *Anglo-Saxon Chronicle* all name the location for the battle as *Woddes beorge* or *Woddesbeorge*. From this, Ingram derived Wanborough, a village just east of Swindon.[36] A generally more popular site, as translated and chosen by Swanton above, is *Woden's Barrow*, an Iron Age long barrow today called Adam's Grave near Alton Barnes in Wiltshire. The barrow is on Walkers Hill, part of a high chalk ridgeline that provides far reaching views across and beyond the Wansdyke a mile or so to the north. *Woden's Barrow* is a good marker for the north-east corner of the British Wansdyke territory, given that it overlooks both the dyke and the upper tributaries of the Hampshire Avon. As such this site had clear strategic importance. It was likely another primary location in the defensive network planned and organised under Ambrosius, where a move by aggressive neighbours into the Wansdyke territory would have been met. The remains of Romano-British huts have been found there as well as Saxon weaponry.

The E manuscript is unique in writing the place-name as *Wodnesbeorge* and this version was emphasised by Godsal to get his Wednesbury site, which we have already dismissed.[37] There is a potentially valid explanation for the difference in the E version that may well lie in confusion arising from a location in Kent. A notable Anglo-Saxon burial was excavated in 1845 next to the village of Woodnesborough, which is about 10 miles east of Canterbury. The existing E version of the *Chronicle* was copied from an original compiled in Canterbury, so this difference of one letter is understandable as a mistake made by a scribe familiar with an important site nearby.

Regarding Wanborough, a battle at this site in 592 would have represented a stand some way inside Gewisse territory, which is assumed to have spread westwards as Ceawlin prosecuted his earlier campaign in the Hwicce territories. A defeat for Ceawlin at Wanborough would most certainly explain why he was driven from his kingdom, but the *Chronicle* text is too open to interpretation for us to conclude that things were that simple. The survival of the Gewisse under Ceol, who ruled for one year alongside Ceawlin and onwards after Ceawlin's expulsion, is made explicit. The continued influence of the Gewisse in the region is evidenced by their longstanding association with Ashdown Park, about 8 miles east of Wanborough. This former power base takes its modern name from *Æscesdun*, a name thought to have referred to a wider surrounding area in Saxon times, perhaps a small kingdom encompassing much of the Berkshire Downs. Perhaps the British did pay a heavy price for Ceawlin's removal as the first line of text implies and Ceol's accession was in some way acceptable to them. Unless more evidence can be unearthed, we cannot choose easily between Woden's Barrow and Wanborough for the site of this battle any more than we can deduce a winner from the equivocal records. *Woden's Barrow* is my personal favourite, but only for the quixotic notion that Ceawlin's adventurism finally came to grief when he messed with the same folk whose ancestors had defeated Ælle. Whatever happened in 592, the removal of Ceawlin seems to have left Ceol, son of Cuthwulf, to rule over a fragile kingdom centred on the chalk hills that overlook the Vale of the White Horse and the Thames beyond.[38]

As if Cerdic and Cynric were not obscure enough, with the downfall of Ceawlin we apparently enter a period of successive West Saxon kings that is even harder to unravel. There can be little reliance on the *Chronicle*, not least when an English medievalist, historian and author as eminent as Ann Williams assesses that its record of the early Anglo-Saxon period is 'largely worthless as history'.[38] In spite of this, what we seem to have discerned thus far is that Cerdic and his line were the leaders of warbands who had long since relinquished any purely Germanic ancestry. Ceawlin's battles were not 'invader versus Briton' encounters but were part of the complex feuding and fighting typical of his era in which localised kingdoms vied for dominance. In 593, the *Chronicle* says that Ceawlin perished along with Cwichelm and Crida. We therefore presume his demise came in yet another battle although no site is named. His legacy as recorded suggests there was no respite from discord. In the *Chronicle* entry for 597, Ceol is succeeded by Ceolwulf, the fifth ruler in the West Saxon Genealogical Regnal List, who is said to have 'continually fought and strove either against the Angle race, or against the Welsh, or against the Picts, or against the Scots'.[39] Such uninterrupted conflict was never the basis for a stable kingdom and, with Ceawlin's initial successes reversed, the Gewisse were under intense pressure.

The seeming failure of the Gewisse to prosper and secure defensible borders inevitably led to opportunism by others. Much of their Thames Valley territory was subsumed into Mercia. The only enduring legacy of the early Gewisse seems to have been a presence at Ashdown, close to the famous Whitehorse Hill, which bears the symbol of Wessex to this day. The role of Ashdown will come more into the light as we attempt to follow the campaigns of Ceawlin's descendants further down the generations and identify their influence on the development of Wessex. As for the Hwicce, archaeological finds confirm that they prospered in the Cotswold region from the latter part of the seventh century, albeit by then as subordinates to Mercia.[40] They are attested to in part by the title *Episcopus Hwicciorum*, used to describe the earliest bishops of Worcester, and by several place-names in the region, for example the Wychavon district of Worcestershire. Little is known of them and the origin of their name remains obscure. The Old English word *hwicce* translates to locker, chest or trunk. It seems a curious name, whether they chose it themselves or had it bestowed upon them. There are variations on a long-standing theory that part of the landscape they lived in resembled a chest. I think the answer is simpler: the name preserved something of their seafaring, expeditionary heritage. There were no inbuilt seats in Anglo-Saxon *céols*, so the warrior at his rowing station would sit on his own wooden chest, which also served as his personal container for possessions including any booty captured. In the Irish version of Nennius, there is a story that echoes the familiar red and white dragon story of Arthurian legend. It has little relevance here except to demonstrate the importance attached to voyages and their attendant articles. But it also hints at the power of the Ambrosius dynasty. The story tells of how a king called Gortigern and twelve druids were having problems constructing a fortress in Gwynedd and decided, as was their wont, to sacrifice a young boy to rectify things. The boy saved himself by revealing to the druids what he knew of a nearby lake. The druids dredged from the lake two wooden chests and a ship's sail. The boy told the druids they would find two maggots, one red and one white, rolled up in the sail asleep:

And the boy said, 'See now what the maggots will do.' They advanced towards each other, and commenced to rout, cut, and bite each other, and each maggot drove the other alternately to the middle of the sail and again to its verge. They did this three times. The red maggot was at first the feeble one, and was driven to the brink of the cloth; but the beautiful maggot was finally the feeble one, and fled into the lake, and the sail immediately vanished. The boy asked the Druids: 'Tell ye,' said he, 'what doth this wonder reveal?' 'We know not,' said they. 'I will reveal it to the king,' said the boy. 'The lake is the kingdom of the whole world, and the sail is thy kingdom, O king. And the two maggots are the two powers, namely, thy power in conjunction with the Britons, and the power of the Saxons. The red maggot, which was first expelled the kingdom, represents thy power; and the white maggot, which occupied the whole sail except a little, represents the power of the Saxons, who have taken the island of Britain, except a small part, until ultimately driven out by the power of the Britons. But do thou, O king of Britain, go away from this fortress, for thou hast not power to erect it, and search the island of Britain and thou shalt find thine own fortress.' The king said, 'What is thy name, O boy,' said he. The youth replied, 'Ambrose,' said he, 'is my name.' (He was Embros Gleutic, king of Britain.) 'Tell thy race,' said the king. 'My father, said he, was a Roman consul, and this shall be my fortress.' Then Gortigern left the fortress to Ambrose, and also the government of all the west of Britain.[41]

Summary

Tales of psychopathic maggots are entertaining but best ignored in assessing the early battles of the Wessex line of kings. To do that we must make a decision on the veracity of the *Anglo-Saxon Chronicle* accounts regarding Cerdic and his immediate descendants. Academics have already set a precedent in this regard by choosing to treat the arrival of Cerdic to Britain by boat as highly suspect. There is general agreement that he more likely originated from the Thames region. The decisions to be made therefore revolve around which battles among those recorded are manufactured and which are founded on real events. Given the chaos that followed the departure of the Romans and prevailed through to the writing of the various chronicles and beyond, none of the identifiable battle sites can be ruled out on the grounds that they lacked military significance. All were potentially significant when the geography and the number of factions involved in fighting are considered. In promoting the deeds of any particular leader, the scribes would have been well aware of this and, potentially, would have chosen the geographical locations that best fitted their version of his story. Today we can only make a best guess at the reality behind their records.

Where locations are concerned, Cerdic's shore is perhaps the most suspect of all given that the account of his arrival by sea looks to be entirely false. That being the case, Cynric's battle at Sarum is equally hard to believe in. Once we get to Barbury on the Ridgeway, and all subsequent Thames Valley and Cotswold locations, we are on surer ground for battle sites because they do correlate with other evidence for the existence of the Gewisse and Hwicce kingdoms. We are also sure that British territory west of the Hampshire Avon and south of the Wansdyke remained stubbornly resistant to the Germanic threat until a time beyond Ceawlin's demise. The next chapters will address the beginnings of the collapse of British rule in Dorset and Somerset, but there is little doubt that the descendants of Ambrosius continued his legacy of coordinated and effective defence against incursion. Through the sixth century, the territory that would later form the heartlands of Wessex was firmly in British hands.

Ceawlin's achievements in particular should be viewed in the light of his war leadership of peoples in the Thames Valley region whose origins can only be guessed at. Through success in battle these peoples collectively came to inhabit a territory defined roughly by the four settlements mentioned as taken from the British in 571. In the east I posit that this involved Ceawlin supporting his brother Cuthwulf in a battle that defeated a Kentish-Anglian force at Wyboston and helped to secure a boundary for the Gewisse on the Great Ouse. Thereafter, Ceawlin campaigned to the west and may have been instrumental in establishing the kingdom of the Hwicce. By the time he was killed, there is no doubt that the combined lands of the Hwicce and Gewisse were severely threatened by several rival neighbours. Whoever they might really have been, Alfred's ancestors had set a standard for tenacity and battling against the odds.

Chapter Eight

The Fall of British Glastenning

The desire to conquer is itself a sort of subjection. – George Eliot

The battle at Chester

With Ceawlin dead and the Gewisse in crisis, the chroniclers should be forgiven for looking elsewhere for news of Anglo-Saxon success. For the early part of the seventh century, events in Northumbria seem to have been of interest to the scribes. The *Anglo-Saxon Chronicle* does not anywhere suggest that what happened in Northumbria had any impact on the rise of Wessex. Yet there is one battle that may have played a part in weakening the British in the South West, just when they needed to be at full strength to meet any threats from Ceawlin's descendants:

> *606. And here Æthelfrith led his army to Chester and there killed a count-less number of Welsh; and thus was fulfilled Augustine's prophecy which he spoke: 'If the Welsh do not want peace with us, they shall perish at the hands of the Saxons'. There were also killed 200 priests who had come there in order pray for the Welsh raiding-army. Their chieftain was called Scrocmail, who escaped from there as one of fifty.*[1]

Bede's earlier version of events is less clear on the date of the battle at Chester. Based on his wording it has been proposed that it was as late as 617. The *Welsh Annals* record that it was fought in 613.[2] Bede wrote that 1,200 monks from the monastery at Bangor were slain there, having come to the field to pray for a British victory. The later *Chronicle* scribes may have baulked at such a scale of atrocity or simply found it to be unbelievable and therefore reduced the number recorded as killed. Æthelfrith was the king of *Bernicia* (Northumbria). He is thought to have invaded Gwynedd around this time in order to subdue his old enemy King Edwin of Deira, who had been given sanctuary there after his family was killed by Æthelfrith. Of potential interest when considering the fortunes of the Gewisse at this time is that the Britons on this campaign were possibly a united force from Gwynedd, Powys, *Pengwern* and *Dyfneint* (Dumnonia) led by King Iago of Gwynedd.[3] Some Welsh accounts say that King Bledric of Dumnonia was killed in this campaign. The presence of the Dumnonian king and his army in North Wales would have weakened Dumnonia, at least temporarily. His death and the inevitable associated losses in his army would have exacerbated this. The Gewisse, or any other group coveting the rich lands of the South West, might have seized on this opportunity to strike at the Britons there.

No one doubts that Chester was indeed the site of this significant battle, so if Welsh records are correct, then Bledric was operating a long way from home. By contrast the Gewisse seem to have continued their incessant warring in the Thames region, against neighbouring kingdoms and northern raiders. To add to their list of enemies it is recorded for 607 that Ceolwulf fought against the South Saxons. No location or result is declared, but this battle indicates that Sussex was once more a power to be reckoned with, and also that the Gewisse were looking southwards. It is the first mention in the *Chronicle* of the South Saxons since the 490 victory of Ælle at Pevensey. Such a lengthy absence from the records is most likely due to the severe consequences of their defeat at Badon Hill. The 607 battle site is impossible even to guess at. There are no records of other activity to place it in context, but it was probably somewhere south of the Thames. Had Ceolwulf been victorious, it is likely that the *Chronicle* authors would have made more of this event and, therefore, we must assume he lost or, at best, achieved a stalemate.

The implied resurgence of Sussex in the early seventh century also raises anew the question of what happened to any remaining British enclaves near its borders. The British kingdoms of Winchester and Silchester were now threatened simultaneously from north and south by the Gewisse and Sussex respectively. Unfortunately, the South Saxons once again disappear from the records. Similarly absent are Ceolwulf's descendants until Æscwine, his great-great grandson, becomes ruler of the West Saxons in the Wiltshire-Hampshire region in 674, a noteworthy resurgence to which we shall return in Chapter Nine. These omissions from the *Chronicle* record are significant. We can infer that another long period of stalemate occurred. The Hampshire Avon frontier was still intact, as it had been prior to and after Badon. The Germanics had still not managed to advance westwards into Dorset or move southwards from the Thames region and breach the Wansdyke.

Cynegils

Ceolwulf's reign was short and little can be deduced from it of military relevance. Just four years after his 607 battle with the South Saxons, his son Cynegils succeeded him. The *Anglo-Saxon Chronicle* makes it clear that he 'succeeded to the kingdom in Wessex and held it thirty-one years'.[4] However, given the conclusions of Yorke and others that the term 'West Saxons' is today considered inappropriate until after Cædwalla's reign ended in c. 688, we should continue to consider Cynegils as having led the Gewisse.[5] Geographically, the pattern of Germanic expansion is often assumed as having been westwards from the Hampshire region across Wiltshire and Dorset and thence into Somerset. Such a spread of influence appears reasonable when based on the *Chronicle's* depiction of early Wessex. But if Yorke and others are correct about the earliest Wessex leaders originating in the Thames region, then it is not so easy to sustain as a theory. The way is therefore open for a more rigorous examination from a military perspective and there are several different threads to be unravelled. Locating Cynegils' first battle is fundamental to understanding how Wessex came to dominate the South West. In order to understand the key events of Cynegils' reign, it helps to realise that he was one of a number of Gewisse rulers called West Saxons in the *Chronicle* who held power simultaneously. Also that he warred with both Britons and Germanics. His first recorded battle was in 614 and subsequent events led to his making of a pact with Mercia:

614. Here Cynegils and Cwichelm fought on Bea's Mount [Béandún], *and killed 2 thousand and 65 Welsh.*

626. Here Eomer came from Cwichelm, king of the West Saxons – he wanted to stab King Edwin, but he stabbed Lilla, his thegn, and Forthhere, and wounded the king. And that same night a daughter was born to Edwin, who was called Eanflæd. Then the king promised Paulinus that he would give his daughter to God, if by his prayers he should obtain from God that he might fell his enemy who had earlier sent the assassin there. And then he went into Wessex with an army and felled 5 kings there and killed a great number of the people.

628. Here Cynegils and Cwichelm fought against Penda at Cirencester, and they came to an agreement.[6]

Edwin had succeeded to the Northumbrian throne in 617 after Æthelfrith's death in a battle with King Rædwald of the East Anglians. The *Chronicle* records that he 'conquered all Britain except for the inhabitants of Kent alone, and drove out the princes, the sons of Æthelfrith', so presumably his move against the Gewisse was part of this overall subjugation.[7] Given that Cynegils and Cwichelm survived the slaughter in 626, we have seven Gewisse 'kings' in action in the extracts above. If five really were killed by Edwin's forces, then the scale of defeat must have severely weakened Cynegils, leaving him open to defeat by Penda, King of the Mercians, two years later. The pact he made in 628 indicates that Cynegils failed to hold on to territories in the Upper Thames region, hardly surprising given that he had incurred the wrath of the Northumbrians and their Mercian clients. It seems the changing fortunes of Cynegils and Cwichelm were in no small measure due to the ill-advised attempt to assassinate Edwin. Thus, despite a notable success in 614, the parlous state of Cynegils' kingdom is in stark contrast to the evident supremacy of the Northumbrians. Penda clearly had freedom to protect his place in the hegemony and got the better of Cynegils and Cwichelm. The treaty with Penda at Cirencester and other evidence that Cynegils paid tribute to Northumbria indicates that the enmity between the Gewisse and their northern neighbours was at least put on hold.[8] The question to be resolved is how this situation developed to allow Cynegils and his immediate descendants to play their roles in the establishment of the kingdom of Wessex.

Cynegils, Cwichelm and Cuthred are recorded as having been baptised at Dorchester-on-Thames in the 630s. The degree to which they would have volunteered for this is questionable and it is likely that they bowed to pressure from the recently Christianised Northumbria. The sequence of baptisms also shows that a Gewisse presence was at least tolerated in the region and we know they continued to hold Ashdown as their powerbase. The treaty with Penda no doubt enforced the payment of tribute and further weakened the Gewisse as an independent power in the Thames region. Given Cwichelm's botched attempt on Edwin's life, it is remarkable that he survived at all. He probably had to buy himself protection and forgiveness.

Through this period and beyond it seems that the Gewisse were sporadically at war with the two powerful Germanic kingdoms to their north whose leaders nonetheless seemed to baulk at the idea of annihilating them. It follows that the Gewisse campaigns to seize territory from the British, beginning with the 614 battle at *Béandún*, were made necessary because they could not hold on to their original territories in any meaningful or independent manner. Such a situation would have suited Northumbria and Mercia given that the Gewisse were their *de facto* proxies in a potentially costly war against the British. The Gewisse might even have been mercenaries in the pay of their northern over-lords. All of this suggests that *Béandún* lies somewhere on the fringes of the original Gewisse territory but certainly not to the north or east where other Germanic kingdoms were becoming dominant. Like the Britons, the Gewisse were being forced to look westwards for a home. *Béandún* most likely estab-lished a new centre of gravity for them, a territory captured from the Britons that wasn't disputed by Northumbria, Mercia or Sussex. In that respect, it could be considered as the first of the significant battles that secured a future for the Gewisse in a region that would later be at the heart of Wessex rather than on its fringes.

Béandún

The events of 614 are a vital piece of the jigsaw regarding the birth of Wessex. Did Cynegils initiate an invasion of the South West or continue the struggle to protect his embattled territories in the Thames region? The answer would be obvious if *Béandún* could be identified easily, but even the name can be interpreted in a number of ways. *Dún* translates as down, moor, height, hill or mountain, *beadu* as war, battle, fighting or strife. Thus, any high feature associated with a battle becomes a candidate. *Béan* actually translates as bean, pea, legume, or any other sort of pulse. There is no evidence to associate any particular settlement with pulse-growing. It might, however, be significant that excavations of Iron Age hillforts have revealed that their inhabitants grew predominantly wheat and barley, but also peas, beans, vetches and lentils. It might be that the name is simply derived from the agriculture that occurred there, and thus it could be near any occupied site where the Britons continued such traditions. Ingram suggested Bampton in Oxfordshire for the location. Swanton associates it with someone called Bea, but in a footnote describes it as unidentified. Extra confusion was later added by those who agreed it was probably Bampton, but in Devon not Oxfordshire. Another suggested translation is Bindon, for which there are several possibilities in England. There is also a Binton and a Brean Down to be considered.

Bampton There are three Bamptons, one each in Cumbria, Devon and Oxfordshire. The case for any of them to have been the site of *Béandún* does not stand up particularly well in etymological terms. Bampton is in any case more probably derived from *Béamdún*, where *béam* translates as tree. On close examination it may have made it onto the list of possible sites for the 614 battle only because Ingram translated *Béandún* into Bampton in 1823. Ingram's aim was to provide a translation of the *Chronicle* from Old English to a more readable Modern English, but place-names are notoriously difficult and he may have been over hasty in this case. Subsequent promotion of the site was inevitable because of the respect his work commanded.

Of the three possible Bamptons we can discard the one in Cumbria immediately. The Devon location however, is sometimes proposed in the context of early Wessex territory being established by Cynegils on an expeditionary campaign. But Bampton in Devon is a long way westwards for a weakened Gewisse to have reached at this time. There is nothing to suggest that the South West Peninsula was anything other than firmly held by Britons. Dumnonia, even though having to recover from the defeat at Chester, is hardly likely to have permitted an enemy force to penetrate so far. Bampton in Devon is some distance from any coast. A seaborne force landing at Exeter, a scenario sometimes proposed, would have found itself some 20 miles to the south of Bampton. Minehead on the Bristol Channel coast is around 15 miles to the north. One would expect in either case some record or evidence of a beachhead being established rather than a direct raid so far inland. Over land from identifiable Gewisse territory the required marching distances increase. It is highly unlikely that Cynegils ever got near to Devon's borders, let alone captured Bampton. His successor, Cenwalh, was demonstrably the first of the Gewisse to make headway into eastern Somerset, but he stopped short of the River Parrett and never got near the Devon border either.

Bampton in Oxfordshire has more in its favour. It is within the assessed limits of the Gewisse territory we have already identified as annexed by Ceawlin and Cuthwulf. It lies 3 miles north of the Thames and about 9 miles south-west of Eynsham, one of the four settlements named as captured by Cuthwulf in 571. The problem with Bampton in Oxfordshire is the difficulty of identifying a likely British enemy. The British kingdom of *Caer Celemion*, centred on Silchester, was over 30 miles to the south-east and *Cynwidion* in the Chiltern Hills a similar distance eastwards. Either or both could have launched an opportunistic campaign in the wake of a power vacuum created by Ceawlin's fall, although such moves would have left their home territories vulnerable. Their preoccupation would have been the protection of their own borders given the mounting threats to their existence. Bampton in Oxfordshire was undoubtedly at the heart of Gewisse territory in Ceawlin's time. As such, it is a possible location for Cynegils to have made a stand in 614, to stabilise his kingdom against a British threat. However, when we look ahead to Cenwalh's battles, we see that Cynegils was more likely to have been pushing at British boundaries rather than vice versa.

Bindon – Devon One mile east of Axmouth on the southern Devon coastline is Bindon, an ancient manor complex close to the cliffs. Axmouth was one of the first villages to be founded by the Saxons when they settled in Devon and Bindon was part of Axmouth Manor in Saxon times. The estuary of the Axe here was much wider in the post-Roman period than it is today and the coastline was considerably further south, having been eroded over the centuries, including in the 'great Bindon landslip' of 1839. This stretch of coast undoubtedly bore witness to raids and pirate activity, but is a long way to the west of any territory that we can safely identify as being held by any Germanic group in 614. As applies to Bampton in Devon, Cynegils would have to have moved from his identified area of operations in the Thames region to the coast and constructed a fleet in order to reach Axmouth by sea. By land he would have had to march an incredible distance through enemy territory. Dumnonia's weakened state in the wake of Bledric's death is often argued as having enabled Cynegils to achieve one or the other of these courses of action. A popular proposal is that Bledric's son, Clemen, was defeated at Bindon by Cynegils and forced to retreat to *Caer Uisc* (Exeter). The proponents of this scenario rely on place-name likeness and interpretation of the *Welsh Annals*. They take no account of the difficulties Cynegils would have encountered in mounting such an expedition, let alone his requirement to hold the territory he already had in the face of increasing threat.

Some who argue that Cynegils campaigned into Devon in 614 cite St Boniface as evidence. According to his biographer Willibald, Boniface was born c. 675 under the name Wynfrith, in south-west Wessex. Early in his life he was schooled in Abbot Wulfhard's monastery at Exeter and this is held up to be evidence of the early Saxonisation of Devon. However, the archaeological record points to a Christian presence in Exeter from late Roman times onwards and Devon has many sites dedicated to Celtic saints. Early Saxon cross shafts are few in Devon and predominantly to be found in eastern parts. It is a big leap of the imagination to say that Cynegils was active in Devon based on the very sparse information we have of Christian Saxons there. All things considered, the case for Bindon in Devon as the battle site for *Béandún* is weak.

Bindon – Dorset Bindon Hill in Dorset is an impressive ridgeline, which overlooks Lulworth Cove to the west and Worbarrow Bay to the east. It rises over 520 feet above sea level at its highest point, allowing extensive views along the cliffs of the Dorset coast and out into the English Channel. Settlements in the area date back to c. 350 BC, when iron workers from central Europe followed in the footsteps of their predecessors who had settled Hengistbury Head some 150 years earlier. Long earthworks are plainly visible on the hill, built to help protect their homes and industry in time of conflict. The remains of Bindon Abbey, founded by Cistercians in 1172, lie some 8 miles inland to the north, near the River Frome at Stokeford. Downriver from Stokeford is Wareham with its ancient quay, the highest point of navigation on the River Frome, which is reached via Poole Harbour. Wareham's history spans 2,000 years and the town is surrounded on three sides by earth bank defences that date back to at least the time of King Alfred of Wessex.

Poole Harbour's importance has already been addressed and seizing Wareham and the Isle of Purbeck would have been a very attractive proposition for a Germanic grouping looking to expand along the Dorset coast. For this reason, Dorset's Bindon has been linked to the 614 battle. The Isle lends itself to defence, being surrounded by sea on three sides whilst presenting a commander with numerous choices of high ground to occupy. On this basis alone, the Dorset Bindon has to be on the shortlist for *Béandún*. The question is whether Cynegils led his people this far south in 614, and used southern Hampshire as the launch-pad for a campaign westwards, a situation that closely mirrors the one we have already described for Ælle at the time of Badon. Such a course of action cannot be ruled out, but it does not sit easily with the identifiable pattern of Germanic expansion into Wessex, which emphasises an early role for North Somerset rather than South Dorset.

Bindon – Somerset A small hamlet called Bindon lies about a mile southwest of Milverton in the Vale of Taunton Deane, Somerset. It has never been suggested as the site for *Béandún* and is mentioned here only for completeness, based on the similarity of the name. Even so, as a site for Cynegils to have clashed with the Dumnonians, it at least has more logic to it than Bampton in Devon, being only 3 miles or so east of the Devon border. Nonetheless, that places it a long way west of the River Parrett. Once we consider the actions of Cenwalh, who succeeded Cynegils, the importance of the Parrett will become more apparent. It is enough to say that this Bindon must take its place on the list of less likely sites for *Béandún*.

Binton Binton in Warwickshire lies half-a-mile north of a crossing place of the Avon, about 7 miles west of Stratford-Upon-Avon. The south bank of the river here is similar to Fretherne in that the river meanders greatly and forms a promontory two-thirds of a mile across and nearly a mile deep. A large village called Welford-on-Avon sits in the promontory and a through-road crosses the Avon by bridge at an area of shallows just to the north of Welford. Binton Hill overlooks the crossing on the northern side. Like Fretherne, the site is an obvious choice for an ancient battle, offering various advantages to a defender electing to position his forces either in the promontory or on the hill to the north of the crossing. It is a possible battle site for a clash whereby Cynegils was operating along the Avon, or seeking to cross the river. The promontory is about equidistant from Gloucester and Eynsham, being some 30 miles in a northerly direction from both. Strategically it fits the bill, in the context of the Gewisse under Cynegils, perhaps together with the Hwicce, trying to either extend or defend their dominions, and clashing with neighbouring Britons. Cynegils would have competed for conquests in this direction with Mercia, which conceivably would have provoked Penda. Militating against this location is the later activity of Cenwalh, which is discernibly to the south towards Dumnonia, and the proximity of the Mercians, which would have deterred the

Gewisse from pursuing any ambitions to the north. The place-name evidence is a little shaky, but one can perhaps argue that the suffix *tún* (village/town) replaced *dún* (down/hill) at some point. Given the survival of the name Binton Hill, this is conceivable.

Brean Down Brean Down is a huge limestone outcrop that protrudes into the Bristol Channel at the southern end of Weston Bay in Somerset. Immediately south of Weston-super-Mare, it is the westernmost outcrop of the Mendip Hills. Three hundred and thirty feet above sea level at its highest, it has far reaching views over the Somerset Levels, the Bristol Channel and across into South Wales. Man has inhabited the Down since the Stone Age. It was an island up to Roman times, surrounded by salt marsh. The Somerset Levels were drained to permit agriculture through the Roman period so the outcrop would have become more accessible. The surrounding area was rich through lead mining in the Mendip Hills. The Romans constructed a temple on Brean Down c. AD 340, adding to its effectiveness as a landmark for mariners in the Bristol Channel, and the promontory may also have served as an observation point to help warn of Irish and other sea-borne raiders. The temple and surrounds were used for burials in post-Roman times, indicating the continued use of the site. There is a hillfort enclosing roughly 1¼ acres at the eastern end of the Down, which dates to the later Iron Age. It is of different construction from most Iron Age hillforts in that more stonework is evident.[9]

Brean Down lies on the fringes of a territory that seemingly flourished in Roman and post-Roman times, but may have become lost or spoiled by later flooding:

> *Stratigraphic and palaeo-environmental evidence at Banwell Moor showed that these reclaimed landscapes were abandoned some time in the late Romano-British or early medieval periods when the North Somerset Levels were flooded and once again became an inter-tidal environment.*[10]

In 1607, the entire region flooded to a depth of 12 feet as far as Glastonbury. The last major inundation took place in 1703. Drainage efforts increased in the eighteenth and nineteenth centuries, which restored the viability of the area for settlement and agriculture.

Brean Down as the site for *Béandún* seems to have a lone champion in Andrew Breeze, who drew attention to the location in 2004. He also seemed to solve a potential problem relating to the name of the site, pointing out that there is no problem with *dún* for down or hill, but that there is no Old English personal name Bea. Neither is Bea from the Celtic, but it may have been corrupted from *Brean*, which *is* Celtic, and linked with the Cornish and Welsh *Bre* for 'hill'.[11] Breeze is not alone in recognising the importance of the area in general through this period. Keith Gardner draws attention to the same region in his 1998 paper entitled *The Wansdyke Diktat?*:

> *What prevented them* [Ceawlin's army] *in AD 577 swinging south into Somerset having taken Bath? Not surely a 'gentleman's agreement' allowing the construction of an agreed barrier? Is it not more likely that the present area of North Somerset, behind a pre-existing Wansdyke, was so powerful a polity as to deter them from even trying? It is suggested by Morris (1973, p.307) that the one local pre-Roman tribe to have survived intact enough for Gildas to have mentioned it by name, the Dumnonii, had formed alliances with the neighbouring 'Welsh' – that is the Britons around the Bristol Channel. This alliance would seem to have been defeated c.AD 614 in a battle near Axminster and, according to Gwent traditions their peace was broken in the same year. Even so it is not until AD 658 that 'Cenwalh fought at Peonna against the Welsh and drove them in flight as far as the Parrett'.*
>
> *Cad Cong was contemporary with all this – or at least with Badon and with Dyrham. Its decline could be attributed archaeologically to the early 7th century – a result of the Saxon defeat of the Dumnonii in AD 614? Do we see in Cad Cong a llys, the court of a local 'Welsh' king, backed by a western alliance; do we see in the adjoining temple at Henley Wood a ghost of Hen Llys, the 'Old Court', and do we see in Wansdyke the northern frontier of a latter day Dumnonia?*[12]

Cad Cong refers to the hillfort on Cadbury Hill near the village of Congresbury, a fort that was the military centre of a small but comparatively rich post-Roman British kingdom that flourished only briefly. Professor Robin Fleming, author of *Britain after Rome – The Fall and Rise, 400-1070*, identifies it as one of three particularly rich, well-organised and competently led fifth/sixth-century British communities, along with those at Birdoswald on Hadrian's Wall and at Wroxeter. The archaeological evidence suggests that it was a community of very mixed peoples who had coalesced under powerful leadership in the uncertain times that followed Roman rule. Tin mines were the source of Cadbury-Congresbury's wealth and 'the British metal' was traded for tableware and amphorae from Byzantium and rare Greek wines.[13] Interestingly, Fleming also notes that the prosperous community at Birdoswald cohered under military leadership and that there is evidence of a similar post-Roman militaristic group at Cirencester.[14] Gardner suggests that Cynegils' battle of 614 was against the Dumnonii and notes the much later flight of the Britons to the Parrett. However, he stops short of proposing the most likely explanation, which is that this battle resulted in Cynegils directly taking control of Cadbury-Congresbury, having fought there rather than near Axminster. I propose that the capture of a beachhead at Brean Down was the first step in pushing the Britons out of North Somerset. It was Cynegils who first led an army south of the Wansdyke to achieve this, and from this tenuous hold Cenwalh was able to make the next gains on behalf of the Gewisse in 658.

The strategic advantages of holding Brean Down to either threaten or preserve a territory extending south from the Bristol Avon are obvious. It would have proved invaluable in dominating the Bristol Channel, the mouth of the River Axe immediately below it, and a large part of the Somerset Levels. A military commander seeking influence south of the Wansdyke would have recognised immediately the importance of holding the Mendip Hills. Add to this the wealth of the Cadbury-Congresbury kingdom and we can envisage how tempting the prize was for Cynegils.

The available evidence suggests that Cynegils and Cwichelm fared poorly against the Mercians and were forced to either migrate or cede territory at some point. The direct Mercian threat to Gewisse interests seems to have been temporarily resolved at Cirencester in 628, suggesting that this former Roman civitas of the Dobunni and its environs were lost by the Gewisse at that time. It is possible, therefore, that the Gewisse had earlier defeated the post-Roman military community identified by Fleming. However, given the evidence that the Gewisse were not West Saxons who arrived from abroad, they might have been part of that community or allied to it. The 628 treaty was clearly in Mercia's favour and it was most probably at this time that Mercia subordinated the Hwicce. So where else would Gewisse interests have shifted if not south towards the Somerset region? The Mendip region stands out as a credible objective for Cynegils, and Brean Down would have secured an initial foothold for the Gewisse in Somerset away from his Mercian oppressors. Such an incursion would explain the demise of British Cadbury-Congresbury at the right time. This scenario provides the most credible explanation for the location of *Béandún*.

The Gewisse – expansion and fragmentation

The idea that Cynegils was displaced from the Thames region and forced to find lands for his people in Somerset is more compelling once the core of early Wessex is identified. West Saxon documents suggest that Glastonbury was the early nucleus for the kingdom. As the seventh century progressed, more and more written records were created, mostly charters that recorded the grants of land made by kings. These documents provide useful clues to when the kings took control of these lands. It must be borne in mind that their authenticity in every case cannot be taken for granted. Nonetheless, the sheer number of early Wessex charters in the Glastonbury region tells its own story of the emerging kingdom. Locations referred to in the charters relating to early Wessex have been plotted on Map 8.

The earliest three charters record gifts of land made by Cenwalh, son of Cynegils, at Meare, near Glastonbury, and Downton in Wiltshire, together with a grant of exemption from secular dues for the see of Sherborne in Dorset. They are recorded in three different Bishoprics, Glastonbury, Salisbury and Winchester. Next chronologically is Centwine's grant of lands at Quantock Wood and *Crycbeorh* to Hæmgils, an abbot of Glastonbury, made in 682. A common assumption for this charter is that *Crycbeorh* was Creechbarrow Hill, near Taunton. However, Creech St Michael and Creech Hill, both closer to Glastonbury, should also be considered. Centwine was apparently not alone in making grants. In his time, gifts are recorded in Wiltshire and Dorset from a Cenred, a Cenfrith and a Baldred. Yorke cites Baldred as part of the evidence for several kings to have shared rule over early Wessex and notes that he is described in the primary sources as '*subregulus*, clearly implying inferior

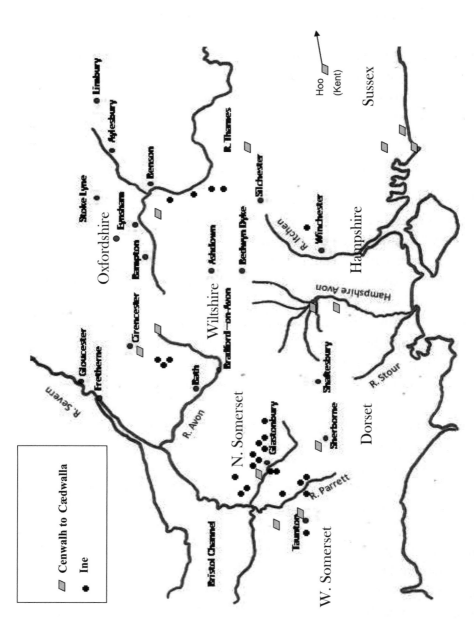

Map 8: Early Wessex Charters

status'.[15] No grants made by sub-kings are marked on Map 8. Charters recording Cædwalla's grants point to more distant locations on the northern and eastern fringes of later Wessex and even as far to the east as Hoo in Kent. Once we reach Ine's reign, there is a particularly remarkable concentration of charters referring to the Glastonbury/Parrett region. The Somerset charters help to define a relatively small area that encompassed the rivers Parrett and Yeo, within which Ine and other Wessex rulers made significant transactions and gifts. This supports a hypothesis that the Wessex territories most closely associated with Alfred's era grew outwards from northern Somerset, a centre of gravity established during the reigns of Cynegils and Cenwalh.

Religious affairs and Cenwalh's role in them is particularly confusing. In the *Anglo-Saxon Chronicle*, other Gewisse kings are recorded as having been baptised whilst he is not. Bede tells us that he 'learned and received the true faith' while in exile.[16] The *Chronicle* covers the conversion of the Gewisse leaders starting with Cynegils, and lauds Cenwalh for establishing a church at Winchester:

> *635. Here Cynegils was baptized by Birinus, the bishop in Dorchester, and Oswald received him.*

> *636. Here Cwichelm was baptized in Dorchester, and passed away the same year.*

> *639. Here Birinus baptized Cuthred at Dorchester and received him as a son.*

> *643. Here Cenwalh succeeded to the kingdom of the West Saxons, and held it 31 years; and that Cenwalh ordered the church at Winchester to be built.*

> *645. Here Cenwalh was driven out by King Penda.*[17]

These lines, and others to be elaborated upon shortly, reveal that Cenwalh led a turbulent life from the start. In turning our attention to his deeds, we must pick up the story once more from the extracts above that record the aftermath of the strife between Cynegils and Penda. With the 628 treaty between the Gewisse and the Mercians presumably still intact, the Northumbrian King Oswald became godfather to Cynegils, beginning the series of baptisms of the

Gewisse at Dorchester-on-Thames. Even the scheming Cwichelm appears to have made peace with Northumbria, perhaps in the wake of his heavy defeat of ten years earlier. Cuthred was the son of Cwichelm and, true to family tradition, he was later to rebel against Northumbria. Bede records that both Oswald and Cynegils rewarded Birinus with this first West Saxon bishopric at Dorchester and that Oswald married Cynegils' daughter on the same day as the baptism in 635.[18] Around this time, Gewisse dominance in the Thames region seems to have been absorbed into the greater power of Mercia and Northumbria combined. The same fate then befell Hampshire. The *Anglo-Saxon Chronicle* implies that Winchester, once Cenwalh had built the church there, assumed importance as a West Saxon centre. This was only a short time before Cenwalh fell out with Penda. We can only surmise that the dominion Cenwalh was driven from in 645 included Winchester.

Despite the entrenched idea that Cenwalh was instrumental in bringing Christianity to the West Saxons, from his actions one has to doubt that he had any interest at all in the Christian faith, let alone in building churches. Rather than making amends with Penda, the next two *Chronicle* records indicate that Cenwalh abandoned any interest in Hampshire and the Thames region and forayed to the west:

> *648. Here Cenwalh gave his relative Cuthred '3 thousands' of land by Ashdown [Æscesdūn]. That Cuthred was Cwichelm's offspring, Cwichelm Cynegils' offspring.*
>
> *652. Here Cenwalh fought at Bradford on Avon.*[19]

Æscesdūn is Ashdown Park, just inside Oxfordshire, 6 miles north-west of Lambourn, Berkshire. Alfred was later to gain a victory there in 871 whilst defending the region against the Danes. Cenwalh must have been confident enough of success elsewhere to give this jewel in the Gewisse crown to Cuthred. It is possible that the gift, which was 3,000 'hides' of land, helped to secure assistance with building the army that Cenwalh then blooded at Bradford-on-Avon in 652. The result of this battle is not recorded, but it seems to have opened the way for Cenwalh to pressurise the British south of the Wansdyke. However, self-imposed domestic issues immediately hampered his ambitions because, from 655 to 658, he was 'in exile for 3 years – Penda had driven him out and deprived him of the kingdom because he abandoned his sister.'[20] Cenwalh, unseated by Penda for the second time, served his exile in East Anglia where King Anna presumably saw to it that he behaved himself. If Bede is correct, it was only at this time that Cenwalh became a Christian, which casts further doubt on his earlier enthusiasm for church affairs as depicted in the *Chronicle*. In any event, the situation eventually resolved in Cenwalh's favour, some time after Penda's heavy defeat in a war with Northumbria:

> 655. *This year Penda was slain at Wingfield, and thirty royal personages with him, some of whom were kings. One of them was Ethelhere, brother of Anna, king of the East-Angles. The Mercians after this became Christians. From the beginning of the world had now elapsed five thousand eight hundred and fifty winters, when Peada, the son of Penda, assumed the government of the Mercians.*[21]

Such losses would have rendered the Mercian leadership ineffective for some considerable time. Bede recorded this battle in more detail. From a military history perspective, Bede's account is bonus material in that it offers a reminder of the roles that climate and terrain can play in warfare:

> *When battle had been joined, the pagans suffered defeat. Almost all the thirty commanders who had come to Penda's aid were killed. Among them Æthelhere, brother and successor of King Anna of the East Angles, who had been responsible for the war, fell with all his men. This battle was fought close by the River Winwaed, which at the time was swollen by heavy rains and had flooded the surrounding country: as a result, many more were drowned while attempting to escape than perished by the sword.*[22]

With Penda gone, Cenwalh enjoyed more freedom of action. Ongoing troubles in Mercia helped maintain this situation. Peada, the new king of Mercia, was murdered only a year after his succession, having 'reigned no while; for he was betrayed by his own queen, in Easter-tide'.[23] Cenwalh's military career was thus revived once his exile ended, and with a spectacular victory at that:

> *658. Here Cenwalh fought at Penselwood* [Peonnum] *against the Welsh, and drove them in flight as far as the Parret.*[24]

The flight of the Britons to the Parrett is much emphasised by historians charting the rise of Wessex. It is usually agreed, as in Swanton's translation above, that this retreat was initiated by a battle at the southern tip of Selwood, the great forest that divided Alfred's Wessex into two parts, West and East. However, Cenwalh's trail of battles tracks him from Ashdown through Bradford-on-Avon to the River Parrett, albeit that his time in exile interrupted his efforts. It is a campaign trail different from what one would expect had he attacked the British at Penselwood, but more logical if he was gaining territory in increments from the Britons and seeking to link with his father's gains in the Mendip region. There is no evidence of any collapse of the British holdings immediately west of the Hampshire Avon at this time. Whilst British kingdoms were undeniably shrinking elsewhere, Britons were holding out in the heights across much of the 'chalk massif' region of South Dorset and Wiltshire, an assessment that is in line with the dearth of early Anglo-Saxon archaeology across most of Dorset and Wiltshire.

Historians have failed to discern a realistic campaign pattern because *Peonnum* is so often presumed to be Penselwood, and Cenwalh's next battle is then listed as having taken place in Shropshire, a questionable progression to say the least. For this reason alone it seems that the obvious Somerset-centric birth of Wessex gets ignored. The *Chronicle* authors are partly responsible because they downplayed the influence that Mercia and Northumbria wielded over Cenwalh. In discussing the ancestry of two ninth-century kings of the Mercian line, Yorke refers to 'a brother of Penda called Cenwalh who is otherwise unknown'.[25] Given that Cenwalh of the Wessex line was a contemporary of Penda of Mercia, it is a little surprising that no connection is made by Yorke, but Williams suggests that these two Cenwalhs may have been one and the same.[26] The *Chronicle*'s Cenwalh of Wessex was Penda's brother-in-law. This implies that he was King of the Gewisse with Mercia's blessing, a patronage that was lost once he discarded Penda's sister. All of which helps explain why Cenwalh's success at *Peonnum* was Pyrrhic, quickly overturned by Mercia's new leader, as we shall discover. First we must examine the case for Penselwood and other locations mooted as sites for the pivotal action at *Peonnum* in 658.

Only then can we see how this battle fits with Cenwalh's subsequent activities. There is certainly no logic in him having fought at Penselwood and next in Shropshire.

The withdrawal of the Britons to the River Parrett

The battles at Bradford-on-Avon and *Peonnum* appear at first glance to be two consecutive steps in a campaign that culminated in driving back the Britons. However, before accepting this there are a few complications. Cenwalh's adversary at Bradford-on-Avon in 652 is not recorded. Given that he incurred the wrath of Penda at that time, it is possible he fought with the Mercians. Æthelweard recalled the battle at Bradford as part of a civil war:

> *A. 652. Four years after, he fought a battle against his own people, at a place called Bradford, on the river Afene.*[27]

Cenwalh had not long given Cuthred the 3,000 hides of land a considerable way to the east of Bradford, so it is difficult to see how he could have been fighting his fellow Gewisse. Given that Cenwalh's exile followed immediately after, it seems more likely that the battle, if it was civil war, was part of the feud between Cenwalh and Penda. There is no mystery about the location of Bradford-on-Avon, which sits on the general line of the Wansdyke boundary (see Map 7). Cenwalh's presence there threatened British territories to the south and it may be that he actually fought Britons in 652. Presuming that Cynegils had indeed established a foothold in the Mendips in 614, the entire North Somerset region was already vulnerable. Cenwalh would have sought to exploit this by displacing more of the remaining Britons in order to expand his father's gains.

Whatever the earlier role of Cynegils was, and whatever the identity of the enemy at Bradford, the clear effect of Cenwalh's campaigning up to and including the battle at *Peonnum* was that the Britons lost territory. A new frontier zone was established with the River Parrett as the defining boundary. Æthelweard confirms the same, albeit that he sows more confusion:

> *A. 658. After three years more, the kings Kenwalk and Pionna renewed the war against the Britons, and pursued them to a place called Pederydan.*[28]

Scholars usually explain the implication that Pionna was a king rather than a place as a mistake. Æthelweard's *Pederydan* is consistent with the *Anglo-Saxon Chronicle* because it refers to Petherton on the River Parrett, which retained a degree of importance as a site through to early Norman times at least. John of Worcester, a twelfth-century monk and chronicler, recorded that a council had taken place at *Pedred* in 1070. Present were the king, the Archbishop of Canterbury, and the bishops, abbots, earls and lords of all England.[29] William of Malmesbury also noted the proceedings of this council and called it the '*concilio apud Pedridan*', usually taken to mean 'council on the Parrett'.

Within the *Chronicle's* heady mix of civil war, treaties, murders and treacherous queens, there is sufficient evidence of an uneasy relationship between the early Mercian kings and the Gewisse, which soured as early as the 620s and deteriorated further when Cenwalh spurned Penda's sister. We must leave that thread temporarily and return to the geographical picture, which is less murky. The effect of Cenwalh's victory in 658 was to push the British west to the River Parrett. From then on the Parrett in all likelihood delineated a new border between Britons and Germanics. Therefore, we are certainly looking for a battle site east of that river. With this in mind, we must return to considering how powerful the Gewisse were in military terms and what the battles of Cynegils and Cenwalh achieved. The most realistic assessment is that, having ceded power north of Wansdyke to Mercia, Cynegils established a fledgling kingdom in Somerset through his victory at *Béandún*. When Cynegils died, control over this kingdom was vested in Cenwalh, who succeeded in expanding its borders. The British kingdom in Somerset displaced by these combined efforts was probably Glastenning, described by the authors of *Post Roman Celtic Kingdoms* as:

> *The territory around and mostly to the west of Glastonbury was a sub-kingdom of Dumnonia, and came under its overall control. The kingdom probably covered much of modern Somerset. From the mid-sixth century its immediate rule was under the king of Dogfeiling, which itself was a sub-kingdom of Gwynedd.*[30]

This assessment concurs with the picture already drawn of a widespread British alliance in the South West. The battle at *Peonnum* in 658 was another significant defeat for this alliance, which had first begun to fracture as a result of the British defeat at Chester some forty to fifty years earlier. When Glastenning fell the alliance, already physically divided by the Bristol Channel, was finished. Dumnonia, with part of its buffer-zone gone, was alone and directly under threat along its border.

Peonnum

Having accepted just how crucial the battle at *Peonnum* was, we are now better placed to look for its location. The name is often shortened to Pen and there are thousands of place-names containing Pen, mostly in Wales. This is not surprising because in Welsh it means 'head' or 'top' and is often used either to denote a high point or the tip of a geographical feature. Pinhoe, north-east of Exeter, has been mooted as the site of *Peonnum*, often in conjunction with Bindon in Devon for the preceding battle at *Béandún*.[31] The problems associated with attributing a Devon campaign to Cynegils and Cenwalh have been covered already. The site most favoured by historians is Penselwood, where the modern boundaries of Dorset, Wiltshire and Somerset meet.

Major derived a short list of candidates for the site of this battle which, rightly in my opinion, ignored Devon:

> *Mr Freeman says, in his* Old English History, *'Peonna is certainly one of our Pens in Somerset,' and while not rejecting Penselwood, he suggests as alternatives Pen Hill, a point of Mendip, or Pen or Ben Knoll, close to Wells. The late Mr Kerslake, however, argued in favour of the identification of Peonna with Poyntington (D.B.* Ponditona*), near Sherborne, primarily on the ground that the Saxons would not have represented the short* e *in Pen by the diphthong* eo.[32]

There are several hills called Pen scattered around the West Country, having retained their names since Celtic times. Among these, Pen Hill in Somerset is a logical objective for a force intent on displacing the Britons from Glastenning. It lies on the eastern end of the Mendips some 4 miles north-east of Wells and 15 miles south of the Wansdyke. Pen Hill today dominates the modern A39, which is forced from its straight course there in order to breach the hilly barrier which, in military terms, guards the main approach route to Wells and Glastonbury from the north. Ben Knowle is another important hill that would have lain at the very heart of an ancient Glastonbury-centric kingdom. Two miles south-west of Wells it is one of a series of outcrops of high ground and there are traces of ancient defences in the area. It affords a view directly across the intervening levels to Glastonbury Tor about 8 miles to the south. Ben Knowle directly overlooks a small fortified mound at the base of its southern slope in an area called Battlebury. This has echoes of the Battlesbury at the base of nearby Brent Knoll, on the eastern slopes of which Wessex fought successfully against the Danes in 875. Just as Mr Freeman identified so long ago, neither of these sites can be ignored.

I can find no particular reason to dismiss Poyntington, near Sherborne, from Major's list other than it seems to sit too far south for an army approaching from the Mendip region and too far west for one heading across northern Dorset. Certainly, in the latter case, Penselwood is more likely as is the Pen Hill that lies a mile west of Fontmell Magna in Dorset. The Fontmell Magna Pen Hill would have been a possible objective in a campaign that sought to expand Germanic influence westwards from the Hampshire Avon frontier, a subsequent step in the earlier Badon campaign had it succeeded at Badbury Rings. It overlooks tributaries of the River Stour to the east but is itself dominated substantially by the much higher chalk hills of Cranborne Chase just a couple of miles to its east. It is quite some distance from the Hampshire Avon, even if one embraces the idea that Cenwalh's actual route into the South West was similar to that which Ælle had envisaged. More importantly, this Pen Hill is much too far from the River Parrett. The same argument, about how far realistically the British are likely to have retreated, comes to the fore when one considers Penselwood.

The village of Penselwood lies on the end of a ridgeline that overlooks the Blackmore Vale. It is sited on the southern tip of the remnant woodlands that once made up Selwood, hence the name. It is a considerable distance from any of the choices for the earlier battle at *Béandún* and is therefore difficult to place in the context of a logical progression of conquest by Cynegils and Cenwalh. Of course, this does not rule it out. But in order to have reached it from the Wansdyke, an army would have had to move unopposed for over 20 miles across the hilly terrain of the Mendips or the Marlborough Downs.

From the Hampshire Avon to the east this distance is increased to 26 miles with the hillforts and high chalk downs of Wiltshire lying in the way. From the Wareham region, the distance increases once more to 30 miles, again with elevated terrain and hillforts to be negotiated. It is very difficult to see how Cenwalh, given his circumstances on return from exile, could have mustered an army capable of moving unopposed to Penselwood in one bound. Despite this, the idea that Penselwood was the battle site has taken root and nowadays seems rarely disputed. The primary reason for this is the name, allied perhaps to the idea that Wessex first expanded westwards from the Hampshire border to the Forest of Selwood. It is thus assumed that this battle allowed the West Saxons to breach the natural barrier of Selwood, which forced the Britons to withdraw across the River Parrett. A 25-mile retreat by the Britons after a heavy defeat might be credible, but not when the territory ceded included the stronghold at Cadbury in Somerset and other defendable forts on high ground. The argument falls apart further given the archaeological evidence that British power was preserved across much of Dorset beyond 658.

Another reason this site might have found a place in history erroneously is its role in later Anglo-Saxon conflicts. When he emerged from hiding in the Somerset marshes, Alfred gathered his armies around a stone erected near Penselwood by his grandfather, Ecgberht, to mark the convergence of the boundaries of Dorset, Somerset and Wiltshire. Alfred marched east to fight, but for 1016, the *Anglo-Saxon Chronicle* records that: 'King Edmund had then gone out [from London] before that, and then rode into Wessex, and all that people submitted to him; and quickly after that he fought against the raiding-army at Penselwood near Gillingham.'[33] The raiding-army was that of the Danes under Cnut, who lifted their siege of London and marched west in pursuit of Edmund, who met them in battle at Penselwood. To continue this theme of possible conflation, in 1001 the Danes won a battle at Pinhoe near Exmouth during a seaborne invasion of the region. Even this battle is sometimes attributed wrongly to Penselwood. Due to these actual battles, Penselwood and Pinhoe have both entered the collective consciousness as ancient battle sites, but neither of them is as strong a choice for *Peonnum* in 658 as the Mendip locations.

The Mendip region is the most credible choice for *Peonnum*, given the strategic picture that emerges from the likely aftermath of the earlier battles of

Béandún and Bradford-on-Avon. Even if one rejects that *Béandún* was Brean Down, it is still evident, given the geographical focus of the early Wessex charters and the displacement of Britons from those areas at the time, that Cenwalh came to preside over a small kingdom in North Somerset around Glastonbury. This was the early nucleus of Wessex. Pen Hill and Ben Knowle, both much closer to Glastonbury than Penselwood, are likely features for the Britons to have chosen to defend as Cenwalh moved south from Bradford-on-Avon seeking to strengthen the Gewisse presence in North Somerset. Pen Hill guards the saddle in the hills, which provides access to the steep combes leading southwards to Glastonbury and Wells. It would have been a natural choice for the Britons to have met an attack from the north. Ben Knowle has at its foot the defensive earthwork called Battlebury, and other earthworks nearby demonstrate that the hills around the Knowle had particular military significance in ancient times. These hills dominate across the levels to the south where there was significantly more surface water in Cenwalh's day.

Britons forced to concede Pen Hill or Ben Knowle would have lost the vital ground at the eastern end of the Mendips. The victors, on the other hand, would have been well-placed to consolidate the chain of hilltops as far west as Brean Down. Any Britons seeking to prevent further loss of territory would have found very little ground to their liking in the inundated Somerset Levels, so the next defensible high ground was 8 to 10 miles south in the Polden Hills. However, in the seventh century, the Poldens formed a promontory, with the estuaries of the Brue and Parrett rivers to the north and south respectively. A retreating army choosing to occupy the Polden Hills would have found itself trapped rather than helped by the terrain. Defeated Britons from the Mendip region would have been forced to withdraw south and east onto safer high ground, or westwards beyond the Parrett as the *Chronicle* describes. Glastonbury and the Polden Hills were ceded to the Gewisse in the wake of their victory at *Peonnum*, a battle that was fought in the Mendips as Cenwalh advanced southwards from the Wansdyke.

Summary

From the arguments put forward, we can surmise a credible scenario whereby a powerbase of the Gewisse shifted from the Thames/Cotswolds region to North

Somerset under Cynegils and Cenwalh. An earlier Gewisse vill remained in place at Ashdown under Cuthred. The battle in 614 at *Béandún* might have been fought at Brean Down when Cynegils established a foothold in North Somerset, forced there because his territories north of the Wansdyke were being lost to Mercia. His ambition was necessarily limited by the size of his army, so he seized a defendable strip of coastal territory outside of Dumnonia proper, consolidating it with a victory at *Béandún* in 614. The British in Cadbury-Congresbury were directly threatened as a result, just as the whole British alliance in the South West was crumbling following heavy losses in the battle at Chester. Cynegils, with Cwichelm, continued to hold territory in the Cotswolds at this time, but they later had to cede it to Penda, at Cirencester in 628.

Cenwalh's betrothal to Penda's sister helped him keep power when he succeeded Cynegils in 643. At some point later on he rejected her and incurred Penda's wrath. Cenwalh had mixed fortunes in his recorded military career, beginning with his fight at Bradford-on-Avon in 652. This may have been a successful battle against Britons, which forced them to yield the Wansdyke. Given Æthelweard's reference to civil war, it might equally have been a loss for Cenwalh, part of the strife with the Mercians that led up to his period in exile. Whatever happened at Bradford, by 658 Penda was long dead and the Mercians in some disarray. Cenwalh's way was clear for a subsequent venture to expand the Gewisse territories into North Somerset, where he had his finest hour at *Peonnum*. Exactly how Wessex power came to be established in the region west of Selwood will remain a matter for debate. I propose that Wessex expanded from Glastonbury, which was captured from the Britons by Cenwalh, who came there from the north via a victory in the Mendips in 658. Locating Cenwalh's subsequent and final battle in 661 may be the key to the whole Cenwalh saga, but the importance of Glastonbury to the early Wessex kings is an established fact, a clue that cannot be ignored.

Chapter Nine

Wessex, Mercia and Dumnonia

In Llongborth I saw the rage of slaughter,
And biers beyond all number,
And red-stained men from the assault of Geraint.

– from 'Geraint, son of Erbin'.

T he establishment of a Gewisse kingdom in North Somerset threatened the Britons of the South West, but not enough to drive every
one of them into Dumnonia or across into Wales. Most of Dorset
and Wiltshire continued to be British through Cenwalh's time. Stenton drew
particular attention to the 'Britishness' of Dorset:

> *There is no evidence as to the date of their* [the West Saxons] *occupation*
> *of Dorset; but no heathen burial-grounds of their race have yet been*
> *discovered in the county, and a large number of its British inhabitants*
> *undoubtedly survived the Saxon conquest.*[1]

Records of the mid-seventh century fighting between Northumbria and
Mercia indicate that these Anglian kingdoms were waging war on a larger
scale than hitherto. By this stage it is clear that bigger armies were campaigning across considerable swathes of territory. Grabbing land piecemeal was no
longer necessary for the most powerful kings, they could unseat each other
wholesale and seize whole kingdoms. But this was not necessarily true of the
Gewisse. The alliances formed by Ceawlin had long collapsed and, despite
some successes under Cynegils and Cenwalh, the Gewisse were fragmented
and marginalised. Cenwalh's kingdom was an enclave that enjoyed little
growth under his stewardship. He was forced to maintain a defensive posture through the early stages of consolidating the territory. It is likely that he
chose the Isle of Glastonbury as his base, primarily to make use of its natural

defences. Map 9 illustrates the likely outcome of the campaigns of Cynegils and Cenwalh in North Somerset.

In Mercia, the betrayal and murder of Peada led to his brother Wulfhere succeeding to the kingdom. The misdeeds recorded indicate that Wulfhere inherited a difficult internal situation that took time to resolve. Occupied in the South West with consolidating against any British counter-attacks, the Gewisse probably viewed events in Mercia with relief and some *schadenfreude*. Perhaps also for the first time, the British in Dorset and Wiltshire began to feel vulnerable. Cenwalh's incursion had fragmented the allied Britons at a time when Dumnonia was weakened. British territory in Dorset, Somerset and Wiltshire was vulnerable to further Gewisse expansion out of Glastonbury. A map study of places associated with the early Wessex leaders reveals how Cenwalh's dominion was subsequently expanded. Somerton lies directly south of Glastonbury, overlooked by the easternmost of the Polden Hills on the River Cary. It is recorded as the first royal vill of Wessex in the South West, but was taken from the West Saxons by Æthelbald of Mercia in 733.[2] This action illustrates the continued enmity between the Gewisse/West Saxons and the Mercians. Sherborne was also one of the first places in Dorset to join the Wessex portfolio. In geographical terms its inclusion reflects a predictable expansion of the fledgling kingdom, along the valley of the River Yeo and its tributaries from the Polden Hills region.

In Cenwalh's time, his domain was bounded by the Bristol Channel and the River Parrett to the west. To the east and south there was clear space for expansion if the British could be prised from their forts in the high chalk downs. With such opportunities beckoning it is ironic, but perhaps wholly to be expected, that Cenwalh was ousted not by a British resurgence but once again by the Mercians who so despised him. There are several interpretations of what occurred. Ingram's translation of the *Anglo-Saxon Chronicle* suggests that Cenwalh was thwarted by Wulfhere and forced to retreat to Ashdown:

> *661. This year, at Easter, Cenwalh fought at Pontesbury; and Wulfhere, the son of Penda, pursued him as far as Ashdown.*[3]

Swanton's more recent translation leaves the whole situation, including the battle site, more open to debate:

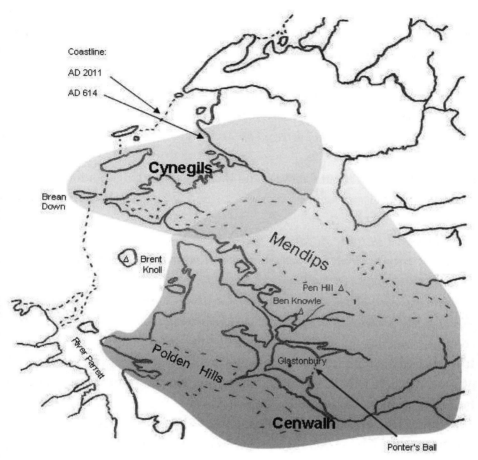

Map 9: Cynegils and Cenwalh in North Somerset (Glastenning) – c. AD 614-661

*661. Here, at Easter, Cenwalh fought at Posent's stronghold; and Wulfhere,
Penda's offspring, raided as far as Ashdown. And Cuthred, Cwichelm's offspring, and King Coenberht passed away in the one year.* [4]

Just as Ceawlin did not actually pursue Æthelberht all the way into Kent in
568, neither did Wulfhere chase Cenwalh across hills and dales to Ashdown,
even if Ingram's 'pursued' is preferred to Swanton's 'raided'. Nonetheless,
Cenwalh's natural refuge in the wake of a defeat was indeed at Ashdown with
Cuthred, to whom Cenwalh had gifted 3,000 hides of land there in 648.

Æthelweard's account of the 661 battle is markedly different from others. In an apparent attempt to obscure his ancestor's failings, he records Cenwalh as triumphant over Wulfhere:

> *A. 661. After three years, Kenwalk again fought a battle near the town of Pontesbury, and took prisoner Wulfhere, son of Penda, at Esc'sdune [Ashdown], when he had defeated his army.*[5]

Bede has this to say about Cenwalh and the state of his kingdom following his return from exile:

> *During which time, the king of that nation, sustaining very great losses in his kingdom from his enemies, at length bethought himself, that as he had been before expelled from the throne for his infidelity, and had been restored when he received the faith of Christ, his kingdom, being destitute of a bishop, was justly deprived of the Divine protection.*[6]

It seems Cenwalh proved careless enough to lose two bishops in a short period of time. Agilbert left the see of Dorchester in 660 and returned to his native France in protest at Cenwalh's decision to make Winchester a second bishopric for Wine, who was also of Gallic descent.[7] Three years later Cenwalh expelled Wine for reasons unknown. Bishop Wine 'took refuge with Wulfhere, king of the Mercians, of whom he purchased for money the see of the city of London'.[8]

All of this confusion, including Æthelweard's outright dissembling, highlights just how difficult it is to assess the birth of Wessex as a Saxon kingdom. Cenwalh's uncertain control over religious affairs indicates that his rule over the Dorchester-on-Thames and Winchester regions was collapsing even before his defeat by Wulfhere. Bede's record of 'very great losses' seems to confirm this. The evidence shows that several kings ruled at any one time over the Gewisse/West Saxons in the seventh century. It might be the case that Cenwalh was not directly responsible for Dorchester-on-Thames or Winchester. The politics are not at all clear from the written records, so we must keep looking for battle sites in order to form an idea of how the various kings' territories waxed and waned.

Posentes byrg

In the *Anglo-Saxon Chronicle*, the battle site for 661 is written in Old English as *Posentes byrg*. It has long been considered to have been Pontesbury, based on the similarity of the name and its translation by Æthelweard, Ingram and others. We should not accept Pontesbury readily as the site of this confrontation. Other traditional suggestions are equally unsatisfactory. This is largely because proponents for recorded battles are too often seduced by a similar sounding name, which they then attempt to fit to a military strategy. This rather unhelpful reverse engineering is prevalent among local historians in particular, who can be over-keen to promote their home regions. *Posentes byrg* presents a particular difficulty because there are very few place-names like it. As demonstrated already with Ceawlin and Wyboston, it is advantageous first to look for some context in which the military activity took place. Who was attacking? Who was defending? What do we know of their existing territory? What were their relative strengths at the time? Wulfhere was clearly on the offensive. The *Chronicle* entry for 661 goes on to make clear that he ranged far from Mercia to punish his foes, not just to *Posentes byrg* and Ashdown, but as far south as the Isle of Wight.[9] He must have been at the head of a powerful army, capable of sustaining itself on expeditionary operations for protracted periods. Cenwalh, on the other hand, lost the battle and his kingdom, lands he had only recently gained that were still under threat from any British resurgence. The Gewisse were discernibly weaker than Mercia and fighting for their very existence. Cenwalh was in no position to be campaigning in new lands and must have been defending his own stronghold.

The limited choice of names similar to *Posentes byrg* has allowed credence to be given to some unlikely locations: Posbury in Devon for example. Posbury is 8 miles north-west of Exeter and 28 miles as the crow flies from Bindon. Those who espouse Posbury as the location for *Posentes byrg* tend to propose Bindon for *Béandún* and sometimes also Pinhoe for *Peonnum*. From this they theorise that Cynegils and his successors campaigned in Devon. The difficulties of this proposal have largely been covered. It implies a Germanic presence in Devon earlier than archaeological evidence suggests. It also infers from the written sources that Dumnonian Britons fled from Pinhoe to the Parrett. That would have taken them 40 miles north-east, an incredibly long retreat which is also in the wrong direction.

In military terms, Cenwalh fighting at Pontesbury makes little sense, given that it would have required him to abandon progress in Somerset and march his army considerably more than a hundred miles to the north. This would have left his embryonic Somerset kingdom very vulnerable. There is no good reason for any group based near the River Parrett to be fighting in Shropshire, let alone Cenwalh's people against Mercia. Most historians reject Æthelweard's version of the aftermath, but no realistic alternative site or context for the battle has been offered. Swanton's translation provides the least speculative picture, telling us only that Cenwalh fought at 'Posent's stronghold'. In all versions the business between Wulfhere and Cenwalh culminates at Ashdown, which clearly remained in Gewisse hands. Logic dictates that *Posentes byrg* was also in Gewisse territory.

We must not lose sight of the evidence that the Gewisse were active around Cirencester, Bradford-on-Avon and Ashdown under Cynegils, Cwichelm and Cenwalh. They were threatened by Mercia to the north. The best opportunities for them to settle in new lands lay to the south, where they had to displace the Britons from North Somerset. How they might have begun that process has been suggested in the previous chapter. There is nothing to suggest that Cenwalh was in the White Horse region at the time of the battle at *Posentes byrg*, only that he ended up there afterwards. The Gewisse seat at Ashdown remained the preserve of Cuthred and his descendants, so it is entirely logical that a dispossessed Cenwalh took refuge there, but only after his defeat. We have already waded through sufficient evidence to place Cenwalh in North Somerset by 661. *Posentes byrg* is most likely to be found there.

Ponter's Ball is an ancient earthwork. It is a linear embankment about a mile to the south-east of Glastonbury Tor. Almost a mile in length, it is aligned north-to-south and crosses a piece of raised ground which, in the seventh century, provided the only access by land to the Isle of Glastonbury (see Map 9). It is designed for defence, to protect the Tor from an enemy approaching from the east, the ditch being on the eastern side. The embankment has been reduced by the passing years but is still 30 feet across and up to 12 feet high in places. Pottery finds have dated the earthwork to the Iron Age, but it may be older. Another bank and ditch, called New Ditch, lies about 3 miles to the south-west. It seems that the two banks formed part of one defensive system at some time. In Old English *byrg* means 'dwellings within a fortified enclosure'.

Posentes does not translate. It is most likely the name of the chief of such an enclosure, as Swanton's translation suggests. The evidence of early settlement on and around the Tor has been assessed as having borne the hallmarks of a military-orientated people.[10] The name Ponter's Ball has been mooted as deriving from the Latin *pontis vallum,* meaning 'bridge over the ditch or moat'.[11] The earthwork could be argued to form a bridge between two stretches of water but is certainly not a bridge over water. It is very clearly an embankment. Ball may seem an odd noun to use at first but not if it is a corruption of the Old English *balc,* which means a balk, beam, bank or ridge. Ponter's, as written on modern maps, can be explained as a corruption of *Posentes* or Posent's. The *balc* would have been part of the defences of Posent's stronghold or *byrg.* Thus, we have a military feature, in an area where Cenwalh was active, the modern name of which can be derived from *Posentes byrg.*

Surviving charters, already discussed and plotted on Map 8, confirm that Glastonbury was a significant location for Cenwalh. That alone makes it a very credible site for his final battle. It was a fortress at the heart of his embryonic kingdom and Ponter's Ball was part of its defensive works. There is nothing to suggest that Britons wrested control of the Polden Hills back from the Gewisse. Whilst the words in the *Anglo-Saxon Chronicle* are vague, they indicate that Cenwalh fought Wulfhere and was ousted by him. The vagueness is deliberately there to mask this crushing defeat of 'early Wessex' by Mercia, in a purge that also accounts for the deaths of the Gewisse leaders Cuthred and Coenberht in the same year. We can assume that they met their end when Wulfhere reached Ashdown, and wonder only how Cenwalh avoided the same fate.

Except for the record of his death in 672, Cenwalh disappears from the literature at this point. Bede's recollections of Cenwalh's continuous ill-fortune at the hands of his enemies support the view that he lost power to Wulfhere. Despite the ousting of Cenwalh from Glastonbury, it is clear that an Anglo-Saxon presence remained in place there and that it was a very important location in the history of early Wessex. With the Gewisse defeated by Wulfhere, perhaps we need to look for Mercians in Somerset as having continued Anglo-Saxon dominance there, even before Æthelbald's punitive expedition to Somerton in 733. Evidence for such a Mercian presence is as startling as it is obscure. It comes from William of Malmesbury's record of his visit to Glastonbury in the early twelfth century, during which he noted the details of some stone monuments in the grounds of the old church there:

> *That which to all men is altogether unknowen I would gladly relate, if I could picke out the truth: namely, what those sharp pillars or pyramides should meane, which being set distant certaine feet from the old Church, stand in the front and border of the Churchyard. The highest of them, and that which is neerer to the Church than the rest, hath five stories, and carrieth in height six and twentie foot. Which albeit for age it be ready to fall, yet hath it certaine antiquities to bee seen, that plainly may be read, although they cannot so easily bee understood. For in the uppermost storie there is an Image in habit and attire of a Bishop; in the next under it, the statue of a King in his roiall robes, and these Letters,* HER. SEXI. *and* BLISWERH. *In the third, these names likewise, and nothing else,* WEMCHESTE. BAMPTOMP. WINEWEGNE. *In the fourth,* HATE. WULFREDE *and* EANFLEDE. *In the fifth, which is the lowest, a portaict and this writing,* LOGVOR. WESLIELAS and BREGDENE. SWELSWES. HWINGENDES. BERNE. *The other Pyramis is eighteene foot high and hath foure floores or stories, in which you may read* HEDDE *Bishop &,* BREGORRED & BEORWALDEE. *What all this should signifie, I take not upon me rashly to define: but by conjecture I gather that in some hollowed stones within are contained the bones of those whose names are read without. Surely* LOGWOR *is affirmed for certaine to be the same man of whose name the place was sometime called* Logweresbeorgh *which now they call Mont-acute. And* BEORWALDE *sembably was Abbat next after* HEMGISELUS.[12]

A number of scholars have tried to interpret what Malmesbury read on this pyramid. It is generally agreed that, whilst the inscriptions would have been very worn by age and weathering, the names presented are those of prominent Anglo-Saxons who were associated with Glastonbury. Sexi may refer to Seaxburg, the second Abbess of Ely, daughter of King Anna of East Anglia with whom Cenwalh spent his time in exile. Perhaps more likely that name recalls Sexwulf, Bishop of the Mercians from c. 664.[13] The third tier of names appears to include Bishop Wine, who sought shelter with Wulfhere after Cenwalh expelled him. Perhaps the most recognisable name is that of *Eanflede* (Eanflæd), inscribed on the fourth tier. She was the daughter of Edwin of Northumbria, the newborn he had devoted to God, in return for assured vengeance on that fateful night in 626 when the Gewisse attempted to assassinate him. She went on to become one of the two wives of Oswiu, who ruled *Bernicia* and defeated Penda at Wingfield. Eanflæd was 'a particularly forceful queen of Northumbria' and later the Abbess of Whitby.[14] The name *Wulfrede*, which appears alongside Eanflæd's on the stone, almost certainly recalls Wilfrid. He was a member of Eanflæd's household and had changing fortunes as the Bishop of Northumbria, spending some of his time in exile. It was this Wilfrid, together with Wulfhere, who ordered that the people of the Isle of Wight be baptised.[15] Wilfrid was also bishop for Mercia in the 690s. *Hate* most likely recalls Bishop Hætla of Dorchester-on-Thames, which by the 670s was under Mercian control.[16] Eanflæd, Wilfrid and Hætla are said to have visited Glastonbury together in 681.[17] The ancient church at Glastonbury burned down in 1184 and in 1539, the later abbey there was destroyed as part of Henry VIII's ruthless programme of dissolution. Its last abbot, Richard Whiting, was hanged on the Tor. The stones that William of Malmesbury witnessed were lost forever.

As a result of the events of 661, the Gewisse we have followed through more than a century of battles were seemingly finished. Cenwalh is rumoured to have been buried at Winchester, but there is nothing to substantiate this. Cenwalh's reign of 'one and thirty winters', as a West Saxon king and commissioner of the old church at Winchester, is the success story that the *Chronicle* authors were keen to portray.[18] In reality, the Gewisse had been on the back foot for some time before Cenwalh was finally eclipsed by Wulfhere. When Bede recorded the 635 baptism of Cynegils, he described him as 'of the West Saxons, formerly called Gewissae'.[19] Yet for 685 and 686, Bede continues to refer to the Gewissae, with Cædwalla as their king. He calls the area around the Solent 'the lands of the Jutes, belonging to the country of the Gewissae', but also describes Winchester's inhabitants as 'Gewissae, that is, the West Saxons, who were in the city of Venta'.[20] The *Anglo-Saxon Chronicle* compilers may have taken Bede's ambiguity as licence to avoid mentioning the Gewisse at all. Thus, we end up with a narrative that serves Alfred's aims and neatly airbrushes any hint of British origins from the West Saxon story.

Mercian dominance

Wulfhere's continued campaign in 661 seems to have met little resistance:

> *661 ... And Wulfhere, Penda's offspring, raided on Wight, and gave the inhabitants of Wight to Æthelwald, king of the South Saxons, because Wulfhere had received him [as god-son] at baptism.*[21]

Wulfhere rewarding the South Saxons marks them clearly as clients of Mercia. Yorke identifies a pattern to this behaviour and notes that 'other members of the Mercian royal house can be identified as assisting in the Mercian control of satellite provinces in the seventh century'. This apparently included the installation of Berhtwald as a '*subregulus* on the borders of the Hwicce and the West Saxons', a region Yorke further defines as North Wiltshire and Somerset.[22] The Abbott of Glastonbury, for a decade or so beginning in 667, was also called Berhtwald and went on to be Bishop of Canterbury. It seems likely that these characters are one and the same. Berhtwald was appointed by Wulfhere to control the region.

There is very little information available on the fate of Cenwalh's people once he lost power. Most likely they remained in Somerset under Berhtwald. It is possible to pick up some clues regarding other remnant factions of the Gewisse. The importance of Ashdown as Cuthred's seat of power and Cenwalh's last refuge is evident. The Thames is only 12 miles directly north of Ashdown and was an obvious physical boundary at some period in time for Cuthred's shrinking territory. For one indicator that Mercia annexed the Thames Valley systematically, we can revisit Ceawlin's early victory to secure the Ouse as a boundary for the Gewisse. As described in Chapter Seven, Ceawlin most likely fought at Wyboston (*Wibbandun*) in 568. Wybba was the second King of Mercia from c. 593-615, son and successor of Creoda. In Wybba's time, Mercia must have regained control of the area in order for his name to be given to *Wibbandun*. Even if one rejects Wyboston as the 568 battle site, there is broad agreement among scholars that Mercia annexed the Thames region in the seventh century, at the expense of the Gewisse and others.

The Second Battle of Badon Hill

The *Welsh Annals* contain the only record of a second Battle of Badon, fought in 665. The expansion of Mercia provides the most likely backdrop for this battle. Three possible sites are all within a relatively short radius of Cuthred's Ashdown. Liddington Castle is 10 miles to the west, Baydon is 4 miles to the south, and Badbury Hill is 16 miles to the north. All of these have been suggested as the site of the original battle referred to by Gildas. As the detailed analysis in earlier chapters demonstrates, the case for them is weaker than that for Badbury Rings in Dorset. For the 665 battle, however, these sites are all possible. They are within identifiable Gewisse territory, long since reduced from its apogee under Ceawlin by this time and crumbling further in the face of Mercia's expansion.

Liddington Castle is the strongest contender for a seventh-century Badon. It is an Iron Age hillfort that lies just under a mile south-east of the village of Badbury, near Swindon. The hillfort is on the Ridgeway, a prehistoric track 250 miles long, which linked the Dorset coast to the Wash. It was in use for some 5,000 years. Liddington Castle nowadays overlooks two modern roads, built over the course of the Roman road known as Ermin Street. South of Liddington, Ermin Street runs along the Og Valley. At Ogbourne St George, it crosses the Ridgeway and meets the Roman road that linked Winchester with Wanborough. Converging on Wanborough from the south-east is another Roman road from Silchester. Liddington Castle was one of several possible bastions that guarded the Marlborough Downs, part of the high chalk region Britons occupied because it was defendable against the encroaching Germanics. The earthwork dominated the key lines of communication described above. As such it helped to protect one approach to Silchester, probably the last British kingdom in the South East to fall to the Anglo-Saxons.

Liddington's position explains why it has long been a candidate for Gildas' Badon Hill. Myres favoured the Wiltshire Downs for the site, suggesting that early Germanic groups from the Thames Valley attempted to capture part of the Ridgeway escarpment in order to expand into British territories.[23] This scenario for the original Badon continues to find favour. At one time the website of the Ivy House Hotel in nearby Marlborough was advertising the feature as 'a Neolithic hillfort known to be the battle site where King Arthur was defeated by the Saxon invaders'. A visiting enthusiast has probably righted that slur on Arthur's reputation by now. The argument for Badbury Rings as the Gildas site is stronger. For the later battle, however, Liddington and the hills around Baydon do straddle those key routes south out of the Vale of the White Horse.

This is where the embattled Gewisse, or possibly some remnant Britons, might have tried to stand against Mercia in the late seventh century. Either way, the remaining Gewisse in the Thames region probably lost Ashdown around this time. What exactly became of them is a mystery, but from this point on it is probably more accurate and understandable if we begin to talk of Wessex and the West Saxons.

The next recorded battle between Mercia and Wessex is of note because it indicates that West Saxons were fighting to defend territory in Hampshire. Seaxburh had succeeded Cenwalh on his death in 672, but only for a year or so. It was Æscwine who succeeded her, marking a switch from Cutha's direct line to that of Ceawlin's other brother, Ceolwulf. Æscwine was the great-great-grandson of Ceolwulf and he took up the cudgel on behalf of the West Saxons through a particularly bloody two-year reign. He died in 676, but not before facing the mighty Wulfhere:

> 675. Here Wulfhere Penda's offspring, and Æscwine, fought at Bieda's Head [Biedanheafde]; and the same year Wulfhere passed away, and Æthelred succeeded to the kingdom.[24]

The chroniclers would surely have made more of this battle had it been a clear West Saxon victory under Æscwine's leadership. Wulfhere probably died in this battle, but once again the *Chronicle* is less than clear on the location and the result. Swanton describes the battle site as unidentified.[25]

Biedanheafde

The favoured site is Great Bedwyn, about 7 miles south-west of Hungerford, on the eastern fringes of Savernake Forest. A sub-king named Cissa, not mentioned in the *Chronicle* but attested to in Abingdon Abbey, is known to have ruled over a territory in the Wiltshire and Berkshire area during the late seventh century. Cissa's stronghold was at Great Bedwyn. His name is preserved in Chisbury hillfort, which overlooks the village. Before Cissa's time a linear ditch was constructed that runs in a south-easterly direction, from the hillfort's southern entrance across the Bedwyn Brook and up the valley-side beyond. It has been mooted to be an eastern extension of the Wansdyke. With Mercia expanding southwards, Bedwyn was a natural place for Æscwine to make a stand in defence of West Saxon lands in Hampshire. Yorke assesses that Cissa was more than likely a sub-king under Ine of Wessex, who reigned from 688.[26] Cissa's status as a Wessex sub-king might have been gained because he fought alongside Æscwine against Wulfhere.

Another suggestion for the site of *Biedanheafde* is Beedon, near Ashdown. Beedon lies on a direct line from Oxford to Winchester, about 6 miles south of the Ridgeway track. In the latter part of his reign Wulfhere ranged too widely to be tracked with any certainty, but his relentless pursuit of Cenwalh and his kin might well have led Wulfhere to a final battle near their stronghold at Ashdown.

Centwine

In 676, Centwine, another son of Cynegils, was made King of the West Saxons on Æscwine's death. Bede classified Æscwine and Centwine among several under-kings who divided Cenwalh's former kingdom between themselves and ruled over the constituent parts for ten years.[27] Berhtwald of Glastonbury and Cissa of Great Bedwyn were probably of this group. Mercia's overall dominance continued through this period, however. Æthelred, who succeeded his brother Wulfhere, was King of Mercia for twenty-nine years. His first recorded act was to overrun Kent in 676, which demonstrates the power he wielded. Centwine and his fellow sub-kings of Wessex probably only survived because Æthelred allowed them to rule their small kingdoms as his clients. Centwine is recorded by Aldhelm, a Bishop of Sherborne who died in 709, as having won three great battles.[28] No locations are given, which is disappointing, given that Aldhelm was a prolific writer. His works include the particular gem entitled *a treatise on the praise of virginity, addressed to the Abbess of Barking*.[29]

The *Anglo-Saxon Chronicle* records that, in 682, Centwine 'put the Britons to flight as far as the sea'.[30] Unfortunately, we are given no indication as to which particular sea the Britons fled to. We do know that Centwine's only recorded charter granted lands at Quantock Wood and *Crycbeorh* to Hæmgils, Abbot of Glastonbury.[31] This charter is of uncertain provenance and may have been conflated with one of Ine's. Where Centwine is concerned, the works of Aldhelm, the *Anglo-Saxon Chronicle* entries and the 682 charter all look suspiciously like attempts to exaggerate his success. Based on the 682 record, some authors suggest that Centwine crossed the Parrett and forced a general Dumnonian withdrawal westwards. Such a feat seems to be entirely out of kilter with later events in the Dumnonian border region, as we will discover.

The majority of evidence indicates that Mercia was supreme among the Germanic tribes in Britain at this time. Yorke assesses that the spread of Mercian political dominance was achieved through the establishment of Mercian ealdormanries in the satellite territories that had once been independent sub-kingdoms.[32] Permitting Centwine and others to rule in this way effectively created a buffer zone against British Dumnonia, comprising small client kingdoms that posed no threat to Mercia.

Cædwalla

At some point these disparate sub-kingdoms coalesced into a more viable entity. This seems to have occurred in the reign of Cædwalla, who acceded to the throne of Wessex in 685, according to the *Anglo-Saxon Chronicle*. The chronology for the period prior to Cædwalla's accession is acknowledged as being particularly confused.[33] This is not surprising when one considers that he is the first of Ceawlin's line to be named as a ruler since Ceawlin himself, a hundred years before. Cædwalla is credited with gaining Wight and southern Hampshire. Assuming he also gained control over Mercia's satellite territories in Wessex, then his lands stretched from the Parrett eastwards to the Solent, which was the border with Sussex at this time. Not content with this, Cædwalla brought Sussex and Surrey to heel in his short reign. In spite of these achievements, Cædwalla is not lauded as much as might be expected in the *Anglo-Saxon Chronicle*. Instead it says that he 'ravaged' or 'spread devastation' in these areas. Even in modern times he is to be found described as 'a cruel and cunning pagan'.[34]

The *Chronicle* introduces Cædwalla in 685 with the enigmatic statement: 'Here Cædwalla began to contend for the kingdom.'[35] Bede provides more detail, stating that Cædwalla was of the Gewisse line and that he returned from exile in 685 and killed Æthelwealh, King of the South Saxons. Shortly thereafter he subdued Sussex entirely and killed Berthun, a former commander under Æthelwealh.[36] Cædwalla was clearly an experienced war leader, capable of tremendous violence, according to Bede. Like his ancestor Ceawlin, he built quickly on his initial success with further swift and violent campaigns:

> 686. Here Cædwalla and Mul ravaged Kent and Wight.
>
> 687. Here Mul was burned in Kent and 12 other men with him; and that year Cædwalla again ravaged Kent.[37]

Æthelred of Mercia had invaded Kent in 676 in a campaign noted for its ferocity, either to enforce his overlordship or to protect his interests in Surrey and London.[38] Kent was effectively two sub-kingdoms throughout this period, East and West. It seems that Mul, Cædwalla's brother, was installed as King of East Kent in 687 and had less than a year to enjoy his office. Mul must have been extremely unpopular with his new subjects, given that they burned him to death and added a dozen of his friends to the fire for good measure. Understandably miffed by this treatment of his sibling, Cædwalla returned to exact revenge. Yet by 694, East Kent was back under the control of Wihtred, a king descended from the Kentish *Oiscingas* line.[39] Cædwalla's reign was short and bloody, but he restored Ceawlin's line to the throne of Wessex, and this time it prevailed.

Alfred's ninth-century scribes were reluctant to hail Cædwalla, probably because 'his name, which is an anglicized form of the British Cadwallon, points to a British strain in his ancestry'.[40] Cadwaladr ap Cadwallon was a king of Gwynedd, said to have 'reigned among the Britons'.[41] His father, Cadwallon ap Cadfan, merited a mention in the *Anglo-Saxon Chronicle*:

> 633. Here King Edwin was killed by Cadwallon and Penda at Hatfield on 14 October; and he ruled 7 years. And his son Osfrith also was killed with him. And then afterwards Cadwallon and Penda went and did for the whole land of Northumbria.[42]

Cadwaladr ap Cadwallon has long been a candidate for 'the real King Arthur', not least because Geoffrey of Monmouth declared him to be last in the line of legendary kings of the Britons.[43] He is said to have been ill for much of his reign and his date of death is uncertain. The *Welsh Annals* claim that he died of plague in 682, but other accounts say he died whilst on a pilgrimage to Rome in 688.

After his death he was pronounced a saint by the Welsh church, and referred to as 'the Blessed'. The accounts of Cadwaladr's final days are very similar to the story told for Cædwalla of Wessex. Cædwalla's rule was short, probably because he was either already old or sick around the time he acceded to the throne. Bede mentions that he was wounded during his Isle of Wight campaign.[44] In 688, when he knew he was dying, he went to Rome to be baptised and died just seven days after the ceremony, still dressed in his 'crisom-cloths'.[45]

The most viable explanation for this is that Cadwaladr of Gwynedd, a Gewisse leader in the mould of Ceawlin, was one and the same as Cædwalla. It was he that united the disparate sub-kingdoms that emerged across Somerset, Dorset, Wiltshire and Hampshire, into the kingdom of Wessex. If there was a distinct West Saxon group in the Winchester area, then it too was subsumed into a Wessex ruled by descendants of the Gewisse at this time. Cædwalla was succeeded in 688 by Ine, who seems to have managed the transition to power fairly well. Bede confirms that he successfully held Sussex in subjection for 'many years'.[46] During the early years of Ine's reign his kingdom seems to have prospered in relative peace. The inhabitants of Kent paid Ine 30,000 pounds by way of apology for burning Mul.[47] Mercia remained unfriendly, but did not attack Wessex again until 715.[48] To complete the quest to find the battle sites that shaped Wessex in its infancy, we must look westwards once more. The greatest threat to Ine's kingdom in its earliest days came from Dumnonia. Britons continued to live in Wessex under Ine, albeit they were not accorded equality in Ine's laws. Any pockets of British resistance in the lands united by Cædwalla and Ine were finally brushed aside or absorbed. But Dumnonia remained independent, under the rule of Britons hostile to Wessex, and thus it was back towards the Parrett that Ine directed his military attention.

Wessex and Dumnonia

There is nothing on record that directly tells how Wessex encroached on Dumnonia. Yorke suggests that the early years of Boniface are significant:

> *The West Saxons must have been in control of the Exeter area by about 680 as the young Boniface received his education in a monastery in Exeter at about that time.*[49]

It seems to me that one monk's presence is not sufficient evidence to place a whole people in the same area. The record that places Boniface in Devon dates from the fourteenth century and is not accepted as factually accurate. In one of his own letters, Boniface states he was born and reared in London. Other written evidence suggests that the West Saxons were slower to colonise Devon. Out of forty-two surviving charters made by Wessex leaders to the time of Beorhtric, who made the last of his three grants in 801, only one refers to land in Devon. That charter is dated 739, when Æthelheard of Wessex granted twenty hides of land at Crediton to Bishop Forthhere of Sherborne in Dorset. Opinion is divided on this charter. It has been described as of 'dubious authenticity', as well as 'basically authentic, but interpolated and rewritten in 11th century'.[50]

Dumnonia did not yield Devon easily to Ine and his allies:

> 710. ... Ine and Nunna, his relative, fought against Geraint, king of the Welsh.[51]

The main protagonists are easily identified. John of Worcester recorded Geraint's life and death in battle against Ine in the twelfth-century *Chronicon*. John of Worcester was born around 670 and is best known for having received a missive from Aldhelm, Bishop of Sherborne. This letter was an attempt by Aldhelm to persuade the Celtic church in Dumnonia to comply with the practices and doctrine of the Church of Rome. Nunna, or Nothhelm, ruled the South Saxons as a sub-king under Ine. The battle recorded in the *Chronicle* for 710 is almost certainly the battle of *Llongborth*, and the one described in *The Black Book of Camarthen*, one of the *Four Ancient Books of Wales*:

> *In Llongborth I saw Arthur's*
> *Heroes who cut with steel.*
> *The Emperor, ruler of our labour.*

> *In Llongborth Geraint was slain,*
> *A brave man from the region of Dyvnaint,*
> *And before they were overpowered, they committed slaughter.*[52]

The Black Book, named after the colour of its binding, is thought to have been compiled by a single scribe around 1250 and the extract above is an English translation. The poem is called *Geraint son of Erbin*, and the hero is portrayed as the most valiant of a number of warriors under Arthur's command. A potential problem with the poem as supporting evidence is that some believe it was written before 710. It has been attributed to Llywarch Hên, or Llywarch the aged, a sixth-century Welsh bard. But Llywarch Hên is as much a figure of myth and legend as he is factual. He is oft said to have been at the court of King Arthur and some records claim he lived to be 150. There is no evidence that he wrote the poems attributed to him and it is now more widely believed that they were composed later, c. 800-900.

What the poem does do is deliberately draw attention to the role of warhorses in the fighting. Eight verses that follow on from the extract above repeatedly refer to swift, long-legged chargers maintained with wheat grain as their fodder. In equine terms this is a high-performance food. The poem suggests that cavalry forces, maintained at some cost, were a prized asset. Despite the valiant efforts portrayed, *Llongborth* was a defeat for the Britons. At Badbury Rings we assessed that the going and terrain was ideal for cavalry and that they were employed to best effect. At *Llongborth* it seems that the fine war stallions were unable to fulfil their military potential.

The Welsh name *Llongborth* means 'ship's port' and, as such, is sometimes taken to be Portsmouth, based on the place-name and the dubious assumption that *Geraint son of Erbin* was written in the sixth century. If the battle was there, then it was fought in 501, according to the *Anglo-Saxon Chronicle*. In this scenario the 'very noble' young British man recorded as killed is assumed to have been an earlier Geraint than the one who fought against Ine in 710.[53] The strategic situation as it developed over the two centuries concerned tells us that the other traditional candidate for *Llongborth*, Langport on the River Parrett, is the more likely location. It was to the Parrett that the Britons withdrew in 658 and there is no convincing evidence that this frontier was breached before 710. In the eighth century, the Parrett was considerably wider and deeper than it is today and Langport was a key crossing point. The importance of the area to Ine is a matter of record:

A little beneath, by Langport, a proper market town, the Rivers Ivel
and Pedred running together make betweene them an Iland called

Muchelney, that is to say, The great Iland, wherein are to be seene the defaced walles and ruines of an old Abbey built by King Athenstane, as writers report. This Pedred, commonly named Parret, hath his beginning in the verie edge or skirt of the shire southward, and, holding on a crooked and winding course thorow Crockherene, in the Saxon tongue Cruecerne, and Pedderton, to whom it gave the name, sometime Pedridan, the Roiall seat of King Ina.[54]

Petherton as the royal seat of Ine could only have become viable after the frontier with the Britons was pushed westwards. Ine's victory at Langport in 710 achieved this. The idea that Centwine brought the Taunton region under his control when he drove the Britons to the sea in 682 is pure speculation, as already noted. The Saxon garrison at Taunton was built by Ine. From Major and others, we can infer that Ine populated his new fortress with warriors from Sussex, who had fought alongside him at Langport:

The settlement of the Taunton district by South Saxons is well known, owing to the sporadic occurrence of distinctive Sussex customs in the Manor of Taunton Deane. The late Mr T. W. Shore says, in his Origin of the Anglo-Saxon Race, that here 'the customs which prevailed were almost identical with those of the Rape of Lewes. This great Liberty in Somerset resembled in its constitution a Sussex Rape in containing hundreds within it.' There are other points also which he notes, and these have been fully recognised by other writers.[55]

Taunton was an outpost, a key part of the defences across a new frontier with Dumnonia. Ine probably settled the South Saxons there to reward them. He gifted them a share of his new territories, which in turn made them responsible for securing part of his western border. The identified connections between Taunton and Sussex, referred to in the extract above, are significant to the understanding of a rather confusing *Chronicle* entry:

722. Here Queen Æthelburh threw down Taunton, which Ine built earlier; and the exile Ealdberht departed into Surrey and the South Saxons, and Ine fought against the South Saxons.[56]

These words are often noted with wry amusement. However, a plausible explanation why Ine's wife saw fit to trash her husband's edifice stares us in the face. It is clear from the final line of the entry that trouble brewed at this time, in the form of a Sussex revolt against Ine's overlordship. Ine most likely had to put down this revolt on two fronts, on the Sussex border and in the west where his former allies turned against him. The South Saxon garrison at Taunton became a threat. On Ine's orders, Æthelburh destroyed it as part of the effort to restore order. This idea was first put forward by Henry of Huntingdon in the twelfth century.[57] The destruction of the stronghold also ensured it could not fall intact to the British, in case they tried to exploit the situation. Ealdberht, a South Saxon atheling of the royal line, may have been in Taunton taking refuge, or even commanding the Sussex contingent there. If so, then his casting-out surely led directly to his 'wretched exile in Surrey and Sussex', as Ingram's translation describes it. It transpires that he would have been wise to keep up his wanderings. He chose instead to make a comeback with the South Saxons in 725, whereupon Ine promptly 'slew' him.[58]

Ine's kingdom was considerably larger and more powerful than any of the scattered territories carved out by his Gewisse ancestors, but his problems remained much the same. Newly acquired territory needed protection and it was essential to maintain the compliance of any allies. Rampaging through kingdoms to punish miscreants, in the manner of Wulfhere, was one thing. Capturing and consolidating territory in order to exercise lasting power was a much harder prospect.

Ine, like Cædwalla before him, died in Rome in 728. The *Anglo-Saxon Chronicle* relates that Ine was succeeded by Æthelheard. He immediately had to face-down Oswald the Ætheling, a prince descended from Ceawlin, who made his own bid for the throne. In 733, the Mercians returned to the heart of Wessex and ousted its rulers from their seat at Somerton. Mercian interference in the affairs of Wessex was renewed, probably because this internal warring among the Wessex factions weakened them militarily.[59]

Summary

Cenwalh's escape from exile and subsequent success in Somerset enraged Wulfhere, who by 661 had raised a powerful enough force to exact revenge.

He marched southwards and defeated Cenwalh at Glastonbury, establishing Mercian control over the former British territory there. In subsequent fighting, which probably included the Second Battle of Badon Hill in 665 and the battle at *Biedanheafde* in 675, Wulfhere drove the remaining factions of the Gewisse from their Thames territories.

Cædwalla's intervention in affairs south of the Thames might have been a response to the threat posed by Mercia to his kinfolk. He united the factions descended from Ceawlin and his brothers. With Sussex subdued and harnessed to his cause, he established a kingdom strong enough to resist Mercia. Ine's inheritance was Wessex, a kingdom by then strong enough to challenge Dumnonia, which was forced to yield the River Parrett boundary when Ine and his Sussex allies combined to defeat the Britons at Langport in 710. Wessex finally took shape as a contiguous kingdom that encompassed most of the lands across the modern counties of Somerset, Dorset, South Wiltshire, Hampshire and Sussex.

Chapter Ten

Conclusions

Unfortunately this earth is not a fairy-land, but a struggle for life,
perfectly natural and therefore extremely harsh   – Martin Bormann

The primary aim of this book has been to locate the battle sites of early Wessex, in order to understand better how the West Saxons established themselves in southern Britain. When writing about the *Adventus Saxonum*, the historians of yesteryear were apt to describe a conquest that removed the Britons wholesale and established new Germanic kingdoms. In modern times, academics tend to argue either for a *coup d'état,* in which new ruling elites displaced existing ones, or for a process of acculturation, whereby different ethnic groups gradually merged. This has come about in part because some of the primary sources for Britain's history are nowadays regarded with healthy suspicion. Earlier historians were not privy to the wealth of research available today and many accepted the material available to them at face value. This led military historians in particular to make unrealistic assumptions regarding the scale of warfare in post-Roman times. In the case of Wessex, the story of a sixth-century West Saxon army marching from the Solent to the Thames region, engaging in successive pitched battles as they drove back the Britons, is based almost entirely on the *Anglo-Saxon Chronicle*. It does not stand scrutiny today.

The factions that struggled against each other in the immediate aftermath of Rome's abandonment of Britain had relatively few warriors to call upon. Fighting was localised and territorial boundaries were usually the flashpoints for early battles. The resources required to sustain larger armies, especially on campaigns into hostile territory, only became available as kingdoms grew in strength. Wessex eventually became the most powerful of the Anglo-Saxon kingdoms, but its origins are the most mysterious and complicated of them all. The military history of early Wessex is much better understood once we recognise the sixth-century rise to prominence of the Gewisse and their actions in the Thames Valley region. It is possible that the Gewisse came originally from purely British stock. It is also possible that they were the descendants of Germanic mercenaries who had lived amongst and interbred with a Romano-British population for generations. The evidence that they intermarried and treated with the early Anglian kingdoms suggests they were at least part-Germanic by the sixth century. Whatever their origins, when Roman governance collapsed, the Gewisse were forced into war like many other groups, initially to fight for their very existence.

Badon Hill

The *Anglo-Saxon Chronicle* does not mention Badon Hill and there is nothing to suggest that Gewisse or West Saxons were present at the battle there. Prior to it we can discern significant Germanic encroachment into Hampshire and the Isle of Wight by Jutes and Saxons, but Badon Hill's real significance is understood only when one considers it as the opening act in a dramatic and protracted saga. It was the first major battle in the wars over those lands that would later be at the heart of Wessex. The prevailing situation in southern Britain at the time of this battle tells us much about why, how and where it was fought.

We know from the archaeology that having settled large parts of Kent and Sussex, Germanic groups began to spread along the south coast. By the late fifth century, they had reached the Hampshire Avon. The Britons across the Avon, particularly in that region comprising the former Celtic kingdom of the Durotriges, were already preparing for war in response to the growing threat. The Germanics had no interest in capturing the decaying towns that Rome had abandoned. It was rich agricultural land they prized. There was no need for Ælle of Sussex to march north and gather an army in the Thames Valley, or to lay siege to Bath. All he had to do to break the deadlock along his frontiers was to cross the Hampshire Avon in strength and defeat the Britons there.

Once the Germanics felt strong enough to mount their campaign, a primary objective was the hillfort at Badbury Rings. It was within realistic striking distance and of military and economic significance. It also played a crucial role in the defensive strategy of the Britons. The British military to the west of the Hampshire Avon was a cohesive, determined and effective force who harnessed the fighting prowess of the British tribes and the descendants of Roman mercenaries and auxiliaries. It was led by Ambrosius Aurelianus, a seasoned commander. When he planned his offensive, Ælle failed to focus sufficiently on the strengths of his enemy. He underestimated the preparedness of the Britons under Ambrosius. When the opposing armies clashed, Saxon overconfidence was exploited and Ælle's military leadership was found wanting. As a result, Sussex and its allies, which probably included Kent, suffered a crippling defeat at Badon Hill, today called Badbury Rings. At the tactical level, a timely and destructive action by British cavalry provides the most realistic explanation for the magnitude of the Germanic defeat.

The exact date for the battle remains unidentified. All we can say is that it was fought some time around the turn of the fifth to the sixth century. The aftermath included the reverse migrations of Germanics that happened around that time, as warriors who survived Badon returned to mainland Europe to fight with Theodoric. The growth of Sussex was severely curtailed, which is why the hitherto powerful South Saxons disappear from the *Anglo-Saxon Chronicle* records for decades. The British remained united and secure in the South West, protected by the network of forts and strongholds they had established along the Hampshire Avon frontier and the Wansdyke – a network that gave presage of Alfred's ninth-century *Burghal Hidage*.

The early Gewisse

The lull in military activity after Badon ended around the time that Ceawlin was a youth. The *Chronicle* suggests that Ceawlin's father, Cynric, reignited hostilities with his attack on Sarum in 552, but the records for this period are highly suspect. The early Gewisse were more likely forging a kingdom in the Thames region, and it was briefly quite a substantial kingdom. It spread north-eastwards in the latter half of the sixth century and came into conflict with the Germanic settlers on the east coast. The Anglian kingdom of Mercia was to become a significant military power in the seventh century. This power arose because successful alliances were forged among the east coast Germanics, a trend started when the *Iclingas*, forebears of the Mercians, engaged in joint military ventures with the Jutes of Kent. These efforts were thwarted to a degree when Ceawlin and Cuthwulf, securing their north-east borders, defeated King Æthelberht of Kent and his Anglian allies in 568. That battle is named in the *Anglo-Saxon Chronicle* as *Wibbandun*. It was probably fought at Wyboston, adjacent to the Great Ouse, and established that river as a natural boundary between the Gewisse and the Anglians.

Despite this early success, Ceawlin's kingdom was surrounded by enemies and difficult to defend. The battle at *Fethan leag* in 584 may have been fought at Stoke Lyne against an incursion into the Thames Valley area by Britons. Fretherne on the Severn is another possible site, in the context of Ceawlin fighting in the Cotswolds as suggested by the *Anglo-Saxon Chronicle* entry for 577. Ceawlin's final battle at *Woddes beorge* in 592 was at Woden's Barrow on the north-east corner of the British Wansdyke territory. Like *Fethan leag*, it was likely to have been part of Ceawlin's attempts to protect a shrinking Gewisse area of influence. There is nothing to suggest the Gewisse were strong enough to mount a serious offensive against the British in the South West at this time.

After Ceawlin's death his people came under increasing pressure from the Mercians and began to lose their Thames Valley territories. They were forced southwards and into conflict with the Britons beyond the Wansdyke. Cynegils led one group – to where is open to question. The only clue is that he fought successfully at *Béandún* in 614. The possibility that this was at Bampton in Oxfordshire cannot be ruled out, in the context of his continuing to defend in the Thames region. If Bampton was the site of the 614 battle, it surely enhances the achievements of Cenwalh, son of Cynegils, who was able to return from exile, breach the Wansdyke and drive back the Britons as far as the River Parrett. It is more likely that Cenwalh achieved this feat at *Peonnum* in 658 because his father laid the foundations. *Béandún* and *Peonnum*, with Cenwalh's fight at Bradford-on-Avon in 652, make more sense geographically and sequentially if Cynegils fought *Béandún* in 614 as part of a campaign to establish a new home for his people in the Somerset region. Brean Down is a possible site for the battle in this context. The British kingdom of Glastenning in that region, centred on Cadbury-Congresbury, was wealthy and would have been particularly attractive as a conquest. Its relative isolation from its allies in Wales and Dumnonia may have contributed to its downfall, especially as the Britons were generally weakened when they lost heavily to Æthelfrith at Chester around this time. The battle at Chester was probably the catalyst for the collapse of that alliance of Britons, forged and led originally by Ambrosius, which had kept the South West secure for over a century.

In 628, Cynegils and Cwichelm of the Gewisse fought against Penda at Cirencester. The relationship between the Gewisse and the Mercians requires significantly more research. It is apparent that Penda of Mercia and his son Wulfhere continually harassed the Gewisse, Cenwalh in particular. On the other hand, there was intermarriage (Cenwalh to Penda's sister) and we see that in 633 Cadwallon, quite possibly a Gewisse leader and father of Cædwalla, went with Penda to ravage Northumbria. The Gewisse were discernibly fragmented, with different groups seeming to have been either allies or enemies of Mercia at the same time. Cenwalh's faction was for a while successful against the British. His battle at *Peonnum* in 658 was probably fought at Pen Hill north of Wells, as he finally displaced the Britons from Glastenning. Glastonbury became the seat of Cenwalh's kingdom, the Britons having yielded the Tor there and the adjacent Polden Hills by withdrawing to the River Parrett.

The emergence of Wessex

Cenwalh's influence after 658 extended to the Dumnonian border, but he was clearly much despised by the Mercians. He was ousted from Glastonbury in the 661 battle of *Posentes byrg* (Ponter's Ball at Glastonbury), as swiftly as the difficult circumstances of Wulfhere's accession allowed. Wulfhere's subsequent dominance across the south was enabled by his sponsorship of numerous client kingdoms. Factions of the increasingly displaced Gewisse survived because they provided warriors to these client kingdoms, a number of which were later to be united by Cædwalla into a recognisable kingdom of Wessex.

Ashdown in the Vale of the White Horse remained a stronghold of the Gewisse under Cuthred but they were not secure there after Cenwalh's defeat. They eventually lost Ashdown to Mercia in Wulfhere's purge, which included the Second Battle of Badon and ended with the battle at *Biedanheafde* in 675. The second Badon was probably fought at Liddington, or one of the other sites close to Ashdown. Great Bedwyn is the most likely battle site for *Biedanheafde*, but it may have been fought at Beedon, near Ashdown. Wulfhere died in 675 as a result of this battle and the threat from Mercia was diminished. The fate of the Gewisse, and thus of early Wessex, hung in the balance until Cædwalla's intervention in 685.

The *Chronicle* seems to be deliberately evasive on Cædwalla's early whereabouts, perhaps because of a British strain in his ancestry or perhaps because he perpetuated his father's friendship with Mercia. He might have turned his attention towards the affairs of the southern Gewisse having suffered setbacks in the north that are unrecorded. What he achieved by entering the fray in southern Britain in 685 is much clearer. In his short reign the kingdom of Wessex was forged in blood and fire. Ine was heir to this legacy and his notable achievements include the maintenance of order after such a turbulent time, and the further unification of disparate groups across his kingdom. Ine had to struggle to preserve fragile Wessex in its infancy. He made a particular effort to reduce the remaining threat from the Britons in the South West. A major part of this was Ine's victory over Geraint of Dumnonia, at the Battle of *Llongborth* (Langport), in 710. Twelve years later, together with his queen Æthelburh, he put down a South Saxon revolt against his overlordship. Mercia remained at bay, but not for long.

Thus, we leave early Wessex much as we originally found the Gewisse, with enemies on at least three borders and, with Æthelheard's disputed succession in 728, also in the midst of a civil war. Such were the challenges faced by the warrior kings of the Dark Ages. Given what we have learned of their exploits, they probably wouldn't have had it any other way. Thousands of warriors lie beneath Britain's turf, having fought for their right to live on it. Among them the 'Englishmen' of Wessex remain lauded to this day, but their origins are more ambiguous than once thought. Such is the mysterious history of Dark Age Britain. I hope this book has at least contributed towards a better understanding, in particular of the kings and warriors who fought in the early wars that shaped Wessex.

The days are gone
of all the glory
of the kingdoms of the earth;
there are not now kings,
nor Cæsars,
nor givers of gold
as once there were,
when they, the greatest, among themselves
performed valorous deeds,
and with a most lordly
majesty lived.
All that old guard is gone
and the revels are over --
the weaker ones now dwell
and hold the world,
enjoy it through their sweat.
The glory is fled,
the nobility of the world
ages and grows sere,
as now does every man
throughout the world.
Age comes upon him,
his face grows pale,
the greybeard laments;
he knows that his old friends,
the sons of princes,
have been given to the earth.

From: *The Seafarer,* an Old English elegy

Endnotes

Chapter One – The Fifth-Century Tribes of Britain

1. Berresford Ellis, 134.
2. Peddie 1997, 67-68.
3. For instance, Laycock 2009.
4. Pryor, 43.
5. Langton and Morris, 10.
6. Text of the 1907 Romanes Lecture on the subject of Frontiers by Lord Curzon of Kedleston, Viceroy of India 1898-1905 and British Foreign Secretary 1919-24.
7. Cook, 10.
8. Haywood, 103.
9. Salway, 189-191.
10. Corney, *The Wessex Hillforts Project*, 133.
11. Tacitus, *Agricola*, 11.
12. Rivet (out of print).
13. Davies, 153.
14. Gildas, ch 23.
15. 452 *Gallic Chronicle* entries for 410 and 441.
16. Bede, *Ecclesiastical History*, I, 15.
17. Ingram, 4.
18. Williams, 2.
19. Kirby, 40.
20. Ibid.
21. Myres 1986.
22. Capelli, Current Biology, Vol. 13, 979–984, May 27, 2003.
23. Article by Mark Thomas of University College London, Michael Stumpf of Imperial College London, and Heinrich Harke of the University of Reading, published 19 July 2006 in The Proceedings of the Royal Society B.
24. Pryor, 149.
25. Swanton, 12.
26. Yorke, 26-27.
27. Ibid, 28.

28. Ibid, 26.
29. Gardner, Appendix 2.
30. Tacitus, *Agricola*, 14.
31. Laycock, 116-117.
32. Bede, *Ecclesiastical History*, II, 5.
33. Swanton, 14.
34. Ibid, 16.
35. Grinsell, 278.
36. Laycock, 65-66.
37. Hunter Blair, 179.
38. Dunning: *Ilchester – A History of the County of Somerset*.
39. Camden, text transcribed by Professor Sutton, of the University of California, Irvine, from Philemon Holland's 1610 translation.
40. Yorke, 157.

Chapter Two – The Hampshire Avon Frontier

1. Gildas, 25-26.
2. Bede, *Ecclesiastical History*, I, 16.
3. For a comprehensive discussion on when Gildas wrote and the meaning of the '44 years', see Robert Vermaat's articles on the Vortigern Studies website (link is in bibliography).
4. *Annales Cambriae* entry for 516.
5. Dumville 1977; Grabowski and Dumville 1984; Charles-Edwards 1991; Green 1998.
6. Green: *The Monstrous Regiment of Arthurs*.
7. Ashley 1998, 214-5.
8. Ashley 2005, 160.
9. Arnold 1988.
10. Internet Article: *Anglo-Saxon Hampshire*.
11. Major, I, 18-19.
12. Ibid.
13. Godsal 1908, xiv-xv.
14. Bede, *Ecclesiastical History*, II, 5.
15. Grinsell, 249.
16. Dark 2000.
17. English Heritage, *Record of Scheduled Monuments*.
18. Grinsell, 281-3.
19. Taylor, 113-119.
20. Cunliffe 1978.
21. Major, I, 12-13.
22. English Heritage, *Record of Scheduled Monuments*.

23. Peddie 1997, 145.
24. Field, 50.
25. Guest 1849, *On the Early English Settlements in South Britain*, an article presented to the Annual Meeting of the Archaeological Institute of Great Britain and Ireland held at Salisbury in July 1849.
26. Godsal 1924, 153.
27. Laycock, 95-96.
28. Myres, 151.
29. Leeds and Harden 1936.
30. Whittock, 186-191.
31. Yorke, 138 – and others.
32. Internet Article: *Anglo-Saxon Hampshire*.
33. Yorke, 131 – and others.

Chapter Three – Doctrine, Organisation and Tactics

1. Swanton, 16.
2. British Army Doctrine Publication, *Land Operations*, 2005, 133.
3. Cassius Dio, *Roman History*, Book 56, Chapter 21.
4. AAP-6, NATO Glossary of Terms and Definitions.
5. Svechin 1931.
6. McCall, 8-10.
7. Holder, 124-125.
8. Makkay, 1996, *The Sarmatian Connection: Stories of the Arthurian Cycle and Legends and Miracles of Ladislas, King and Saint*.
9. Bachrach, 166-171.
10. Tacitus, *Germania*, 6.
11. Ibid.
12. 'Rob' Roberts – Master-at-Arms (Medieval Re-Enactment Group).
13. Peddie 1997, 184.
14. Haywood, 93-110.
15. Sidonius, VIII, VI, 13-14.
16. Jones, *The End of Roman Britain*, particularly Chapter 3 in regard to limiting factors on maritime operations.
17. Godsal 1908, 110.
18. Waller, 4-5.
19. Arnold 1997.
20. Peddie 2005, 73-4, 122.

Chapter Four – The British in the South West

1. Huntingdon c. 1129.

2. Biehl.

3. Wood, 50.

4. Stenton, 65.

5. United States Army Doctrine Publication (ADP) 6.0 – *Mission Command*, 1 – 5.

6. Homer, *Iliad* 10.206-10.

7. Ibid. 9.66-68, 80-88.

8. Xenophon, *Cyropaedia*, 5.3.44.

9. Ammianus, 28.3.

10. Pryor, and others.

11. British Army Field Manual, 2007: *Formation Tactics*, para 404.

12. Vegetius, Book 3.

13. British Army Field Manual, 2007: *Formation Tactics*, paras 117-8.

14. Vegetius, Book 3.

Chapter Five – The Badon Campaign

1. Tacitus, *Germania*, 14.

2. Haywood 1999.

3. British Army Field Manual, 2007: *Formation Tactics*, para 301.

4. The purpose of a feint is to distract the action of an enemy force by seeking combat with it. The purpose of a demonstration is to distract an enemy's attention without seeking contact.

5. Peddie 1997, 143-151.

6. Ellison, A and Rahtz, P A R 1987: '*Excavations at Whitsbury Castle Ditches, Hampshire, 1960*'. Proc Hampshire Fld Club Archaeol Soc, 43, pp. 63–81.

7. *Anglo-Saxon Hampshire*.

8. Eagles 2004.

9. Ashe, 32-24.

10. Papworth 1995 and 1996.

11. *Anglo-Saxon Chronicle* entry for 491.

12. Huntingdon, translated by Thomas Forester c.1853.

13. Maxfield, 157-60.

14. Guest, Vol II, 189.

15. Pech and Durden 2003.

16. Ibid.

17. Wood, 57.

18. Blake and Scott 2002, 161.

19. Godsal 1908, 171.

20. Geoffrey of Monmouth, *The History of the Kings of Britain*, Book IX, Chapter III. Translated by J.A. Giles, D.C.L.

21. Griscom, Acton and Robert Ellis Jones, eds., *The Historia Regum Britanniae of Geoffrey of Monmouth*, (London: Longmans, Green and Co., 1929), p. 219.

22. Morris, 113.
23. Haigh, 291–292.

Chapter Six – The Siege of Badon Hill

1. Nennius, *Historia Britonnum*, 50.
2. Papworth, M, 2013, Archaeology National Trust SW – Category Archives: Badbury Rings, *Arthur, Badon and Badbury*.
3. *Annales Cambriae* entry for 516.
4. Pikoulis and others, 1.
5. Internet Article: *The Vistula Ulans at Albuera, May 1811*.
6. Makkay, 1996, *The Sarmatian Connection: Stories of the Arthurian Cycle and Legends and Miracles of Ladislas, King and Saint.*
7. Tacitus, *Germania*, 6.
8. Nennius, *Historia Britonnum*, 50.
9. Ammianus, XXXI, 12.

Chapter Seven – Cerdic to Ceawlin – The Early Gewisse

1. Stenton, 7–8.
2. Bede, II, v.
3. Encyclopaedia Britannica.
4. Finch-Crisp.
5. Bede, I. 237
6. Sir Charles Oman, in *A History of England Before the Norman Conquest* (1904) provides a particularly good overview of the difficulties that arise from the *Anglo-Saxon Chronicle* entries between the years 495 and 530. See Oman, 223–227.
7. Æthelweard, I, ii.
8. Swanton, 15 (footnote 11).
9. Giles, 7.
10. Swanton, 16–18.
11. Yorke, 131-2.
12. Ibid, 132.
13. Hunt, A, *Cunedda as Vortigern*.
14. Arnold, 26.
15. Guest, 31–32.
16. Yorke, and others.
17. Swanton, 18.
18. Ibid, 19.
19. Marren, 37.
20. Crawford and Dodd, 7.
21. *Anglo-Saxon Chronicle* entry for 584.

244 Badon and the Early Wars for Wessex, circa 500–710

22. Oman, 221.
23. In Old English the letter c is pronounced with a k sound if it comes before a back vowel (like o or a) or another consonant. If it comes before a front vowel (like i or e), or at the end of a word following a front vowel, it is usually pronounced like Modern English ch.
24. Swanton, 18.
25. Sims-Williams 1983.
26. Stenton, 44.
27. Swanton, 20.
28. Ingram, 16.
29. Godsal 1924, 195-247.
30. Gibson 1570, *Commentariolum*, ed. 1731.
31. Elrington and others, 29-36.
32. Marren, 38-42.
33. Gelling, 238-9.
34. Swanton, 20.
35. Ingram, 16.
36. Ibid.
37. Godsal 1924, 195.
38. Williams, 2.
39. Swanton, 20.
40. Williams, 16.
41. Todd (ed. & tr.) 1848, *The Irish Version of Nennius.*

Chapter Eight – The Fall of British Glastenning

1. Swanton, 22.
2. Nayland 2006, *Dating the Battle of Chester.*
3. Pengwern was immediately to the east of Powys and extended west into the Midlands.
4. Swanton, 22.
5. Yorke, 132.
6. Swanton, 22-25.
7. Ibid, 24.
8. Higham, 74ff.
9. Burrow 1976.
10. Rippon, 39.
11. Breeze 2004.
12. Gardner 1998.
13. Fleming, 34-35.
14. Ibid, 37.
15. Yorke, 143.

16. Bede, *Ecclesiastical History*, III, 7.
17. Swanton, 26.
18. Bede, *Ecclesiastical History*, III, 7.
19. Swanton, 28.
20. Ibid, 32.
21. Ingram, 19.
22. Bede, *Ecclesiastical History*, III, 24.
23. Ingram, 19.
24. Swanton, 32.
25. Yorke, 118.
26. Williams, 29.
27. Æthelweard II, Ch VII.
28. Ibid.
29. John of Worcester – *Chronicon* entry for 1070.
30. Internet Article, *Post Roman Celtic Kingdoms – Glastenning*.
31. Hoskins, but see also Morris, 307.
32. Major, 45.
33. Swanton, 149.

Chapter Nine – Wessex, Mercia and Dumnonia

1. Stenton, 63.
2. Williams, 54.
3. Ingram, 21.
4. Swanton, 32.
5. Æthelweard, II, Ch VII.
6. Bede, *Ecclesiastical History*, III, 7.
7. *Anglo-Saxon Chronicle* entry for 660.
8. Bede, *Ecclesiastical History*, III, 7.
9. *Anglo-Saxon Chronicle* entry for 661.
10. Rahtz 1975 in Ashe, 111-122.
11. Mann, 16.
12. Camden, *Somerset-shire*, 15 (quoting from Malmesbury).
13. Bede, *Ecclesiastical History*, IV, 6.
14. Yorke, 37
15. *Anglo-Saxon Chronicle* entry for 661.
16. Kirby, 49.
17. Watkin.
18. *Anglo-Saxon Chronicle* entry for 643.
19. Bede, *Ecclesiastical History*, III, 7.
20. Ibid, IV, 15-16.
21. Swanton, 32.

22. Yorke, 136.

23. Myres, 159-160.

24. Swanton, 34.

25. Ibid, 35.

26. Yorke, 144.

27. Bede, *Ecclesiastical History*, IV, 12.

28. Ehwald, 14-15.

29. Wood Stephens, 6.

30. Swanton, 38.

31. S 237.

32. Yorke, 124.

33. Ibid, 133.

34. Internet Article: *Orthodox Europe – Latin Saints of the Orthodox Patriarchate of Rome*.

35. Swanton, 38.

36. Bede, *Ecclesiastical History*, IV, 15.

37. Swanton, 38.

38. Yorke, 30.

39. Ibid.

40. Stenton, 69.

41. Nennius.

42. Swanton, 25.

43. Geoffrey of Monmouth, *Historia Regum Britanniae*, XII, 14.

44. Bede, *Ecclesiastical History*, IV, 16.

45. Ingram, 23.

46. Bede, *Ecclesiastical History*, IV, 15.

47. *Anglo-Saxon Chronicle* entry for 694.

48. *Anglo-Saxon Chronicle* entry for 715.

49. Yorke, 137.

50. S 255.

51. Swanton, 42.

52. *Black Book of Carmarthen XXII*.

53. Swanton, 14.

54. Camden, *Somerset-shire*, 4.

55. Major, I, 76.

56. Swanton, 42.

57. Henry of Huntingdon, 112.

58. Ingram, 25.

59. Williams, 24.

Bibliography

AAP-6, *NATO Glossary of Terms and Definitions*.

Arnold, C J 1997: *An Archaeology of the Early Anglo-Saxon Kingdoms*.

Ashe, G 1980: *A Guidebook to Arthurian Britain*.

Ashley, M 1998: *British Monarchs*.

Ashley, M 2005: *The Mammoth Book of King Arthur*.

Bachrach, B S 1969: *The Origin of Armorican Chivalry*, Technology and Culture 10.2 (April 1969).

Berresford Ellis, P 1978: *Caesar's Invasions of Britain*.

Biehl, M L 1991: *A Short History of Arthurian Archaeology*, written for *Archaeology of Europe*, University of Minnesota. http://www.jammed. com/~mlb/arthur.html, accessed 6 July 2011.

Blake, S and Scott, L 2002: *Pendragon – The Definitive Account of the Origins of Arthur*.

Breeze, A: *The Anglo-Saxon Chronicle for 614 and Brean Down, Somerset*, published by Oxford University Press in Notes and Queries, Volume 51, Number 3, September 2004 , pp. 234-235.

British Army Doctrine Publication 2005: *Land Operations*.

British Army Field Manual Vol 1 Part 1 2007: *Formation Tactics*.

Brooks, N 1989: *The formation of the Mercian Kingdom* in **Bassett, S (ed.)**, *The origins of Anglo-Saxon Kingdoms, Studies in the Early History of Britain*, Leicester: Leicester University Press, pp. 159-170.

Burrow, I 1976: Excavation report – Brean Down Hillfort, Somerset, 1974. Proceedings of the University of Bristol Spelaeological Society 14:2 (1976), 141-154

Camden, W 1610: *Britain, or, a Chorographicall Description of the most flourishing Kingdomes, England, Scotland, and Ireland*, London.

Campbell, A (ed. and tr.) 1962: Æthelweard, *Chronicon – The Chronicle of Æthelweard*.

Capelli, C et al 2003: *A Y Chromosome Census of the British Isles*, Current Biology, vol. 13, 979-984, 27 May 2003.

Chadwick, N 1971: *The Celts.*

Cunliffe, B 1978: *Hengistbury Head.*

Dark, K 2000: *Britain and the End of the Roman Empire.*

Davies, N 2000: *The Isles: A History.*

Dumville, D 1985: *The West Saxon Genealogical Regnal List and the Chronology of Early Wessex.* Peritia 4, pp. 21-66.

Eagles, B 2004: *Britons and Saxons on the eastern boundary of the civitas Durotrigum.* Britannia, 35, pp. 234-240.

Ehwald R (ed.): *Aldhelmi Opera.* MGH auct. antiq. XV (Berlin 1919).

Field, N H 1992: *Dorset and the Second Legion*, Dorset Books.

Fleming, R 2010: *Britain after Rome – The Fall and Rise, 400-1070.*

Gardner, K 1998: *The Wansdyke Diktat? – A Discussion Paper*, first published in *Bristol and Avon Archaeology 1998.*

Gelling, M: *The place-names of Oxfordshire. Parts I and II*, English Place-Name Society, Vols 23 (1953) and 24 (1954)

Giles, J A 1906: *Old English chronicles: including Ethelwerd's chronicle, Asser's Life of Alfred, Geoffrey of Monmouth's British history, Gildas, Nennius, together with the spurious Chronicle of Richard of Cirencester.*

Godsal, P T 1908: *The Storming of London and the Thames Valley Campaign – A Military Study of the Conquest of Britain by the Angles.*

Godsal, P T 1924: *The Conquests of Ceawlin, the second Bretwalda.*

Grinsell, L V 1958: *The Archaeology of Wessex.*

Guest, E 1849: *On the Early English Settlements in South Britain*, article in *Memoirs Illustrative Of The History And Antiquities Of Wiltshire And The City Of Salisbury* published by Robson, Levey and Franklyn of London for the 1849 annual Meeting of the Archaeological Institute of Great Britain and Ireland.

Haigh, D H 1861: *The Conquest of Britain by the Saxons*, John Russell Smith, London.

Harrison, K 1976: *The Framework of Anglo-Saxon History to AD 900.*

Haywood, J 1999: *Dark Age Naval Power – A Reassessment of Frankish and Anglo-Saxon Seafaring Activity* (second edition).

Higham, N J 1995: *An English empire: Bede and the early Anglo-Saxon kings.*

Holder, P A 1982: *The Roman Army in Britain*.

Hoskins, W G 1960: *The Westward Expansion of Wessex*, Leicester U.P.

Hunter Blair, P 1963: *Roman Britain and Early England, 55 B.C.-A.D. 871*.

Ingram, Revd. J 1823: *The Anglo-Saxon Chronicle* (e-book edited by Anthony Uyl -Translation by Rev. James Ingram (London, 1823) with additional readings from the translation of Dr. J. A. Giles (London, 1847) – ISBN: 978-1-77356-200-1 published in Woodstock, Ontario, Canada 2018.

Jones, M E 1996: *The end of Roman Britain*.

Kirby, D P 2000: *The Earliest English Kings*.

Langton, J and Morris, R J (eds.) 1986: *Atlas of Industrializing Britain 1780-1914*.

Laycock, S 2009: *Warlords – The Struggle for Power in Post-Roman Britain*.

Leeds, E T and Harden, D B 1936: *The Anglo-Saxon Cemetery at Abingdon, Berkshire*.

Major, A F 1913: *Early Wars of Wessex: being studies from England's school of arms in the West*.

Mann, N R 2001: *The Isle of Avalon: Sacred Mysteries of Arthur and Glastonbury*.

Marren, P 2009: *Battles of the Dark Ages*.

Maxfield, V A *1989: The Saxon Shore, a Handbook*.

McCall, J B 2002: *The Cavalry of the Roman Republic: Cavalry Combat and Elite Reputations in the Middle and Late Republic*.

Miles, D 2006: *The Tribes of Britain*.

Monmouth, Geoffrey of c.1136: *The History of the Kings of Britain*.

Morris, J 1973: *The Age of Arthur; a History of the British Isles*.

Myres, J N L 1986: *The English Settlements (Oxford History of England)*.

Oman, Sir Charles 1904: *A History of England Before the Norman Conquest* (Bracken Books 1994 edition).

Papworth, M 1995: *Excavation of Romano-British Settlement at Shapwick, Dorset*, Proceedings of the Dorset Natural History & Archaeological Society 117.

Papworth, M 1996: *Resistivity Survey, Badbury Romano-British Temple*, Proceedings of the Dorset Natural History & Archaeological Society 118.

Payne, A, Corney, M and Cunliffe, B 2007: *The Wessex Hillforts Project: Extensive Survey of Hillfort Interiors in Central Southern England*. English Heritage.

Pech, R J and Durden, G 2003: *Manoeuvre warfare: a new military paradigm for business decision making.* Research paper published in journal, *Management Decision,* vol. 41, no.2 pp.168-179.

Peddie, J 1997: *Conquest – The Roman Invasion of Britain.*

Peddie, J 2005: *Alfred: Warrior King.* Sutton paperback, ISBN 0 7509 3796 3.

Pikoulis, E A and others 2004: *Trauma Management in Ancient Greece: Value of Surgical Principles through the Years.* World Journal of Surgery 28, 425-430.

Pryor, F 2006: *Britain AD: A Quest for Arthur, England and the Anglo-Saxons.*

Rahtz, P et al: *Medieval sites in the Mendip, Cotswold, Wye Valley and Bristol Region.* Bristol Archaeological Research Group field guides no 3, 9.

Rippon, S 2006: *Landscape, Community and Colonisation: The North Somerset Levels During The 1st To 2nd Millennia AD,* CBA Research Report 152. York, Council for British Archaeology.

Rivet, A L F 1958: *Town and Country in Roman Britain.*

Robinson, S *1992: Somerset Place Names. Dovecote Press*

Salway, P 2001: *A History of Roman Britain.*

Sawyer, P *Anglo-Saxon Charters: An Annotated List and Bibliography.* London, 1968.

Sims-Williams, P 1983: *The Settlement of England in Bede and the Chronicle,* article in Anglo-Saxon England no. 12 (1983).

Snyder, C A 2003: *The Britons.*

Stenton, F M 1971: *Anglo-Saxon England.*

St. Joseph J K 1961: *Aerial Reconnaissance in Wales.* Antiquity XXXV, pp. 270-271.

Svechin, A A 1931: *Strategiya.*

Swanton, M (ed) 2000: *The Anglo-Saxon Chronicles.*

Taylor, J 1998: *Oxford Journal of Archaeology, Volume 17, Number 1.*

United States Army Doctrine Publication (ADP) 6.0 – *Mission Command.*

Waller, R 2006: *Archaeological Resource Assessment of the Isle of Wight: Early Medieval period.* Isle of Wight County Archaeology Service.

Watkin, A 1945: *The Glastonbury "Pyramids" and St. Patrick's "Companions".* Downside Review lxii, 30-41.

Whittock, M J 1986: *The Origins of England: 410-600.*

Williams, A 1999: *Kingship and Government in Pre-Conquest England, c.500–1066*, part of Palgrave Macmillan's 'British History in Perspective' series.

Wood, M 1981: *In Search of the Dark Ages.*

Wood Stephens, Very Revd. W R 1907: *The Bishops of Winchester Part I.*

Yorke, B 1990: *Kings and Kingdoms of Early Anglo-Saxon England.*

Internet Articles

Crawford, S and Dodd, A: *Anglo-Saxon Oxfordshire*, http://thehuman-journey.net/pdf_store/sthames/Oxfordshire%20combined%20Early%20Medieval.pdf, accessed 20 Feb 2011.

Dunning, R W. *'Ilchester'. A History of the County of Somerset: Volume 3.* British History Online. http://www.british-history.ac.uk/report, accessed 14 August 2010.

Elrington C R and others (eds), 1972: Cf. Finberg, Glos. Studies, 53. From: *'Newnham: Introduction'*, by **Kathleen Morgan and Brian S Smith**, *in A History of the County of Gloucester: Volume 10: Westbury and Whitstone Hundreds* (1972), pp. 29-36. URL: http://www.british-history.ac.uk/report.aspx?compid=15749, accessed 6 July 2011.

Gibson 1570, *Commentariolum*, ed. 1731. (quoted in the Journal of the British Archaeological Association (Volume 31 p.18) read at http://www.ebooksread.com/authors-eng/british-archaeological-association/journal-of-the-british-ar-chaeological-association-volume-31-tir/page-18-journal-of-the-british-archae-ological-association-volume-31-tir.shtml, accessed 5 September 2010.

Green, T 2009: *The Monstrous Regiment of Arthurs*, www.arthuriana.co.uk/historicity/arthurappendix.htm, accessed 20 Jan 2010.

Hunt, A: *Cunedda as Vortigern*, www.vortigernstudies.org.uk/artgue/guest-dan3/htm, accessed 6 July 2011.

Makkay, János: *The Sarmatian Connection – Stories of the Arthurian Cycle and Legends and Miracles of Ladislas, King and Saint*, http://www.kavehfarrokh.com/persianate-civilizations/arthurian-and-european-culture-and-an-cient-iran-eire-an/the-sarmatian-connection-stories-of-the-arthurian-cycle-and-legends-and-miracles-of-ladislas-king-and-saint/, accessed 19 November 2012.

Nayland, C 2006: *Dating the Battle of Chester*, http://www.carlanayland.org/essays/dating_battle_chester.htm, accessed 19 July 2017.

Papworth, M: Archaeology National Trust SW – Category Archives: Badbury Rings, *Arthur, Badon and Badbury* – October 27, 2013 – https://archaeolog-ynationaltrustsw.wordpress.com/category/badbury-rings/, accessed 5 May 2017

Todd, J H *(ed. and tr.) 1848: The Irish version of the Historia Britonum of Nennius.* http://www.ucc.ie/celt/ published/T100028/index.html, accessed 17 July 2009.

Various Authors: *Post Roman Celtic Kingdoms – Glastenning*: http://www.historyfiles.co.uk/KingListsBritain/BritainGlastenning.htm, accessed 19 November 2012.

Vermaat, R: Articles on Gildas, www.vortigernstudies.org.uk/artsou/gild-when.htm, accessed 21 July 2011.

Unknown: *Anglo-Saxon Hampshire*, http://thehumanjourney.net/pdf_store/sthames/Hampshire%20early%20medieval.pdf, accessed 14 February 2011.

Unknown: *The Vistula Ulans at Albuera, May 1811*, http://www.napolun.com/mirror/web2.airmail.net/napoleon/Albuera_1811.html, accessed 14 February 2011.

Unknown: *Orthodox Europe – Latin Saints of the Orthodox Patriarchate of Rome*, http://www.orthodoxengland.org.uk>, accessed 3 Sep 2009.

Ancient Historical Sources

Ammianus, M c. AD 378: *Res Gestae.*

Asser c. AD 893. From *Asser's Life of King Alfred.* ed W H Stevenson, Oxford, 1904.

Bede c. AD 731: *Ecclesiastical History of the English Nation.*

Dio Cassius c. AD 164–229: *Roman History.*

Gildas c. AD 540–570: *De Excidio Britanniae et Conquestu.*

Homer c. 800 BC: *The Iliad*

Huntingdon, H c. AD 1129: *Historia Anglorum.*

Malmesbury, William of c. AD 1130: *De Gestis Pontificum Anglorum.* (William of Malmesbury, *Chronicle of the Kings of England.* From the translation by Rev. John Sharpe, 1815. J.A. Giles, editor. London: George Bell and Sons, 1904)

Nennius c. AD 830: *Historia Brittonum.*

Sidonius c. AD 480: *Letter to his friend Namatius,* from Book VIII Ch. VI as translated by Dalton, O M in 1915.

Tacitus AD 98: *Agricola.*

Tacitus AD 98: *Germania.*

Various authors c. AD 970: *Annales Cambriae.*

Vegetius AD 390: *Epitoma rei militaris.*

Worcester, John of, c. AD 1140: *Chronicon ex chronicis* (also attributed to Florence of Worcester (both were monks at Worcester)).

Xenophon, c. 430–355 BC: *Cyropaedia.*

Index